Mahatma Gandhi and His Philosophy

Mahatma Gandhi and His Philosophy

B.M. SHARMA

RAWAT PUBLICATIONS
Jaipur • New Delhi • Bangalore • Guwahati • Kolkata

ISBN 978-81-316-0845-6

Published by
Prem Rawat for **Rawat Publications**
Satyam Apartments, Sector 3, Jawahar Nagar, Jaipur 302 004 (India)
Phone: 0141 265 1748 / 7006 Fax: 0141 265 1748
E-mail: info@rawatbooks.com
Website: www.rawatbooks.com

New Delhi Office
4858/24, Ansari Road, Daryaganj, New Delhi 110 002
Phone: 011 2326 3290

Also at *Bangalore, Guwahati* and *Kolkata*

Typeset by Rawat Computers, Jaipur
Printed at Chaman Enterprises, New Delhi

Contents

Preface

Mahatma Gandhi represents a long and venerable tradition of Indian history, which can be epitomised in virtues, like penance, self-sacrifice and creative commitment. He was adored by all as an ancient sage, a medieval synthesizer and a modern Mahatma. He is a widely known episodic figure whose name is familiar to all the three generations of Indians, nay the world society. Some greatmen are great for the people of their own times. Others may be universal and they exhibit traits of social values. Mahatma Gandhi falls in the latter category.

Gandhi as a multifaceted personality contemplated about the universal good of mankind. As a visionary, he took care of even minor issues as the shortest spells of history which is testified by the fact that even. Just a day before his dastardly assassination on 29 January 1948, he wrote:

'India is yet to achieve her social, ethical and economic independence. As we shall advance towards the goal of self-governance our civil prowess will be more and more effective than that of the military might we may possess.' He set very high and extremely noble ideals of ethics in politics. As a strategist, he evolved a politics of attaining long range sovereign power through political movements of the masses. He quite successfully applied them in the Indian context. He envisaged a world, wherein varied conflicts could be resolved by non-violence. The contemporary world, torn by violence, fear, terrorism, crime and disintegration looks to the philosophy of non-violence as an effective restraint for future. In his own words:

> Non-violence is the oxygen of social and political life. It is the bedrock of liberty. There is no room to compromise or cut down on its scope. It is like water for the survival of life. I never heard of water being diluted.

Gandhiji was an ardent follower of truth and non-violence. He stood for a new organisation around which a new social order may be reconstituted in India. His message was there not only in words but also his entire life itself was his message. He was not a prophet or an oracle but primarily a कर्मयोगी (man of action). He did not strive to establish any school of philosophy but he talked of truth and non-violence, which implied achieving national independence by moral means. That is why he kept on revising his own ideas and actions. His personality was so towering that books cannot define it. But then, he himself believed that books are more valuable than jewels or pearls. The jewels exhibit outer glamour but the books cleanse the conscience. Hence every book on Gandhi is welcome because it represents a humble effort to take the illumining ideas of his life and actions to the lay readers.

The present study is an attempt to comprehend Gandhi's philosophy and his entire life sprawling in a variety of popular movements of decades. The contexts have been so arranged that the holistic nature of the Gandhian thought becomes self-explanatory in its context. There are eight chapters. The first chapter presents his life, parentage and childhood to explain the impact of these factors in the formative phase of his childhood. These sources are valuable and they conclusively shaped his public life in later years. The second chapter explores his not so well known efforts of establishing Ashrams, which were the training institutes to prepare Satyagrahis. It not only reveals Gandhi as an organiser but also a great experimenter of his novel ideas. Gandhi's social thought has been taken up for scrutiny in the third chapter. It explains his worldview of society and presents a penetrating analysis of future human society in the

East and the West. The 'Sarvodaya Samaj' of Gandhi has been put in a theoretical perspective. Trusteeship doctrine along with 'Swadeshi' is the subject matter of chapter four. His varigated political philosophy has been examined in national and international contexts in the fifth chapter. The sixth chapter has been devoted to 'Secularism', a vexed question of Indian politics and as a philosophy has been explained in terms of its practices by the Mahatma. The spiritualisation of politics is a vague term, but the Mahatma lived this way. It elucidates how can a secularist be religious in the Gandhian way. Chapter seven clarifies the Gandhian concept of 'Gram Swaraj' and how can Panchayati Institutions be revitalised without pernicious impact of caste and crude power. It has the potential of strengthening 'ethical factors' and arrest disintegration which threatens consumptive rural development of western variety. The last chapter evaluates the Gandhian credo of truth, non-violence, Sarvodaya, Satyagrah and Gram Swarajya in the overall context of multiple challenges of the millennium. It further includes the analysis of contemporary trends of liberalisation, privatization and globalisation in the light of trusteeship and Swadeshi doctrines along with their dynamism and relevance for the world society.

The book represents a humble attempt to appraise and appreciate Gandhian musings in a novel and original manner. The scholars, librarians, research workers and intellectuals who have contributed to the 'newness' of this enterprise are many and without individually naming them, I express my sincere gratitude to the academic fraternity and own up the responsibility for the endeavour. The discerning readers alone should judge the quality of this work.

1

Gandhian Philosophy

A Conceptual Study of Fundamental Principles, Origins and Influences

The scope of Gandhian speculation is quite comprehensive and multi-dimensional as Gandhi was not a mere leader, thinker and a social reformer, but he was an activist, a saint and a creative writer who gave a new twist to politics and philosophical speculation of all times and climes. He was an apostle of world peace, shaped in the Indian mould of truth and non-violence besides being an epitome of love and saintliness. He was a strategist par excellence. Although his thought and action had a specific context of Indian freedom struggle but his philosophy cannot be circumscribed in the parameter of modern India. He talks of perennial human values and was a protagonist of the best of humanism, which is eternal. All problems whether that of the West or that of the third world, their solutions reflect a touch of Gandhi directly as well as indirectly. The Gandhian philosophy and its study seems like a precondition to perceive and conceive the structure of a new society and a new human being in flesh and blood.

Gandhiji's ideas and thoughts pertain to varied fields of human activity. His social philosophy is apparently more relevant and inspiring in the context of Indian ethos. The Mahatma showed this kindly light to build a new world on the basis of principles of truth and non-violence. He has been called a 'Pure Karam Yogi' because it is incorrect to recognise him as a pure political thinker of European variety. In essence he was a

Man of Action, who tested and practised his ideas on the criterion of practice. He kept on abandoning all that was not practical. He could not come out with a complete or a final philosophy. He called his activities as search of truth[1] which were not a dogma or a gospel of any religion. He boldly and clearly maintained, 'I do not want to leave a thought or a school of philosophy under my name. Whatever I maintain today, I may revise or change tomorrow. I have nothing new to teach. Truth and non-violence are as ancient as hillocks and mountains.'[2]

He suggested and articulated several movements known as Satyagrah, Non-cooperation, Civil Disobedience and Quit India. They were original ideas and they influenced not only the Indians but also all sorts of people all over the globe. His charismatic personality lent grace to these movements. Most of his ideas were not even coherently organised, but were being tested as mass experiments. Some of his ideas and concepts throw a floodlight on global environs and often bring light, novel directions and a fresh floor of energy to the stress-ridden world of today. To name a few, they can be enumerated as under:

1. Induction of ethical principles in the practice of politics and economics of society.
2. Advocacy of a neo-concept of religion.
3. Non-possession of property and its relationships with owners and users.
4. Establishment of a non-violent society of human beings.
5. Rejection of narrow and negative Nationalism for the establishment of a global and fraternal Society of Humans.
6. Cooperation in place of competition.
7. A *Lokneeti* to replace *Rajyaneeti* of violence and deceit.

While viewing social problems in perspective, philosopher Dr Radhakrishanan maintains that 'Philosophy is that invisible foundation on which stands the structure of a civilization.'[3]

It is literally true. Philosophical premises may not be seen by the naked eye of the mind, but there is nothing in human behaviours and structures that cannot be linked to these basic foundations. The social activities rotate around the hub of social philosophy. Knowledge and science have their origins in this life philosophy of the living beings. Mahatma Gandhi was a unique human being, who inspired and motivated 30 crore Indians to agitate and shook the very foundations of the British Raj in India. He absorbed the most potential religious convulsions of the last 2000 years into politics and rendered them into a mighty force of human and social action.[4]

Rena Full Miller calls Mahatma Gandhi a real social revolutionary.[5] If we agree with Karl Manheim about the fundamental conditions of social reconstruction then Gandhi emerges as a real social revolutionary. Manheim believes that a rebuilding of the individual is a condition precedent for rebuilding a society.[6] Mahatma Gandhi did not strive to reorganise a part of society, but he aimed at total reorganisation and complete rebuilding of human society. He was not a mere social reformer.[7] He was striving to reorganise and rebuild human society according to his principles. He accepted ethics as the fundamental principle of human life. Opposing all extremities he shaped them into an ethical mould. His religion is a synonym for ethical code. He built a bridge between ethics and politics and argued that end and means in politics have to be pure and congruent. He accepted politics consistent to ethical dogmas and professed to the extent that 'Forgo the end if the means are unholy.' He never separated life into compartments like, social, political, economic and religious. He accepted the essence of life as a composite whole. In his judgement all religions have a common goal. He was a protagonist of religious liberalism and religious tolerance. His religious approach to politics implies that political actions should be tested on the Criterion of Ethics. He called the world ephemeral and transient. Hence it is imprudent to reject spiritual values for social development. He used to say that politics devoid of religion is a death trap which pushes the soul to a fall. *Geeta* is correct in asserting 'योग: कर्मसु कौशलम्'. Be efficient and excellent in action as it is yoga. Religion does not teach man to be actionless. Only a man of action is the Man of

God and a true believer of truth. He writes 'My integrity has dragged me into the field of politics and I can say this with utmost humility and without hesitation that those who see no relationship between politics and religion do not know the meaning of religion.'

Mahatma Gandhi presented Indian values in his thought and tried to replace deceptive immorality of politics by establishing love, truth, non-violence and cooperation in public life. He envisaged an equalitarian society. It underlines sovereignty, justice, education, electoral system in international affairs to the extent that he becomes an apostle of stateless world of Marxian variety. According to him cordiality, ethics and change of heart are more important than acquiring power in the political process. He shunned violent means and stressed upon non-violent techniques of socio-political change.

Gandhi: A Profile

Mahatma Gandhi was born at Porbandar in Gujarat on 2 October 1869. His father and grandfather were well known for their honesty, strictness, love and justice in entire Kathiyawad. His father Karam Chand Gandhi served as Diwan of Rajkot, Porbandar and Vokandv state. The family had migrated to Rajkot in 1876 where Gandhi had his early schooling. He was not a promising student and always ranked as middle class student who was deeply rooted in truth, integrity and a boy of principles. This gave him character. In 1881, he entered the High School. Gandhiji had narrated an incident of his first year in High School in his autobiography. It explains his principled stand on issues. Mr Jiles, an inspector of schools from education department had come to inspect the first year students. He asked students to write five words and Gandhi misspelt one term 'Kettle'. The teacher kicked him with his shoe suggesting that he may copy it from the slate of other students near by. Gandhi understood the feeler but his position was that a teacher should not allow copying in the class. On the departure of the inspector the teacher pointed out the mistake but the child Gandhi was not prepared to copy the term. A similar event of his childhood can be cited from his autobiography. His father purchased and presented a book to him entitled *Shrawan's Devotion to His Father*. Gandhi read it and he was highly impressed by the fact that Shrawan Kumar had put his parents in a 'Kawad' and had taken them on the pilgrimage. Similarly a drama entitled *Harish Chandra* touched him to the core and he resolved to be honest and truthful. At this time, when he was 13 years of age he was married to Kasturba. He confessed that in 1884–85 one of his friends forced him to eat meat. He immediately sought apology from his father. In 1887 when he completed secondary education his family arranged to send him to London for legal education at the Bar. He returned as a Barrister in 1891, but because of his dedication to truth and justice he remained a failure at the Bar. He was planning to quit the Bar. Then in 1893, he got on offer to fight out a case from Dada Abdulla and Company of South Africa for a remuneration £ 105. He went to South Africa and this opportunity changed a shy Gandhi and into a vibrant one who started advancing in the field of livelihood as well as made a mark in legal profession. At this time he was just 24 years of age and started fighting for the Rights of the Blacks. To quote Gandhi this experience made him a Karamyogi. He felt 'Reborn' and his struggle for 21 years in Africa made him a Mahatma. It was here that he forged his weapons of truth, non-violence and satyagrah. He experimented with them and his struggle was crowned with success.

Influences on Gandhian Thought

Gandhi was not a systematic thinker and he did not pursue the study of fundamentals of politics in a classical manner. He was a motivated teacher who had a message to communicate. Unlike Shankaracharya or Kant he was not a mere thinker but he can be compared with Socrates and Buddha who delved deep in analysing human problems and offered viable solutions from the field. Politics of South Africa and India was the laboratory wherein he tested his principles for truth and non-violence.[8] He waged a mass movement in the country and liberated India from the bondage of the British. This was not his seminal contribution but his major accomplishment, i.e. to have forged the weapon of non-violence. He taught the human kind that a colossal empire can be challenged without any weapon power and success can be accomplished by sheer force of a non-violent struggle.

These are two cardinal principles of Gandhian thought. Firstly, his ideology pertains to human beings and he was above all sorts of sectarianism. Secondly, he seems deeply influenced by Hindu religion to which he was honestly committed. Gandhian thought is all comprehension, but Gandhi never wanted to leave any ideology behind. In his own words:

> There is nothing like Gandhian and I have no desire to leave a legacy behind. I do not claim to have created new ideas or principles. My effort has been to speak eternal truths of daily life and analyse them in my own way. Whatever precepts I have developed and the conclusions that I have reached to are all tentative. I may change them tomorrow. I have nothing new to teach. Truth and non-violence are as old as hills or rivers. I have strived to experiment in my own way to the best of my capability. My life has been an experiment of truth and non-violence. The truth is that I have discovered non-violence in the pursuit of truth. My philosophy which you call Gandhian is very much implicit in the doctrines of truth and non-violence. Do not call it Gandhian because it does not propound any ideology.

These Gandhian ideas stand based on the pillars of truth and non-violence. In fact, Gandhism, if any, is a mere compendium of universal principles for all for the establishment of a Sarvodaya Society. It sees divine element in all beings. This divinity can be envisaged in the pursuit of truth and non-violence in political and social life. In essence Gandhism is a way of life, a special kind of lifestyle, which can be employed in the solution of all national and international problems that emanate from violence and false ego. The spiritual standard, which evaluates social issues, should be applicable to political and economic realms also. The varied aspects of Gandhism can be lumped into one fundamental bond. It is a sufficient condition to make it a philosophy. The critics allege that Gandhism keeps changing. Gandhi himself had cleared this confusion. 'People say I have changed my ideas. It is not true. The circumstances have changed. Being a Satyagrahi I react to changed situations. Answer to this question can be traced in his book *My Experiments with Truth*. Gandhiji believed that truth is a lifelong pursuit. Gandhi had an experimental outlook towards life and body, whose experiments are bound to have changed ideas. That is why Gandhi's ideas kept changing and he openly denied the concept of Gandhism. Still people want a consensus to develop around his fundamental beliefs.[9] The present century has rendered Gandhian ideas more relevant in the context of freedom struggles in developing countries. Those who have struggled or are struggling with Gandhian techniques have come out triumphant. South Africa could establish a democratic republic on Gandhian principles under the leadership of Nelson Mandela. The non-violent struggle under Aung San Suu Kyi in Myanmar has borne fruits. The Gandhian principles are not inspired by any one religion and the people all over accept them and if one can coordinate them with reality, they become alive and dynamic.

It is true that Gandhi's family shaped his primary socialisation but he could not become a prisoner of so called Hinduism or Vaishnavism. Primary socialisation made him a saint politician. Family offered religious liberalism and the Vaisanav mother taught him the sensitivity of pain felt by others.[10] He was all praise for the truthfullness and religious boldness of his mother. He very humbly confessed 'whatever piousness I have preserved, it is a contribution of my mother, not of my father.'[11] She was too religious to touch food without a prayer. Temple worship was her daily creed. She evoked respect for truth and love, which child Gandhi emulated without questioning. The first lesson in tolerance was a maternal legacy. While proceeding to England his mother took a pledge from him and he confronted incessant challenge in being truthful. It made him resolute and uncompromising all through his life. To fight for principles against odds was a virtue, which bears the imprint of his father's personality.[12] Although tolerance was a parental virtue in the Gandhi family, Gandhi's father used to argue about his religious beliefs with Parasi and Muslim friends. The tenderhearted

Mohan Das used to listen and enjoy these discussions with an open mind. In later life the wife Kasturba rehabilitated this virtue of tolerance in an emotional sense. Gandhi writes about the role of his wife as under:

> The unparalleled tolerance of my wife made her triumphant in every domestic conflict. She was my teacher in the areas of art and non-violent cooperation. Her ignorance was innocence, which was nothing but truth.

Gandhi's nurse Rambha taught him the role of religion in public life. He imbibed the spirit of religion and learnt to separate the grain from the chaff. She dinned in his ears 'God is never happy with external shows, but a true devotion and acceptance motivates you to fight falsehood, Gandhiji has acknowledged this debt of nurse Rambha in unequivocal words. He writes:

> 'It was my Governess Rambha who introduced the name "Rama" in my life the seed which she showed in my juvenile soil never wrinkled or died. Even today the name of Rama is my strength. I accept Rambha Bai's debt.'[13] She visualised Rama as a historic character, but more as a God with out any beginning. Because of Gandhi's respect for Ramcharitmanas, some people may believe that his Rama is the son of king Dasrath. But this is not true. Gandhi has clarified this confusion. 'My Rama or Rama of my prayers is not the historic character born in the palace of king Dasrath. He is an eternal, unborn and unparalleled power, I worship him, he is not an emperor of Ayodhya.'[14]

Gandhi was deeply influenced by Sur, Tulsi, Meera, Narsi[15] and innumerable saints of medieval period. Even Islam and Christianity stirred his spiritual domain.[16] Gujarat had a huge population of Jains. Gandhi interacted with them and non-violence of Jain saints caught his attention. 'अहिंसा परमोधर्म' was Gandhi's doctrine also. He researched into Jain philosophy and admired the intellectual curiosity of Jain saints. Kawalya needs grace of God. Gandhi never believed in god personified but accepted the incarnation theory with hesitation. He found Non-Duality Doctrine (अद्वैत सिद्धान्त) acceptable but he remained a 'theist' with firm belief in God. In fact he was more influenced by Ramayana of Tulsidas than the one composed by Balmiki. His Ram Rajya Concept is a borrowing from Ramcharitmanas. Geeta was the most decisive influence on his thought. He saw the lessons of truth, non-violence and ethics in the story of Geeta. He called it a reference book of spiritualism. Nishkam Karmayoga and Satyagrah he developed from the doctrines of Geeta. To stay away from unreal (असत्) and action, ethical perfection through social control and the essence of Shanker's philosophy became the core premise of his beliefs.[17] Gandhiji had said 'whenever I find myself in utter darkness and failures and depression takes me over, I find Bhagwat Geeta as the beacon of light.' He maintained that Geeta reconciles the conflict between salvation and worldly life. The message in that religion should rule the worldly affairs and whatever one cannot practise in daily life is not a religion. He never accepted Hindu scriptures in totality, but kept rejecting the distortions, exaggerations and the unethical. He accepted Veda, Upnishads, the Geeta and Purans as interpreted by his rationality.[18] He never accepted Hinduism as the only and the best religion of the world. He has said that Vedas alone are not the divinely inspired scriptures, but Bible, Quran, Zendresta are no less inspired by God.[19]

According to Gandhiji, 'all religions have one goal but they suggest varied ways to reach to this common goal.[20, 21] He believed that their moral codes are based on common principles.' My moral religion contains all those rules when encompass the entire humanity.[22] Thus Hinduism provided a spiritual outlook to Gandhian ideas. He confessed that Hindu scriptures fulfilled his spiritual needs.

The inspiration of Mahatma Gandhi can be traced back to Christianity, Jain Buddhism philosophy, Islam and the writings of philosophers like Thoreau, Ruskin and Tolstoy.[23] Christian religion left a profound impact on his ideas. He writes:

> 'Bible to me is a scripture very much like *Geeta* and *Quran*. Sermon on the mount stirred my heart and I used these lines in practice of my life philosophy.' Win evil by good. If someone

slaps on one cheek put the other one in front. Give love to your enemy let him harm you. You keep helping him if he is hungry offer him food. If he is thirsty, quench his thirst.[24] He learnt this from the Lord Jesus 'Oh God! Forgive them, they know not what they are doing'. Additionally Ruskin's *Unto this Last,* Tolstoy's *The Kingdom of God is Within You* had a deep and abiding influence on his life. Emerson was another source and Ruskin convinced him about equality of labour. *Grown of wild Olive* and *Unto this Last* by John Ruskin changed his life philosophy of physical labour. Ruskin convinced him about dignity of labour and inspired his thought process.[25] His writings brought a constructive change in his life.[26] He translated Ruskin's *Unto this Last* into Gujarati under the caption *Sarvodaya.* American thinker Thoreau suggested him the idea of civil disobedience, non-cooperation and stateless society. The idea of people's good was installed in his mind by these philosophies. His Satyagrah doctrine was bodily borrowed, along with several programmes of Thoreau's civil disobedience movement. He admired Tolstoy for his philosophy of a non-violent state. State represents violence and cannot be conducive in the growth of human life and virtues. Like Tolstoy Gandhiji also condemned war, supported pacifism, advocated non-violent protests, suggested respect for physical labour and inculcation of ethical values in personal and public life. His secretary Pyarelal writes 'Tolstoy influenced Gandhi's total outlook towards life. His ideas about art, religion, economics and politics bear his imprint.'

Thus Gandhi freely borrowed from all religions, philosophers ad writings of men of which peace, truth and non-violence were the essence of all these sublime thoughts. The Bhagwat Geeta was a perpetual source of strength and inspiration in his life.

Mahatma Gandhi and South Africa

'My life is my message' said Gandhi. His life was dedicated to the service of humanity. Commencing from South Africa his life by the year 1948 became so illustrious that Albert Einstein while paying a homage had to say, 'Coming generations will scarcely believe that a man of Gandhi's description could have ever walked in flesh and blood on this earth.' His personality began taking shape in South Africa. His first experience in South Africa shook him to the core. With a first class train ticket in his wallet, the train authorities threw him out of rail compartment reserved for the whites. Asserting for his right to equality he was physically beaten, which literally changed his life. He resolved to fight against injustice. His response was that he with argument, appeal and struggle will awaken 'Reason' and will not accept racial arrogance. It was not a question of self-respect only but it was an issue linked with the respect and dignity of human race.[27] The legal case did not satisfy him. His conclusion was 'Pursuit of Justice' will ruin both the litigants. 'Vakils' (lawyers) will thrive and bitterness will continue even after winning or losing. So he decided to settle the case outside the court. In this particular case Gandhi's client Abdulla won the case, but the other side became a pauper. So Gandhiji persuaded his client to accept money in instalments. In his quieter moments, he reflected on the case and wrote 'I have realised the correct meaning of an advocate I know now the divine side of human nature. An advocate should unite the divided sides of the case.'[28]

In 1896 he came to India and when he informed Indians about racial discrimination in South Africa, the Africans resented it. He was attacked by Africans and he fell a victim to racial violence. When the South African government promised to punish the culprits, Gandhiji pardoned them by saying that he carries no ill-will for Africans in his heart.[29]

Beginning of Public Career

His three years at Bar made him a successful lawyer and an influential political leader from India. He addressed the labourers, wrote memos to South African government and articles in newspapers. He was determined to improve the conditions of Indian community. When he was returning home after the Abdulla and Company case the Indian co-nationals requested him to continue his struggle in Africa. Gandhiji reluctantly agreed and resolved to launch a non-violent protest against unjust white laws.[30] On 15 March 1998 he met Chamberlain, the then colonial secretary in London and submitted a memorandum against

British policy in South Africa. To organise his protest activities, he founded the Natal Indian Congress on 22 August 1894 and became its honorary secretary. He opposed all sorts of discriminations and planned to offer a Satyagrah. These Gandhian Movements in Africa can be classified in three categories:

1. *From 11 September 1906 to 30 January 1907:* It started from Johannesburg and ended with an agreement with General Smuts.
2. *On 16 August 1908:* Smuts agreement was violated and identity cards were burnt by Indian emigrants.
3. *From 28 October 1913 to 22 January 1914:* Final violation of Gandhi from Smuts Pact. Gandhi marched from Natal to Transvaal.

After the Boer War the Indians were prevented from going to Transvaal and registration was made mandatory under Asiatic Registration Bill. Registration in Transvaal was compulsory and photographs had to be affixed. Gandhi was shocked to read these rules in *Transvaal Gazette*. It was highly humiliating and registration for Indians above the age of 8 was compulsory. The police could check it any time by invading upon the privacy of their homes. The registration documents could be checked any where, any time. Gandhi struggled quite hard, but did not succeed. So he resolved to launch a Satyagrah. The discrimination was called 'Apartheid' or Racism. Some of these abominable laws were as follows:[31]

1. All non-white individuals were to be registered compulsorily.
2. Their fingerprints were collected for identity purposes.
3. They could not move out freely in the streets. Even roads were earmarked.
4. Non-registration could be challenged in a law court.
5. A thumb impression was essential for a commercial licence.
6. On visiting to India and returning to South Africa reregistration was essential.
7. Their residential colonies and markets were separate.

8. The blacks could not participate in socio-cultural activities with whites.
9. The non-whites paid a tax of 3 £ for the colour of their skin.
10. Marriages between whites and non-whites were illegitimate. Even black marriages were not acceptable in some situations.
11. The property rights of blacks were conditional and white officials could dispossess them.

On 11 September 1906 Gandhi called a meeting at Empire Theatre in Johannesburg and resolved to fight these discriminatory practices. Addressing people here he thundered, 'I have been left with only one course. I will like to die than to surrender. Even if all of you leave me lonely, still, I will fight to the finish.'[32] This pledge was called the commencement of Satyagrah.[33] Gandhi preferred to call it a Satyagrah of love and non-violence.[34] Gandhi took the oath that he will never yield and asked the people to suggest a name for the movement through his paper *Indian Opinion*. People suggested *Sadagrah* (सदाग्रह) and Gandhi named it as *Satyagrah* (सत्याग्रह).

The First Satyagrah Movement

The Transval legislature, not withstanding Indian opposition, passed the Asiatic Registration Bill. Gandhi had to launch his Satyagrah movement. It created a storm in the tiny colony and Gandhiji was sentenced to two months of imprisonment on 10 January 1908. When the Satyagrah was at its peak General Smuts extended his land of friendship towards Gandhi for a pact.[35] The proposal was that if all Indians accept registration voluntarily, then he will cancel the law. Gandhiji accepted it and he was freed from the jail with his followers. When Gandhi entered for registration in the office, a Pathan, named Meer Alam assaulted him but several Europeans intervened and saved his life. When Gandhi gained consciousness, he asked for registration and appealed to the British to release Meer Alam. Despite all this the Asiatic Registration Bill could not be cancelled.[36] It disappointed Gandhiji.

The Second Satyagrah Movement

Gandhi decided to change the form of his protest movement. His decision was that Indians will burn the 'Holi' of their registration papers. Several Indians burnt their cards and they started moving without them. Some opted for jail.[37] The movement spread to Natal. The jail torture did not dampen their enthusiasm. But the Satyagrahis felt economic hardships. In this emergency a German citizen Kallenbach came to Gandhiji and offered his 1,000 acre farm gratis for the Satyagrahi activities. It was named as Tolstoy Farm and it became a new experimental ground for Gandhian ideas. The farm had Satyagrahis from all religions. They all worked physically quite hard and Gandhi felt encouraged. The doctrine of non-violence was tested with rigour. Here he established a primary school. Physical labour was compulsory but education of heart and character was experimented upon. Gandhi maintained that if he and the teachers lie then they have no right to demand truth from the students. He felt that he was learning from those, whom he was teaching. Hence he should be honest for the good of his pupils.[38] The Tolstoy farm experience contributed to the theory and practice of Satyagrah. The strict discipline of the farm hardened these people to the extent that jail atrocities became bearable. The Tolstoy farm taught to be happy in poverty and adversity. It created a strong citizenry against the physical prowess of Transvaal government. The Satyagrah lasted for 4 years or so. In between Gopal Krishna Gokhale visited South Africa as a government quest in 1912. The Smuts Government had released all Satyagrahis in 1911. Gokhale assured Gandhi that Asiatic Registration Act will be cancelled. But Gandhiji knew that it was not easy and would never happen. Gokhale appraised Gandhi about the harrowing conditions in India. He invited Gandhi to India and while welcoming Gandhiji to his native soil Gokhale admitted that Gandhi had indomitable energy to convert average people into warriors and martyrs. He openly said that people cannot do wrong acts, nor can they think of them, in the presence of Gandhi.[39]

The Last Phase of Satyagrah

The Asiatic Registration Bill continued on the Statute Book even after Gokhale's visit. Then an event declaring the marriage of an Indian couple void by Supreme Court caused a furore in entire South Africa.[40] It implied that all Hindu, Muslim and Parasi marriages of people of Indian origin are illegal. This decision was given by a Judge of Supreme Court of the Cape Colony. It annoyed non-Christian women and they came forward to join Gandhi's movement in large numbers. The Satyagrah movement got new life. At this juncture the labourers rose in revolt. Gandhi preached his non-violence and the government used army to repress. Hundreds of poor labourers were killed. The Indian help poured in. A missionary named C.F. Andrews donated his entire property to Gandhi. Satyagrah started catching up and Gandhi was released from jail on 13 December 1913. A commission was constituted but Gandhi's demand of inclusion of an Indian member was rejected. Gandhi told his followers that the struggle was against enemies of humanity. He defended it as a religious war of conscience.[41] Gandhiji marched to Durban on 1 January 1914. This time the white employees of African Railways joined the strike. Seeing the sensitivity of the problem Gandhiji withdrew his movement saying:

> 'My Satyagrah does not have any aim to humiliate anybody. Nor do I want to hurt any person. I do not wish to win by ruining any group. A Satyagrahi must change his opponents by honesty, sacrifice and by dint of soul force. Our Satyagrahis do not want to take advantage of governments adversities. We seek no unscrupulous alliances.'[42]

General Smuts was moved by this Christian technique of a Hindu and he signed a pact with Gandhi on 30 June 1914. The Muslim and Parsi marriages were legitimised and tax on Natal workers was exempted. It was decided that Indian labourers will not be allowed entry after 1920. When it became the law Gandhiji called it Magna Carta. He wrote in his paper *Indian Opinion*, this kind of Satyagrah can revolutionise social modes and the military and totalitarian regimes will leave the colonies.

The South African Satyagrah movement was a political experiment in non-violent change. This groomed a shy and an immature barrister into a bold leader of colonial movement. Non-violence as a weapon was invented here, which later on Gandhi employed for the solution of problems of his motherland.[43] White returning to India from South Africa Gandhiji presented a pair of shoes to General Smuts. They were manufactured by him in jail. Reflecting on the event general Smuts had written, 'He has used them as sandals, although he never thought that he can deservingly wear them.' Smuts has written, 'It was my good fortune that I had the privilege of opposing a man, whom I view with utmost respect. He never ignored the human side of events. He was never angry, never rated anybody and kept his cool and humour even in extremely trying situations. His style and emotional ways were in contrast to the hard and barbaric powers of our times.'[44]

This kind of feeling was expressed by Gilbert Murray in a different way. Murray writes, 'One should be cautious from a man, who does not get disturbed by sensory perceptions. He who does not care about leisure, admiration and personal interests. Such a person concentrates on what he thinks is correct. He is a dangerous and tormenting kind of an enemy. He has triumphed over his body and his soul is beyond the mundane pleasures and pains of his physique.'[45]

Gandhiji started his political career from South Africa. Here he experimented with truth and came out triumphant. This made him an Asian leader on the African soil. B.R. Nanda, his biographer writes that 'Africa did comparatively much less than what Gandhi did for Africa'. Africa changed Gandhi's personality. He established Natal Indian Congress when he was just 25 years of age. In 1908, when he took a trip from London to South Africa, he authored his celebrated treatise *Hind Swaraj*. It stands translated in all important languages of the world.

India: Gandhi's Field of Action

As advised by Gokhale, Gandhi on return from Africa started studying the Indian situation, conditions of people and points of view of Indian leaders. He accepted Gokhale as his political mentor.[46] Like Africa, Gandhi planned his small and huge movements through his ashrams. These ashrams were training centres where Satyagrahis were trained and prepared for action. In South Africa, Tolstoy and Phoenix Ashrams were established by Gandhiji himself. They explain his organisational acumen. This gave him practical insights in social dynamics and gradually he became a Mahatma.[47] Here follows a brief resume of his Indian movements.

Champaran Satyagrah

It was started by Gandhiji on 10 April 1917. Here, Gandhi for the first time experimented with the non-violence of the brave and the complete men.[48] The farmers in Champaran were forced to do Indigo planting. Later on when artificial colours were invented and used, this kind of farming became non-productive. The British government started realising a tax to make up for the loss.[49] So Gandhi made an enquiry to know the truth. He took affidavits from farmers. The British government saw a threat to law and order and asked Gandhiji to leave Champaran. He bluntly declined. He had to go to the court. Gandhi accepted his guilt and maintained that he obeyed the higher law of his conscience. The governor confessed his mistake and sought Gandhi's cooperation. Gandhiji was made a member of Champaran Farm Inquiry Committee which removed difficulties like 'Tinkathia' (It was a system which was introduced by the British Government in Champaran. It was opposed by the Indians under the leadership of Mahatma Gandhi). It was Gandhi's victory without much effort.

Kheda Satyagrah

Kheda is a district in Gujarat. In 1917, it suffered from floods, and in 1918 drought caused famine and plague. The governments did not exempt revenue realisation. On 4 February 1918 Gandhiji declared Satyagrah in Bombay. He asked Sardar Patel to prepare people and they refused to pay revenue. The government started the repression game. This movement was launched from Nadiad where the Anand Ashram was set up for the purpose.

After four months the government ordered non-realisation and non-eviction of farmers from the land. This concluded the movement with success.

Non-cooperation Movement

Gandhiji had brought a unique political method and philosophy from Africa. It proved its utility in India too.[50] He was not cooperating with British government on matters like Jalianwala Bagh and Rowlett Act. So he established a new organisation under the banner of Satyagrah Sabha. As its President, he called a strike on 30 March 1919 to oppose the Rowlett Act. Programmes like prayer meetings, mass fasting, boycott, etc. were planned to awaken people. The date of 13 April 1919 was fixed to launch the protest in the Jalianwala garden by some 2,000 people. It was here that General Dyer opened fire on peaceful protesters and a large number of people lost their lives. So on 18 April 1919 Satyagrah was postponed. Another issue that hung fire was Khilafat and the government policy towards Turkey was humiliating to Indian Muslims. Gandhiji made a big issue and asked Indian friends to return British medals and honours. On 1 August 1920 Gandhiji returned his 'Kaisar-i-Hind' title to Lord Chelmsford, the then Viceroy of India. Students and women joined in large numbers. Swadesh programmes and constructive work was emphasised. The movement presented the positive and negative sides of the protest before the people.

Positive Side of the Movement

1. Establishment of national schools and colleges.
2. Panchayats to resolve family conflicts.
3. Propagation of Swadeshi at mass scale.
4. Development of handicrafts.
5. End of untouchability.

Negative Side of the Movement

Whatever British institutions were available in socio-economic fields were boycotted. The government machinery was rendered dysfunctional.

The non-cooperation campaigns soon spread all over and people rose in open revolt. Gandhi became apprehensive of violence and he began to plan a Civil Disobedience Movement from Bardoli.[51] In the mean time on 5 February 1922, a procession of Satyagrahis burnt the police station of Chauri Chaura, burning 21 policemen alive. Gandhiji was shocked and he took the movement back. The people criticised this bold decision, but Gandhiji was unperturbed. The movement was withdrawn at a time when it was at its climax. Subhash Chandra Bose became unhappy. He wrote, 'Gandhiji provided a strong organisation in 1921. He made the movement active and national. He inducted a revolutionary fervour. Slogans were invented and the country was agog with national sentiment. Hindi replaced English as the language of protest. Khadi became the livery of freedom fighters.[52] Thus the non-cooperation movements of Gandhi evoked nationalism in the country and the elitist agitation became a people's movement for the first time.'

Civil Disobedience Movement

The entire country was in angry mood. Jawaharlal Nehru and Subhash Chandra Bose were the outstanding leaders of the movement. It was resolved that if the government does not grant dominion status to the colony by 31 December 1929, then the Congress will declare Complete Independence as its goal. At appointed time in 1929 at the bank of river Ravi the Congress flag was unfurled and Congress resolved to celebrate 25 January as Independence Day for India. Then Gandhi prepared a charter of demands.[53] He declared that only ashramites, who are disciplined shall participate in the agitation. Gandhi addressed a letter to Lord Irwin calling him a dear friend. He requested him to find a way out. Gandhi presented his total scheme of non-violent fight against the mighty power of British Raj.[54] On 12 March 1930, he with a group of 79 Satyagrahis marched from Sabarmati Ashram to Dandi to break the Salt Law. The 241 mile long march was covered in 24 days. On 5 April when he reached Dandi at the sea coast he picked up salt pebbles and broke the law. It was the beginning of a non-violent movement in the entire country. People were asked to loot salt godown at Dharsaua.[55] But Gandhi was arrested and Congress was declared as an illegal body of traitors. This intensified the civil disobedience movement. The English rulers lost their moral right to rule the colony. The British government rained terror, but no Satyagrahi cried or complained. The agitation made India impregnable and Britain felt her impotence.[56] The civil disobedience created economic problems.[57] On 25 January 1931 Lord Irwin entered into a pact with Gandhi and all political agitators were released from jails. The pact withdrew the salt ordinance and salt making at the sea shore was permitted.

On 28 December 1931 Lord Willington came to India as Viceroy. He reissued the ordinance and Gandhi restarted the civil disobedience. Again Gandhi was arrested and the jail going Satyagrahis touched the unprecedented figure of 1 lakh and 25 thousand. Gandhiji was released on 8 May 1933 and the agitation was postponed for 11 weeks. Then individual disobedience was started and later terminated on 7 April 1934. It was a totally non-violent protest under Gandhi and it shook the very foundations of British Raj in India. Subhash Bose compared Dandi March of Gandhi with Paris return of Napoleon from Elba.[58] It pressurised the British to incorporate provincial autonomy in the Government of India Act, 1935.

Quit India

After Civil Disobedience, Gandhi took a little vacation and devoted himself to the constructive programme of social reform. He encouraged Congress to participate in 1937 elections under 1935 reforms. In 1939, when the Second World War started, English government made India a party without involving Indian leaders. He advised Congress leaders to quit and join the revived civil disobedience movement. In July 1942 Congress passed the Vardha Proposal in its Bombay Session on 8 August 1942. Gandhi's 70 minute long memorable address called as 'Do or Die' became a household slogan. He was arrested with his team of leaders and the agitation spread with added vigour. Aruna Asaf

Ali lead this movement. Communal riots started. Gandhi was allegedly blamed for them. He was so unhappy that he decided to go on a 21 day fast on 10 February 1943 as a token of atonement. The wave of repression and suppression was let off on the people. Then on 6 May 1944, Lord Wavel arrived as new Governor General. His first act was to let Gandhi off from the prison.

Thus Quit India was the third mass agitation of his career and the British Government put all its might to repress it. At this time the partition demand of Muslim League started communal carnage in north India. Gandhi saw the end of his handiwork. He tried his might best to combat communalism. His fast unto death technique also failed. He kept working in Nao Khali with Khan Abdul Gaffar Khan and Maulana Azad, but in vain. His fast unto death on 2 September 1947 helped to ease the situation in Delhi and Calcutta.[59] But the tragedy of partition could not be averted. He firmly refused to accept partition and did not accept any post in the government of free India. Power seekers played the game and the great man had to play a martyr in the midst of political chicknary.

Notes

1. Erikson, Erik H., *Gandhi's Truth: On the Origins of Militant Non-violence,* New York: Norton, 1969; London: Faber & Faber, 1970, p. 391.
2. B.P. Sitaramayya, *The History of Indian National Congress,* Padma Publishing Ltd., Bombay, 1964, p. 348.
3. Kalki, July, 1948, p. 29.
4. Romain Rolland, *Mahatma Gandhi,* Allen & Unwin, London, 1948, p. 3.
5. Rene wrote, 'Gandhi believed that love thy neighbour, he Converted the political organisation into a moral organisation in history, *Lenin and Gandhi,* Bowman and Vance, London, October, 1927, p. 256.
6. Karl Mannheim, *Man and Society,* Kegan & Paul, London, 1946, p. 15.
7. *Young India,* 12 May 1920: 13 July, 15 August 1925.
8. Ganesh Sharkar Vidyaarthi, Karamveer Gandhi's Udghosh, p. 6.

9. M.K. Gandhi, *An Autobiography: The Story of My Experiments With Truth*, Navajivan, Ahmedabad, 1940, p. 2.
10. Gandhi's mother Putli Bai was a Paranami, She combined Islam and Hinduism in her worship.
11. Mahadev Desai *The Diary of Mahadev Desai* Vol. I, Navajivan Publishing, Ahmedabad, 1932.
12. Mahatma Gandhi, *Brief Autography*, Sasta Sahitya, New Delhi, 1995, p. 1.
13. Ibid., p. 26.
14. *Harijan*, 28 April 1946. ·
15. Bhajan of Narsi Mehta influenced Gandhi.
16. J.M. Brown, *The White Umbrella in Indian Political Thought*, Jaico Publishing House, Delhi, 1964, pp. 108–10.
17. Y.G. Krishnamurty, *Gandhian Era World Politics*, Popular Books Depot, Bombay, 1943, p. 66.
18. V.G. Roy, *Gandhian Ethics*, p. 4.
19. *Young India*, 6 October 1921, p. 317.
20. एकं सद्विप्रा वहुआ वदन्ति, अग्निं यमं मातारेश्वान माहु:
21. M.K. Gandhi, *Hind – Swaraj*, Sasta Sahitya, Delhi, 1958, p. 49.
22. Romain Rolland, *Mahatma Gandhi*, National Yiddish Book Centre, London, 1924, p. 28.
23. G.N. Dhawan, *The Political Philosophy of Mahtma Gandhi*, Ch. I.
24. Mahatama Gandhi, *Brief Autobiography*, Sasta Sahitya, Delhi, p. 39.
25. Ibid., p. 76.
26. Ibid., p. 76.
27. B.R. Nanda, *Mahatma Gandhi*, Unwin Books, London, p. 33.
28. M.K. Gandhi, Brief Autobiography, op. cit., p. 168.
29. Louis Fisher, *The Life of Mahatma Gandhi*, Garuda, London, p. 72.
30. Quarantine Bill, Trade Licence Bill, Immigration Bill, etc.
31. D.B. Mathur, *Congress and Apartheid*, Aalekha Publishers, Jaipur, p. 17.
32. B.R. Nanda, op. cit., p. 96.
33. Ibid., pp. 112–13.
34. Ibid., p. 154.
35. Gandhi, *Satyagraha in South Africa*, Navajivan, Ahmedabad, 1961, p. 102.
36. Ibid., pp. 173–181.
37. Gandhi was sent to jail for two and three months.
38. B.R. Nanda, op. cit., p. 75.
39. Louis Fisher, op. cit., p. 140.

40. M.K. Gandhi, *Satyagrah in South Africa*, op. cit., p. 276.
41. Louis Fisher, op. cit., p. 148.
42. Ibid., p. 149.
43. Asha Rani, *Gandhian Non-violence and India's Freedom Sturggle*, Shree Publishing House, Delhi, 1981.
44. Louis Fisher, op. cit., p. 152.
45. Ibid., p. 153.
46. Gandhi, *Gokhale: My Political Guru*, Navajivan, Ahmedabad, 1959.
47. Geoffrey Ashe, *Gandhi: A Study of Revolution*, Heinemam, London, 1968, p. 66.
48. *Harijan*, 4 November 1939.
49. Rajendra Prasad, *Satyagrah in Champaran*, Navajivan, Ahmedabad, 1946, p. 46.
50. M.G. Polak, *Mr Gandhi: The Man*, Allen & Unwin, London, 1931.
51. *Young India*, 19 January 1922.
52. Subhash Chandra Bose, *Indian Struggle Part II*, Thacker, Spink & Co., Kolkata, 1948, p. 112.
53. *Young India*, 13 February 1930, Calcutta, 1948.
54. M.M. Verma, *Gandhia's Techniques of Mass Mobilisation*, R.K. Gupta and Company, New Delhi, 1990, pp. 84–160.
55. Web Miller, *I found No Peace*, Simon and Schuster, New York, 1936, pp. 192–96.
56. *Hindustan Times*, 4 November 1929.
57. *Young India*, 11 December 1930.
58. Subhas Bose, op. cit., p. 255.
59. Louis Fisher, op. cit., ch. 8.

2

Gandhian Ashrams

Laboratories for Experiments with Truth and Non-violence

The ashrams established by Mahatma Gandhi are comparable with laboratories where he used to experiment with his lifestyle and commitment to non-violence.[1] These ashrams used to lend discipline and awareness to hundreds of disciples engaged in launching movements. They enlisted economic and moral support for the cause. Gandhiji believed that simplicity, mutuality and hard work in ashrams can develop temperance necessary for social reforms. He was inspired in this area by the example, of ancient gurukuls, forest lodges, Christian Therapist Association of South Africa,[2] Ramakrishna Missions of Vivekanand, Servants of Indian Society of G.K. Gokhale and Henry Thoreau. He strived to establish a system based on truth and non-violence which could train and groom workers for the establishment of an ideal society. He thought of opening a formal training college and then decided to name this chain by the term 'Ashram'.[3] His idea of an Ashram was to train volunteers in non-violence, civil disobedience, self-help and Satyagrah and then go to the society to encourage people in this direction.

The establishment, organisation, training programme and their evaluation by Gandhiji demonstrate his skill, interest and disposition in the science of management. The Ashrams worked as laboratories and the inmates were the objects of study and experiment.[4]

These Ashrams were based on the principle of Global family. All distinctions of high and low, caste or creed were non-existent there.

Gandhiji was basically a member of joint family and his mother Putali Bai was a great influence on his life and thought. Prayer, worship, fasting, 'prasad', vegetarianism, temperance and self-help were what all the inmates practised in groups.

All the Ashrams of Mahatmaji were linked with his Satyagrah in South Africa and then in India. He believed that social service always needs introspection and all inmates should see and do what they believe in their daily lives. This training of Satyagrah proved to be a strong moral support in the civil disobedience movement in India.

The primary socialisation of Gandhiji, oriented him the doctrine that 'Man must live with humanity and for humanity.' He established the Ashrams as independent units so that the inmates could live for mankind and also with mankind. The Ashram was like a joint family system in which the members shared their experiences without any servants or helpers.

There is an old saying that saints live in Ashrams. They may also live in forests and caves but the Ashramites are the people who live as disciplined lot in the society. The Ashrams had rules and regulations and Gandhiji never relaxed any rule for anybody to maintain the family atmosphere in the Ashrams.[5] The Ashram was a life of collectivity and Gandhiji accepted it as a religious duty very much inbuilt in human nature.[6] The inmates were expected to discover their inner selves here. Love, truth, equality, non-violence apart, they practised the precepts that all men are the children of God. All humans were to be governed by fraternal love and no distinction should be perceived in human interactions.[7]

Phoenix Settlement (1904)

When Gandhiji arrived in South Africa in the year 1895, he was neither a Mahatma nor a popular leader of any consequence. He knew nothing about the place. But his struggles spanning two decades, converted the affluent anglicised barrister into a successful popular leader of the masses. He cherished an innate desire to lead a public life. By 1903, he could collect a group of people who could lead a cooperative life in a planned manner.[8] Gandhiji organised a group named *Indian Opinion* and they resolved to serve the Indian community in an organised manner.[9] The Plague epidemic in Johannesburg gave him the plan to implement Ruskin's idea of *Unto this Last* in the agricultural community of Indians. He purchased an agricultural farm at Durban for this purpose and decided to run *Indian Opinion* on cooperative lines.[10] The employees were given an advance salary of one month and whatever was worked out as profit towards the end of the year was equally distributed among them. The experiment commanded respect and changed the qualitative life of the workers.[11] The land of Natal was named as Garden Colony and Europeans and Indians were made to live together. Together they worked and appreciated each other's lifestyles. The fraternal coexistence of two cultures was very much liked by the co-owner of the press and he sold his share to Gandhiji.[12] Later on another piece of land was purchased on the bank of river Piesang near railway station which was fourteen km away from Durban. It was an investment of one thousand pounds by Gandhiji. Later on five thousand pounds were invested by the Phoenix community on a cooperative basis.[13] It was named as Phoenix Settlement. Legend has it that the bird Phoenix dies only to be reborn. Gandhiji thought his only to be reborn. Ashram will be immortal in history.[14]

The *Indian Opinion* press was shifted from Durban to Phoenix in October 1904. The building material was donated by the residents and the labourers and artisans worked on the press building. Friends of Gandhiji built the structure in one month and the green grass presented a scenic background.[15] Millie

Polak writes that Gandhiji was more concerned about hard work rather than the artistic beauty of the structure.[16]

The press machine was carried to Phoenix from Durban with great difficulty. Three rivers were crossed and 16 bullocks dragged the machine. Albert West had the wheel with four labourers to make publication possible.[17] The newspaper became presentable.[18] Gandhiji knew the art of taking work from unwilling workers. West prayed for the project and created a climate of cooperation in the Ashram. The paper became self-sufficient and people on rent were dropped. The paucity of funds and resources was felt but the paper continued to appear as a one page daily from Phoenix. The settlement had other pressures also.[19] The children of imprisoned Satyagrahis were kept in the Ashram. This added to economic burden. Mahatma called this time an opportunity to introspect his spiritual powers. He not only improved the publication but made sincere efforts to educate people and serve the community. People were advised not to quarrel[20] and not to waste resources. All worked together to bring the settlement out from the morass.[21]

Gandhiji was too busy to look after the settlement from London. So he passed on his responsibility to his associate Magan Lal Gandhi. Gandhiji's absence weakened the situation because people had a personal affiliation with Gandhiji. But the Phoenix settlement continued and was extended in the form of a suburb. More houses were constructed on purchased land. John Cordis built a vapour bath tub. The new inmates kept coming. Gandhiji asked Kasturba and also told his nephew Gokuldas to stay in the Ashram.[22] On reaching Johannesburg, Gandhiji told Henry Polak about Ruskin's influence and his book *Unto this Last*. A happy Polak joined Gandhiji's project. He resigned from his position as Deputy Editor of *The Transvaal Critic* and started working for *Indian Opinion*. Polak and West lived together in a bungalow, cooked their own food when their parents were in London. Both of them were unmarried. Later Polak was called by Gandhiji to assist him at Bar and later on they agreed to marry also on the advice of Gandhiji.[23]

Pywell Best, whom Gandhiji called Granny used to teach tailoring to women. She was an informed music teacher also. Polaks were an ideal couple and the inmates also started calling their spouses from India. Gradually the Phoenix Settlement became a village.[24] By now Gandhiji had not matured his concept of celibacy, but he did insist on simplicity and self-sufficiency. He economised on his personal expenses. He used to wash his own clothes and did the hair cut also on his own. 'Do your own' was the way of life in the settlement. A flour mill to grind wheat was purchased. The children of the settlement joined the elders in this task. It became a part of children's play and even toilets were to be cleaned by all in rotation. In fact, it was a training in character building.[25] The story of Phoenix explains Gandhiji as a barrister, a public figure and a spokesperson of the Indian community. He prepared scripts for publication and financed subscription upto £5000 per annum. He became an outstanding lawyer in no time. His western friends got impressed by his ideas and creativity. A German architect Kallenback and a bishop Josephdak surrendered their assets to Gandhiji and began to live in the settlement. The settlement was agog with discourses on Geeta, Upanishads, and preachings of Tolstoy.[26] The gifts received by Mahatma were deposited in the settlement although Kasturba was opposed to this.[27]

The biographers of Gandhiji accuse that the Phoenix settlement ran on authoritarian lines and Gandhiji was the owner of the newspaper and the agriculture farm like a feudal lord.[28] But the charge is frivolous because the inmates loved the Mahatma and his charismatic personality who could dissolve differences with smiles. Strict discipline, physical labour, non-violence and non-possession was very strongly stressed in the Ashram.[29] It is also wrong that Gandhiji ignored his wife and children. It is argued that Gandhiji imposed his decisions on others but his charismatic style and self-sacrifice can be held responsible for this kind of behaviour. This lifestyle drastically changed in 1906 but the Geeta was his workbook to search the truth. He strived to develop equanimity and selfless service in all and was a tremendous success since the beginning. He developed Phoenix Settlement on these lines and made it a centre of excellence for education, health and agriculture. Consequently, the Phoenix Settlement became a seminary of Satyagrahis who kept working for the Gandhian mission even after his departure to India.[30]

On Gandhiji's return to India the ownership of Phoenix Settlement and Indian opinion were handed over to a Trust. The inmates of Phoenix could not earn their livelihood from land and the press job too was inadequate and unexpanding.[31] The problems multiplied. West continued with his carpentry training[32] but the animal wealth suffered a setback. Polak's wife was unhappy with the life of temperance at the settlement so the couple left for Johannesburg.[33]

The life at Phoenix became dull and the rooms of Gandhiji became mere prayer houses. Phoenix provided Satyagrahis who could bear hardships[34] but the South African government declared non-Christian marriages illegal. Gandhiji transferred 16 families to Tolstoy Farm. Police harassed them there also and ultimately the eight year old Satyagrah came to an end in 1913. Gandhiji and Kasturba left Phoenix in 1914, on the invitation of Gopal Krishan Gokhale who visited them in 1912. The settlement people were reluctant to bid goodbye to the Gandhis, but the Mahatma could pursue Chagan Lal Gandhi and West to run the system in his absence. Several inmates and Gandhiji's son came to India and Gandhiji visited them at Shanti Niketan of Gurudev Rabindranath Tagore in 1915. Later on Gandhiji got involved in national movement and his son Manilal Gandhi completely changed the concept of the settlement at Phoenix. The financial crisis and sickness of senior manager encouraged Inkatha tribes to damage the property and the settlement was crushed to ground.[35]

Tolstoy Farm (1910–13)

It was established as a supplement to Phoenix project. In the second phase of South African struggle, the poor Indian families were to be rehabilitated at Tolstoy Farm for emergency relief.[36] Gandhiji conceived of it as a cooperative family village of Satyagrahis at Transvaal, where they could be self-reliant, simple and one with nature. For this, Kallenbach purchased a farmland of 1100 acres and handed it over to Gandhiji for the dwelling of the Satyagrahis free of cost till 30 June 1910.[37] Gandhiji tried to save the Phoenix project by developing this extension project at Transvaal.

Establishment

Gandhiji always stressed upon collectivity of social life. Housing was to be common and together they worked on the farmland for productive purposes. It offered an opportunity to Indians in South Africa to lead a non-material kind of life. This farm was away from urban filth and mechanical life of cities. Kallenbach gave the name Tolstoy to the project. He was a Jew and had the impact of Kibbutz Movement[38] on his ideas. Keebut system believed in a free living of men and women but the Tolstoy farm was to maintain the segregation.[39] It was to be shaped as a training institute for physical labour and an exploitation free lifestyle with minimum wants. Simple food and sincere labour to earn bread was the principle which was experimented.[40] To live with nature was ideal and physical work could be enjoyed better than material temptations of life. A part of the land produced oranges, almonds, vegetables, etc. for the food and livelihood of the inmates. The water system was arranged in colourful springs and eminent architects built dwelling tenements around for a pleasant living with nature. Small training centres for carpentry and tannery were established and small shopkeepers could run kiosks on the spot. This could yield reasonable income to make the Tolstoy farm self-sufficient.[41] There were no servants on the Farm and every inmate worked quite hard to give results. The inmates performed their respective jobs with care. It was a vegetarian colony although Muslims and Christians were quite a part of the huge population. Kallenbach and Gandhiji presented the model of simple living and high thinking. Fasting and food habits were quite restrained. People used to celebrate all religious festivals with joy. The Geeta was the source of inspiration for all. Labour economy and self-sufficiency were the watch words of the life of farm. The inmates had to improve their forbearance and capacity to suffer and sacrifice. Kallenbach enjoyed gardening and others spent time in the healthy surroundings of the garden without much ailment. There were no doctors and nature care was experimented upon by the use of soil, water, food control or fasting.[42] The Ashramites were not expected to travel to the cities and they usually walked or travelled by third class in trains. It cultivated simple living and hard work. Walking was done by Gandhiji who used to get up at 2 am and travel on foot to Johannesburg and back, which was a walk of 21 miles. Most of the commodities were made available in the canteen and even hand machines were installed to grind flour and prepare bread.

People enjoyed this group life in which nothing was imposed against their will. It was a clean place to live. On return Gandhiji attempted to carry it to villages, cities and jails. This way of life transformed luxury loving individuals like Kallenbach into an expert professional who studied about snakes to rid the potato crops from the menace of reptiles. He used to argue with Gandhiji on religious matters. Geeta recitation and bhajan singing was a daily ritual. Everyone was free to worship the way he or she liked. When Gandhiji and Kolenbach saw the crude milching methods of milkmen, they stopped taking cow milk of the farm.

The second phase of South African Satyagrah came to an end in March 1911. But Gandhiji wanted to compensate Kallenbach for the investment he had made in Tolstoy Farm. He asked Magan Bhai to stay on the farm[43] and the Ashram style of Phoenix was repeated at Tolstoy Farm also. But by 1913 the Tolstoy Farm had to be closed and several disciples of Gandhiji shifted back to Phoenix. They played a significant role in the coming Satyagrah for which they received training at Natal. In fact Tolstoy experiment reformed the Phoenix initiative[44] and later on Gandhiji confessed that eight years of long political struggle was impossible without the rigorous training of Phoenix and Tolstoy Farm. The Tolstoy Farm symbolised unity, sacrifice and power.[45]

Informal Education

Gandhiji can be called a great educationist by virtue of his Tolstoy experiment. In his judgment, Ruskin, Emerson, Thoreau were great teachers of mankind. Emerson stressed on character and the spirit of man. Tolstoy has called physical labour the foundation of spiritual development and expression of faith. Ruskin deeply respected all kind of labour. Gandhiji had tremendous respect for these luminaries even before he crossed the shores of India. Voluntary labour, dignity of work and character building were the tenets of Gandhian ethics.[46] People may disagree with him but for Gandhiji, the moral and spiritual training was the essence of education.[47]

Tolstoy Farm was better organised than Phoenix Ashram to impart quality education to inmates. It was a laboratory for educational experiments. He himself has written 'The Tolstoy Farm was a family and I was the father figure for all the inmates.' Kallenbach and Pragji assisted Gandhiji but most of the training work in carpentry, smithry, cookery, etc. was done by these associates.[48]

In 1968 when Erickson visited Tolstoy Farm, she could not even discover its location. The Indian community there had purchased the original farm houses.[49] When Gandhiji finally left South Africa in 1914 his idea and experiences had been tested on the touchstone of time. His temperance gave him an image and Tolstoy Farm was the home of Satyagrahis who used to monitor Satyagrah from there. The criticism of modern western civilisation which Gandhiji had attempted in his *Hind Swaraj*, it was essentially based on his firsthand experiences at Phoenix and Tolstoy Farm.

Satyagrah Ashram (1915–33)

The people who came from Phoenix Settlement to Shanti Niketan of Rabindranath Tagore were subjected to different kinds of educational experiments by Gandhiji. This resulted in the idea of a new Ashram around Ahmedabad.[50] This Ashram was to be named as 'Satyagrah Ashram'. Its foundation was laid on 25 May 1915. Gandhiji felt that his birthplace Gujarat offered a better opportunity of service to the countrymen. Ahmedabad was a centre of knitting and weaving since early times. The generous Gujaratis came with handsome offers of investment. The original idea was to have the Ashram at Kochrab village near Ahmedabad. A Gujarati advocate from Ahmedabad offered his 'Residential Estate' to 25 inmates of Gandhiji for their social service activities. Gandhiji selected the name 'Sevashram' in preference to other names like Tapovan, Seva Mandir, etc. because the Ashram represented a lifestyle dear to his heart. Gandhiji drafted the code of conduct and discussed it with friends. In its constitution, he called it a 'community of religious people'.[51] By 'Dharma' he implied 'Truth' and 'Non-violence' because they were essential ingredients of Satyagrah.

The Organisation of the Ashram

The 'Satyagrah Ashram' at Kochrab had no servants. Vegetarian food, physical labour, social service, temperance, prayer, etc. were conformed to meticulously. The inmates had to take nine vows vis-á-vis:

(1) Truth
(2) Non-violence
(3) Temperance
(4) No-temptations
(5) No-stealing
(6) Non-possession
(7) Boycott of foreign goods
(8) Fearlessness
(9) Opposition to untouchability[52]

According to Gandhiji, they should not be viewed as expressions of Hindu Traditionalism.[53] He was a strong opponent of social evils like child marriage, devdasi system, and animal sacrifice. He promoted equal treatment to all including children. The allurements were denied to children but the minimum was assured and insured to everybody. When he opened the gates of Ashram to untouchables, a strong opposition greeted him.[54] But he stood calm like a rock and tried to win their hearts. Even his wife Kasturba did not agree with him. But he made everybody to see reason and the world could see the practice of an ideal by frail humans.

For five years it went on quietly, but when the opportunity came in 1920, the Ashramites proved true to their vows and performed the miracle on the basis of their training and experience.

Sabarmati Ashram

Unfortunately the plague epidemic attacked Kochrab and the lives of family members of the Ashram got endangered. This made Gandhiji and Panja Bhai Heerchand to think about shifting the Ashram to the bank of river Sabarmati which was 4 miles away from Kochrab. Gandhiji liked the location[55] and Magan Lal Gandhi was asked to build thatched houses, school, kitchen, library and weaving place in the area. The dwelling place for the Gandhi family was near the river. The inmates who came to live here were trained in various 'practices' of truth (*satya*), non-violence (*ahimsa*), student life (*brahamcharya*), non-stealing (*aasteya*), non-possessiveness (*aparigrah*) and physical labour. Gandhiji built this Ashram in view of the needs of the poor and the deprived sections of Indian society and showered his affection, compassion and parental love to those who came to live here.

The Ashram developed on ethos of social service. There were 150 inmates in the Ashram[56] to begin with and they hailed from different provinces professing various religions. 'Unity in diversity' of the Indian culture was the way which Gandhiji practised in the communal living of the Ashram.

Life in the Ashram commenced at 4 am and functioned like a clock till 9 pm when the bell rang to rest. Prayers from all religions, Bhajans, Ram Dhun and Geeta recitation were conducted from 4.20 to 5 am. In the evening 19 'Shlokes' from Geeta and Ram Dhun were sung by the group.[57] This was the medicine which kept the inmates healthy and happy. They sang while fasting and Gandhiji preferred to give up anything but the daily ritual of recitations which were more important than food. On 30 January 1948, he was slightly late for his prayers. If the assassin would have given him sometime he would have said 'God must punish me because I have been delinquent in my prayers.'

His concept of prayer was something nourishing for the soul. It cleanses the mind and removes its static state in sleep. It removes fatigue and offers an opportunity to repent for our mistakes. To remember God before retiring to sleep is the best medicine that heals the body and the soul.[58]

There were no servants in the Ashram and all inmates cooked their own food and cleaned toilet by rotation. Except for the sick there were no exceptions. Gandhiji himself participated in these activities. Training for jobs like knitting, weaving, spinning, dairy and tannery, etc. were provided by the inmates. There was no hierarchy and tasks were allotted without discrimination. They did not know each others' caste and shared pains and pleasures like a family.

The gates of the Ashram were open to Harijans. Dadu Bhai, Dani Babin and the infant Laxmi were admitted to the Ashram as the first Harijan family. The event stirred the town of Ahmedabad and the people withdrew their financial support for the Ashram. The inmates also got divided. Gandhiji advised restraint and patience to all. He planned to go to the Harijan colony. A philanthropist came and presented 13,000 rupees to Gandhiji as his token of repentance. Gradually the situation limped back to normal.

Gandhiji was a father figure to the Ashram family and resolved conflicts like a patriarch. He used to explain petty details about dietary habits for hours. He attended patients with affection and care. Even lepers were sponged by him. The patients explained details and he showed them the way. He served food like a mother and groomed everybody into a productive relationship. He practised the ideal of global family and all inmates were also open to share community living with each other.

'Spinning wheel' had a special functional role. In *Hind Swaraj* Gandhiji claimed that he can eradicate the poverty of India through this 'spinning wheel', which symbolised cottage industry. The road to freedom passes via stomach. The members of Ashram never had such an experience before. The 'Charkha' was brought from Kathiawad and Palanpur and the trainers also came from there. Magan Lal Gandhi learnt the art of weaving and the inmates resolved to wear khadi in place of manufactured best of the mills.

Gandhiji regarded Charkha as the tool of political, social and economic freedom although the appeal has not reached the masses till now. If the country would have accepted this wheel philosophy, the economy would not have languished in backwaters.

Imam Sahib, an old colleague from South Africa and his daughter Ameenabahan and son-in-law Gul Marsoot Quereshi came to Sabarmati and preached the relevance of khadi to Hindus, Muslims, Parasis and Christians alike. Muslim women used to observe 'Parda' and Charkha was a very safe way of earning a living for these women in veils. Most of the weavers were Muslims[59] who were poorer than the Hindu weavers.

Gandhiji developed the Ashram into a training institute of sorts. Each inmate was a trainee as well as a trainer. He knew the art and was willing to learn the new art.

Rules of the Ashram (Vrat)

The Ashram was a laboratory for experiments with truth and non-violence. The inmates were expected to observe the following rules – truth, non-violence, fearlessness, tolerance, indigenisation, non-possession, no-stealing, etc. Most of these are prescribed by Hindu scriptures. But some of them have been redefined by Gandhiji in his own way.

Truth

Truth is synonymous with God. It is not relative. No principle of life is complete without truth. Ideas, action and language need truth and politics is no exception. One has to suffer for truth, it gives tolerance and generosity.

Non-violence

Truth and non-violence are supplementary to each other. The two are inseparable. Abandonment of prejudice against inmates is non-violence. It is pure love.[60] It is not a religion of saints but of common man.[61]

Temperance

Implies love of God and search of truth. It controls senses. It is difficult but not impossible. It controls ideas and behaviour.

Control over Tongue

Temperance disciplines loose talk. To love God one should control his or her ideas along with the use of their tongues.[62] Denials and sacrifices are more decisive than enjoying.

No-stealing and Non-possession

Theft is not stealing other's property but acquiring unwanted things. If people give up amassing unwanted goods, poverty will disappear. Non-possession is not starvation but avoiding the avoidable.

Bread Labour

One should do physical labour to live. Mere mental labour is parasitism. Ruskin and Tolstoy shaped his ideas and he linked them with the precepts of the Geeta which says 'Eating without yagya (physical labour) is a theft.'

Fearlessness

This renders man to be strong and he cannot be polluted by temptations. Total fearlessness comes by staunch faith in God. It saves the society from being pushed into depredation.

Swadeshi

It represents that feeling which commits us to love the things nearer in preference to things remotely placed. One should follow the religion of his family but if it has evils, he should purify it. In politics also we should eradicate the evils that have entered the system. The same applies to economic living. The doctrine of Geeta too says that 'Swadharma' is great and 'Pardharma' has its pinpricks. In cultural affairs those who are geographically far away, cannot be imitated. Discover your values and do not imitate the west. He said, 'I do not want walls around my house ... the wind from all cultures should blow freely but they should not sweep me off my feet.'[63] He opposed the blind following of the west rather than western ideas.[64]

Elimination of Untouchability

Mahatma called untouchability a blot on the fair name of Hinduism. All people are children of God and discrimination is shame. The Ashram believed in fraternity and love to all. The Harijans lived with other inmates and toilet cleaning was a human job rather than Harijan livelihood. Nobody is low. It is a sin to orient people into this kind of mental slavery which is inhuman and barbaric. Even animals do not have it.

Tolerance

Co-existence is the law of life. People with differing styles must intermingle and learn to live and love one another. It is possible only when people have restraints, tolerance and flexibility of outlook.

Constructive Programmes of the Ashram

In addition to the rules for leadership training the Ashram was involved in the following programmes of social reconstruction:

1. Communal Harmony
2. Elimination of Untouchability
3. Prohibition
4. Khadi Promotion
5. Rural Development
6. Basic Education
7. Adult Education

Condition of Women

Women upliftment was an essential part of Gandhiji's constructive programme. Women played an equal role in the working of the Ashram.[65] Service of the lepers, propagation of Hindi, service of cows, cleanliness campaigns and economic self-sufficiency were some of the constructive programmes which Gandhiji launched from the Ashram.

At Sabarmati, old, children, foreigners, educationists, religious leaders, Sanskrit scholars, intellectuals and atheists all lived in harmony. These diversities after Gandhiji's exit created problems for Magan Lal Gandhi. Gandhiji solved these complaints and did not allow the grievances to get out.[66] Because of Gandhiji's absence from the Ashram, indiscipline began to grow. The loyalty of the inmates was too personal and therefore the substitutes in his absence had genuine difficulties. But then as it worked out the time healed and ironed out the differences.[67]

The Ashram shifted its emphasis on khadi from agriculture. It required trained and skilled weavers. Gandhiji saw the relevance of khadi in Indian economy[68] and established a chain of Khadi centres in the country on the pattern of Sabarmati. His followers cooperated and the number increased. Some of these Khadi Ashrams acquired name because of the dedication of Rajgopalachari at Puduplayam[69], Jagatram at Vedachi, Sardar Patel at Bardoli, Acharya Kriplani at Banaras and Vinoba Bhave at Vardha.[70] Gandhiji conceived Sabarmati as a coordinating agency and a medium of extension and publicity.[71] Here he felt that 'one step should be enough' for the long journey. His associates did not agree with him. Gandhiji was busy elsewhere all the time and even his nephew Prabhu Das felt that Sabarmati without Bapu was lifeless. India was different from South Africa because of caste behaviour and intolerant relations among various groups. Gandhiji worked hard but failed to establish harmony and parity. He used the good offices of Magan Lal Gandhi who was not keeping good health. In May 1925 when Gandhiji came to Sabarmati after his imprisonment of 22 months, he felt that the management of Ashram has dried up his spiritual resources and it was more difficult than the viceroyalty of India.[72] So he resolved to take one year leave from politics and constituted a committee of trustees to run the Ashram. The committee consisted of Jamnalal Bajaj, Rewa Shankar Javeri, Mahadev Desai, Imam Shahi, Bawazeer and Chagan Lal Gandhi. The workload took the life of Magan Lal and he passed away in April 1928. Gandhiji called it the loss of his right arm as he was a devoted and tested Satyahrahi of Gandhi's convictions.[73]

During the rest of the year Gandhiji discouraged foreigners to come to Ahmedabad. He performed the daily chores of weaving and prayers, etc. He lectured on the Geeta and edited *Navjeevan* and *Young India* from Sabarmati Ashram. He replied to letters and entertained guests. Chagan Lal Joshi took over the unfinished tasks of Magan Lal. The trustee committee always consulted Gandhiji although he was not its member. Gandhiji demonstrated that there can be power without being in formal seat of power.[74] He performed varied roles and accepted the good and weak points of his personality.[75]

The inmates from Europe obeyed his orders as religious responsibility. They called themselves his disciples.[76] Medaleen Slede, the daughter of an English Naval Officer came to the Ashram through Romen Rolland and Gandhiji gave her a new name 'Meera Ben'. Her simple ways and honest devotion earned her the image of a 'Meera'. She spoke Hindi, cleaned toilets and weaved all day long. Even Gandhiji felt embarrassed by her hard work. She was not happy with the management of Sabarmati, wrote long letters to Gandhiji and strived to run it on the lines of Vardha Ashram.[77]

Gandhiji discouraged long stays at the Ashram. But people did not listen and this lead to the violation of the disciplined life. There were complaints of corruption and conflicts. People could not dine together. He was of the opinion that 'the key to Swarajya is with women folk.' He handed over stores, relief work and Khadi training to women but they indulged in petty factionalism and frauds. The quarrels about and around women broke rules of the Ashram and Gandhiji's vows could not improve matters. People indulged in sex, accumulation of wealth[78] and the vow of celibacy became a joke not only with married couples but even unmarried ashramites. What Gandhiji wanted to have in society, he could not practise it in this Ashram. The inmates developed guilt complex. Gandhiji sat down with them and pussued them to resolve their problems.[79] He assigned all Ashram responsibilities to his third son Ramdas on the eve of his marriage. There were reports about suicides and even embezzlements of Ashram funds. He established separate houses for the teachers but the inmates opposed it. Gandhiji was very much pained on the failure of his experiment and he tried to convert the Ashram into an 'Industrial Centre' in 1928.[80] The functions had increased to the extent that the Ashram was given the shape of a township. He could not believe that his own nephew Chagan Lal embezzled ten thousand rupees. Gandhiji quietly owned his mistakes and deficiencies and resolved to close the Ashram and establish something new.[81]

Civil Disobedience Movement

Like Satyagrahas of South Africa, the participation of Sabarmati Ashram in civil disobedience movement of Gandhi earned such a fame that all criticism and stigma of past was just washed away. Earlier also the Sabarmati Satyagrahis participated in Champaran, Ahmedabad and Bardoli movements. But this time civil disobedience and salt satyagraha were totally under the stewardship of Mahatma Gandhi. The Dandi March commenced on 13 March 1930 with 78 Saryagrahis from Sabarmati and they all proved the worth of their salt. Gandhiji published their names in *Young India*. The march of 241 miles was completed in 24 days. Gandhiji prayed to God for the well-being of all.[82] The Satyagraha was a crowning glory of the Indian masses who showed temperance, discipline and persistence. The local institutions welcomed the Satyagrahis and Sarpanchas of 390 villages resigned and joined the march. The numbers swelled and the world looked at the Mahatma with expectation. Thousands of these people prepared salt and broke the law in official gaze. Foreign clothes were burnt. Liquor shops picketed and everybody including women braved lathis of atrocious policemen and suffered imprisonment.[83] Gandhiji was arrested. He called it the triumph of Sabarmati discipline and ideals. People demonstrated courage, valour and commitment to a cause.[84] The constructive programme became a reality.

Gandhiji was kept in Yarvada prison, which he called a temple and started writing letters to the inmates. In 1931 when released he went to Sabarmati and lived there. He was criticised for it.[85] The contribution of Ashram made history and Gandhiji got strengthened by the sacrifice. Other persons also returned to the Ashram after sometime and settled down there.[86] Later the 'Gandhi-Irwin Pact' and the Round Table Conference took away Gandhiji from among the Ashramites but he assured them to be mentally with them all the time.[87] On return from London on 28 December 1933 he was rearrested and put in Yarvada jail again. Premaben and Narain Das Gandhi managed the Ashram in his absence. Still Gandhiji was dissatisfied with all the three Ashrams he established. Meera Ben continued to complain about frauds, deceptions and criminal events. The anarchy reached to criminal proportions.[88] He was informed about the decline.[89] Two of his confident Satyagrahis were caught red handed in debauchery. Gandhiji called them ill and sent for medical treatment.[90] Jealousy, hostility shook everybody but Gandhiji struggled.[91] He undertook a fast for self-purification on 8 May 1933. The British government released all detenus when he decided to observe the fast.[92]

One more reason of closing the Sabarmati Ashram was British government's intention to seize the institution. The Ashram was not paying the taxes for last two years. The government had already usurped the property and Gandhiji was advised to close the Ashram. Thousands of Satyagrahis appreciated Gandhiji's predicament, but he advised the donors to refrain from charity. He handed over the productive units of the Ashram to Knitting-Weaving-Association and Cow Service Group. He advised the inmates to carry the message and ideals of the Ashram.[93] With the passage of time the Ashram was reduced to rabble and only a few Harijan families kept sticking to it. Today the Ashram has a green garden around and urbanisation has nibbled the land. It has converted the pulsating heart of a nation into a cemetery for pilgrimage.[94] Today it is a National Tourist Centre.

Constructive Programme

Gandhiji launched his Swadeshi programme to make the country self-sufficient in clothes. He established knitting centres and started protest movement against manufactured fabrics of Ahmedabad mills. Women and weaker sections joined the movement. He personally knit threads and felt that his dream of Hind Swaraj is coming out true.[95] He strived to capture sari market and made khadi the symbol of freedom. Even his critics agreed that the programme was a tremendous success. Several competitions and exhibitions were organised and national prizes were awarded. The All India Gau Samvardhan Sangh worked in the field of dairy products since 1927. Rural milkmen were trained. The allied industries were supported by manure and removal of untouchability programme got momentum.

Educational Programme

Gandhiji thought and worked for a scheme of Indian education to liberate the upper and middle class from the grips of western education. He thought of reforms started by Dayanand, Tagore, Gokhale and others. He invited Kaka Kalelkar for consultation.[96]

He conceived of a university for national service. His 'Phoenix' and 'Tolstoy Farm' experiments were in the background. He did not agree with Tagore on fundamentals. His Champaran Satyagrah started with this educational experiment. Ultimately, the experience was not positive in Gujarat Vidyapeeth. As the educated people did not respond enthusiastically. Knitting and weaving were not liked by anglicised Indians. The scheme of 'buniyadi talim' (basic education) ultimately got launched at Vardha Ashram.

Disintegration of the Ashram

Gandhiji treated his Ashrams as education-cum-training institutes for Satyagrahis. The Sabarmati was different from Phoenix and Tolstoy Farm. It was too rigid in matters of ideology and discipline. These experiments worked as long as Gandhiji was available to lead but he could not delegate the responsibility to any worthy successor. *Young India* and *Navjeevan* tarnished the image. The castist society could not rise up to the ideals of universalism. But still the role of Sabarmati inmates in making the cadres for future Satyagrahas was enormous. The success of Civil Disobedience Movement was largely because of these trained cadres of Satyagrahis. But the Ashram could not become self-sufficient and the donors could not keep them surviving. The contribution of Ashram for rural development can be called substantial and their failure was due to several reasons including their expansion.

Sevagram

The Ashram which was established by Ramneeklal Modi on 14 January 1921 was handed over to Vinoba Bhave by Mahatma Gandhi. He was called the spiritual successor of the Mahatma. Vinoba was an active member of Kochrab Ashram, was trained at Sabarmati and he established the Ashram at Sevagram to serve the rural folks.[97] Only basic functions were assigned to this Ashram.[98] It was kept non-political so that volunteers may learn management. This time the emphasis was on individual learning and local reforms. But then the Congress organisation showed little interest. Gandhiji was disappointed and kept searching for workers willing to serve the villagers.[99] Here he met Jamnalal Bajaj, an eminent industrialist from the Marwari community. He came out with massive financial support for the programmes. Bajaj joined 13 out of 20 social reform organisations. This could save Gandhiji's projects from political influence. He knew it that political movements cannot be sustained for long. So he established Harijan Sevak Sangh in 1933. But Harijan seva was different from Khadi project. The high caste Hindus opposed it tooth and nail because it recruited high caste Hindus for cleanliness and attempted to open school, temples and tanks for untouchables. Gandhiji stood like a rock and all protests ended with a whimper.

In 1934 while leaving the membership of the Congress Party Gandhiji established All Indian Village Industries Association. Though Pt. Nehru was personally unhappy but Gandhi's opposition was in principle, because Congress was not willing to accept his rural development programmes. Rural service and Harijan welfare was dear to him and he dedicated himself to this by leaving the Congress organisation. On closure of Sabarmati, several inmates shifted to Vardha with Vinoba Bhave. Gandhiji changed his plan and declared to avoid the earlier mistakes. The Gujarat Vidya Peeth launched its programme of adopting villages for rural literacy. The office of Rural Industries Association started functioning at Vardha and J.L. Bajaj took the responsibility of funding the project. To commemorate the memory of Magan Lal Gandhi, Jamana Lal Bajaj donated an orchard of 20 acres for forestry. Gandhiji named it as Maganbadi and handed over its administration to J.C. Kumarappa a noted economist with Gandhian persuasions. This Sevagram area was specially chosen by Madam Slade (Meera Ben). While at Maganbadi she used to cross a very dirty area called 'Sindi',[100] she along with Mahadev Desai, the new editor of *Harijan* took the cleanliness project[101] and sweeped roads every morning with other volunteers. The rural folks did not listen. Then Gandhiji went there in person and proposed to have earthen toilets with a facility to sell manure.[102] In 1935, Gandhiji had indifferent health and he decided to live in Sindi. It was a Mahar village. Untouchables and other people built a small cottage of bricks here for Meera Ben. She took water from a Mahar house and the other castes felt outraged. But like Gandhiji she took her cudgels and ultimately people could see reason in her sacrifices.[103]

Jamnalal Bajaj was not only an industrialist of Sevagram but was a Marathee revenue official receiving 75 percent of the income from the village. About 220 acres of land was with the Malgujari while the rest of 1550 acres was fragmented among small jamindars.[104] Meera Ben started living in a cow shed. Another volunteer named Gajanan worked with her in Sindi. She used to believe that village life is source of genuine beauty.[105] Meera felt unhappy when she was not allowed to see Gandhiji in the hospital under instruction from Jamnalal Bajaj. When she met Gandhiji he told her to continue her work in Sindi.[106] Gandhiji was shifted to Ahmedabad hospital and Meera Ben thought that the original relationship had dried up.[107] People did not like her possessiveness of Gandhiji. Though ill, he decided to live in Sevagram[108] against the wishes of Jamnalal Bajaj. Later on Bajaj relented and built a bamboo cottage to protect the ailing mentor from heat. On his return from Nandi hills he again took to develop Sevagram as an ideal village.[109] His charismatic personality inspired all, although he always wanted that work should go on without him. Soon Sevagram developed into a new Ashram. This time visitors were discouraged, yet people including Viceroy of India kept visiting him.[110] Sevagram road was full of mud till 1940.[111] Meera Ben had her hut one mile away in Bareda. Balwant Singh and Munna Lal Shah remained in the Ashram. The secretaries of Gandhiji, Mahadev Desai and Pyarelal had their cottages near Bapu Kuteer. A leprosy patient Parchure was nursed here by Gandhiji himself.[112] By 1942 the Ashram expanded and Jai Bhai Rusrumgi added one more house to the buildings. To quote J.C. Kumarappa 'Sevagram soon became the de facto capital of India.'[113] Sevagram had no post office and people were not used to do things for themselves. It annoyed him a great deal.[114] By 1936, he was 68 years old and felt too weak to travel. In Sabarmati Ashram he was the father figure but Sevagram made him a mother of the Ashram.[115] It was a new and different kind of experiment in community living.[116]

The castist behaviour of Ashramites was unbearable[117] and Gandhiji decided to close it.[118] Disease was the order of the day and all efforts by Sushila Nayar could not save it. The financial crunch killed the spirit of the inmates and the motely crowd converted it into a bunch of unemployed criminals following no rules. Khadi, Harijan welfare continued and Meera Ben helped in drafting the curricula of basic education with Zakir Hussain. The main points of the scheme were:

1. A seven year national education, free and compulsory for children.
2. Medium of instruction should be the mother tongue.
3. Education around physical and productive labour.
4. Paid teachers on roles.

The Zakir Hussain Committee submitted its report on 2 December 1937.[119] It was adopted by several institutions and governments in 1938. Sevagram launched the project as an alternative to expensive English medium education. But this also failed and became a dead letter after the advent of independence in 1947.

Sevagram demonstrated that nothing worked in Gandhian Ashrams unless Gandhiji monitored them in person. He was always there but he could not translate his ideas into action. He reiterated on doctrines of the Geeta and exhorted upon moral and spiritual qualities of men, but people worked only as a part of personal loyalty to the master.

Gandhiji did not like to leave Gandhism behind. He openly disclaimed it. His ideas were reflected in his lifestyle, but the followers did not follow it. Like idol worshipping the Gandhian ideals were ritually accepted and could not reach to the action philosophy of Geeta. His grandson Arun Gandhi comments that 'his Ashrams today are show pieces and they reflect nothing which can be called Gandhism.'[120]

It is true that the concept of human evolution in Gandhian thought is humanitarian and hence revolutionary. He wanted to release the full potential of man and experimented it in his Ashram living. His dream of a just society could not get fully materialised by eating vegetarian food or cherishing noble ideas.

The parts of Ahimsa gave him a code which everybody admired but did not follow. His South African experiment could not emancipate Indians and failed to unify the divided society. He accommodated all religions in his Hindu fold of beliefs and could make some important social reforms.

NOTES

1. Mark Thomson, *Gandhi and his Ashrams*, Popular, Bombay, 1993, p. 4.
2. The Therapist saints lived in Pinetown, Durban, 16 miles away on a hill, ibid., p. 38.
3. Gandhiji used the term 'Settlement' for 'Phoenix' and 'Tolstoy Farm' for farm and 'Ashram' for Sabarmati.
4. B. Sinha, *Bapu ka Ashram Parivar*, Navajivan, Ahmedabad, 1972, p. 5.
5. Ibid., pp. 5–8.
6. M.K.Gandhi, *Ashram Jeevan*, Navajivan, Ahmedabad, 1962
7. Ibid.
8. Gandhi was not happy with family guests in his home.
9. Andrews CF, 'Mr. Gandhi at Phoenix', *Modern Review*, Vol. XV, 5 May 1914, pp. 563–564.
10. M.K. Gandhi, *An Autobiography: The Story of My Experiments With Truth*, Jonathan Cape, London, 1966, pp. 1945–1946.
11. Ibid., p. 246.
12. Ibid., p. 246.
13. Ibid., pp. 246–247.
14. Thomson Mark, op. cit., pp. 47–48.
15. M.K. Gandhi, *An Autobiography: The Story of My Experiments With Truth*, p. 258.
16. Polak M.G., *Mr. Gandhi: The Man*, Vora and Company, Bombay, 1949, p. 67.

17. Albert West, 'In The Early Days with Gandhi', *Illustrated Weekly*, 31 October 1965, p. 252.
18. Ibid.
19. Letters to Magan Lal Gandhi, November–December 1909, *CWMG*, Vol. X, pp. 8187.
20. Ibid.
21. Ibid.
22. Prabhu Das Gandhi, *My Childhood with Gandhi*, Navajivan, Ahmedabad, 1957. p. 39.
23. Ibid., pp. 39–40.
24. A. West, op. cit., pp. 258–259.
25. M.K. Gandhi, op. cit., p. 259.
26. Ibid., pp. 255–256.
27. Ibid., pp. 183–185.
28. Robert Payne, *The Life and Death of Mahatma Gandhi*, Boddy Head, London, 1969
29. M.K. Gandhi, *An Autobiography: The Story of My Experiments With Truth*, p. 231.
30. Mark Thomson, op. cit., pp. 57–61.
31. Albert West, op. cit., pp. 1912.
32. Ibid.
33. Polak, op. cit., p. 41.
34. West, Albert, op. cit.
35. Ibid.
36. Mark Thomson, op. cit., pp. 63–70.
37. The second Satyagrah in Africa was against the Asiatic Registration Bill. M.K. Gandhi, *Dakshin Africa Men Satyagraha*, Navajivan, Ahmedabad, 1938, p. 188.
38. Kibbutz Fistini was a Jewish Settlement which believed in working on of the principles of Rural Economic System, Religious-brotherhood and Dignity of Labour.
39. E.H. Erikson, *Gandhi's Truth*, Faber and Faber, London, 1970, pp. l00–101.
40. *Harijan*, 29 June 1935.
41. These experiments are reflected in Civil Disobedient Movement.
42. These steps of 'Back to Nature' resulted in the establishment of Nature Cure Hospitals in India.
43. Letter to Magan Lal, 9 March 1911, op. cit., p. 446.
44. 'Golden Jubilee', *Indian Opinion*, Vol. 1914.
45. M.K. Gandhi, *Satyagrah in South Africa*, op. cit.

46. M.S. Patel, *The Educational Philosophy of Mahatma Gandhi*, Navajivan, Ahmedabad, 1953.
47. Polak, op. cit., pp. 53–54.
48. Mahatma Gandhi, *Hind Swaraj*, Navajivan, Ahmedabad 1938, pp. 15–22.
49. E.H. Erikson, op. cit.
50. Gandhiji requested Gokhale to assist him in the establishment of Ashram, but in vain.
51. The term 'Ashram' was used for the first time for the Sevashram.
52. Nanda, B.R., *Mahatma Gandhi*, Allen & Unwin, Bombay, 1965, p. 91.
53. An euthanasia case was given an injection of poison, for which Mahatmaji was criticized.
54. Dudabhai, Deenaben and Laxmi were a Harijan family and the Ashram confronted troubles because of their admission.
55. Sabarmati was the place where Mahrishi Dadhich donated his bones. It was on the bank of the river and near the jail premises.
56. The eminent people in the jail were Vinoba Bhave, Kaka Kalelkar, Appa Sahib, Ganga ben Vaidya, Prabhawati, Meeraben, Durga, Maniben, Magan Lal, Mahadev Bhai Desai, Ravi Shankar, Belaben, Ameenaben, Kallenbach, Chacha Khan, Babu Rajendra Prasad, Mahadev Desai, Mashruwala, Jamnalal Bajaj, Ramneek Lal, Hemprabha, Annasahib, Paramhans Vallabh, J.C. Kumarappa, Amrit Kaur, Akbar Bhai, Uma Babaji, Morris Friedmen, Jafar Hussain, Mahadevi, Hari Bhai and Khanda Amma.
57. Balwant Singh, op. cit., p. 101.
58. Ibid., pp. 101–102.
59. Ibid., p. 42.
60. *Young India*, 9 March 1920.
61. Ibid., 11 March 1920.
62. M.K. Gandhi, op. cit., p. 334.
63. Romain Rolland, *Mahatma Gandhi*, op. cit., p. 117.
64. *Young India*, 11 August 1927.
65. Women were regular and special members in the Ashram.
66. Gandhi to Magan Lal, 20 January 1918.
67. Address to Ashramites, 17 February 1919.
68. Gandhi to Magan Lal, 1 June 1919.
69. *The Hindu*, 23 March 1925.
70. Thomson, Mark, op. cit., p. 113.
71. *Navjeevan*, 27 December 1925.
72. Ibid., 15 February 1925.

73. *Navjeevan*, 29 April 1928; *Young India*, 26 April and 24 May 1928.
74. *Young India*, 8 November 1928.
75. *Navjeevan*, 1 November 1925.
76. Letters by Harvard, 29 November 1928 and by J.B. Spilman, 20 October 1926.
77. Mark Thomson, op. cit., pp. 119–120.
78. Ibid., p. 123.
79. Ibid., p. 124.
80. Ibid., pp. 125–127.
81. Letter to Chagan Lal Joshi, 6 May 1929.
82. Address to Satyagrahis, 11 March 1930.
83. Letter to Vasumati Pandit, 2 February 1931.
84. Letter to Gangaben Vadya, 2 February 1931.
85. *Bombay Chronicle*, 16 April 1931.
86. Letter to Chagan Lal Joshi, 15 April 193I.
87. Letter to Chagan Lal Joshi on 25 July 1931.
88. Letter by Meeraben to Gandhiji, 22 April 1933.
89. Letter to Naraindutt by Gandhiji, 17 March 1933.
90. Letter to Premben Kantak by Gandhiji, 26 March 1933.
91. Letter to Meeraben by Gandhiji, 24 Match 1933.
92. *Harijan*, 6 May 1933.
93. *Hindu*, 27 July 1933.
94. Mark Thomson, op. cit., pp. 137–138.
95. Letter to Magan Lal by Gandhiji, 1 June 1919.
96. Kalelkar, *Illustrated Weekly of India*, 31 May 1959.
97. The Village 'Segaon' was named as 'Sewagram'.
98. *Young India*, 17 November 1921.
99. The Civil Disobedience Movement was postponed on 7 May 1933 by Gandhiji.
100. Meeraben, *The Spirits of Pilgrimage*, Longman, London, 1962, p. 192.
101. *Harijan*, 15 March 1935.
102. Ibid.
103. *Harijan*, 22 March 1935.
104. *Harijan*, 1 February 1936.
105. *Harijan*, 28 December 1935.
106. *Bapu's Letters to Meera*, 1942–48, Navajivan, Ahmedabad, 1949.
107. Ibid.
108. *Bapu's Letters to Meera*, 1942–48, Navajivan, Ahmedabad, 1949, op. cit., p. 293.
109. See note no. 97.

110. Viceroy Lord Lothian proposed to cross this way to meet Gandhiji.
111. J.L. Bajaj made a bullock cart available to Jawaharlal Nehru to travel.
112. J.P. Narayan, op. cit., pp. 17–18.
113. R.V. Shrav, *Gandhiji Ashram and Other Institutions in Vardha,* Sevagram, 1969, p. 1.
114. *Harijan,* 5 September 1936.
115. Chimanlal Shah, Interview held at Sevagram, Vardha, 24 March 1981, See Mark, Thomson, op. cit., p.200.
116. Pyarelal, op. cit.
117. Letter of Gandhiji about Krishan Chandra, 22 March 1941.
118. Letter to Meeraben by Gandhiji, 13 May 1941.
119. *Harijan,* 30 October and 11 December 1937.
120. *Gandhi Marg,* Vol. IV, 2, 1960, p. 122.

3

The Social Philosophy of Gandhi

Born individual all men are 'social animals'. Some 2500 years ago Aristotle, the father of Political Science used this term. According to him human beings are the best beings among the living creatures, but when this man abandons law and justice, he becomes the worst of all animals. If someone can live without society or believes that he does not need help from others then he is either a beast or an angel.[1] The reality is that man has existence only in society. His programme and development indicate that his progress is just social. Man and society are so much interdependent that one without the other cannot survive and progress. Individual without society is like an animal and the vice versa makes the society meaningless and anarchic. To achieve a human goal in social order, a system of society is a condition precedent.[2] This system should be conducive to remove obstacles to growth and push him forward. Mahatma Gandhi called such a social system as 'Sarvodaya'.[3] He explains this system in great many details. It is a spiritual way to attain a spiritual goal. For this he discovered a technique of Satyagrah which implies self-suffering to make others happy. Truth and non-violence are the cardinal principles of this social order.

The essence of Gandhian thought in is Indian philosophy which influenced his thought process from the beginning to end. Still, he was not a blind supporter of Indian social system and Indian culture. He protested against the perversions and struggled quite hard to revise and change them more than any other thinker or activist.

Gandhiji believed that an ideal social system has to rest on equality, between man and man and between man and woman. No discrimination can be acceptable here. Such a society will comprise of people, who will be moral, patriotic and enlightened. This system will be free from all external impositions rooted in ignorance. It shall be free from communal rigidity, religious inquisitions and irrationality. People will have maximum opportunities to develop their personality. He attacked upon social evils and struggled to renovate the dilapidated structure of Indian society. Adopting the Indian tradition he accepted social change as a more relevant variable than political change. Although he seems obsessed with the idea of political freedom from the British, but this does not mean that he ignored the social reforms. He continued with both and struggled simultaneously to achieve the twin ends of his political career.

Relationship between Individual and Society

Individual is in the centre of Gandhian thought. He accepted individual as the end and did not envisage any conflict between individual and the society. Individual is above everything and his dignity and self-respect have to be protected at all costs. His entire philosophy rotates around individual liberty and individual development. He found it inevitable and found an organic link between the two. In fact, it is the same consciousness that manifests in both. It is not a comparative question who should precede whom. Individual consciousness if so facto generates social consciousness and as it grows the contradictions start disappearing.[4] This relationship between individual and the society is a relationship like that of a water drop and the ocean. Oceans are made of drops but every drop has its independent identity. Yet, the two are inseparable. We are like tiny drops in the vast ocean of divine humanity. The essence of his philosophy is that every living element has to be adjusted within totality which is the majesticity of the Divine Almighty.[5]

We are the part and parcel of this truth. Gandhiji asserted that this experience did not find any difference between the individual and the societal developments. Society depends upon its individual members. The saying goes that 'A chain is no longer stronger than its weakest link.'[6] Hence Gandhi defined 'social service' as individual freedom and individual liberty in his judgment was dedication to the society. To quote him in original 'Individual liberty makes the individual willfully dedicated to the society. If this is taken away, he will lose dignity and society will decline. Society can never be built on the negation of freedom of the individual. To deny freedom is against human nature. Just as a man cannot be converted into an animal by affixing horns and a tail similarly man does not stay human without mind and consciousness. Even the opponents of liberty demand liberty for their own selves.'[7] Hence 'dedication to society cannot be imposed from outside nor can it be the consequence of political obligation or social discipline. It is a spontaneous command of the inner being.'[8]

Gandhiji talked about the externals of the human body. But he did not remain confined to the present. He suggested how one can improve his nature and develop it in conformity to his capacity. His position was that even the loftiest individuals, as long as they stay in their physical self, they are incomplete. Every individual has high potential for growth, because all men are alike by nature. Nature apart, they have one soul, which renders the possibility of development, somewhat uniform. Human nature being unstable is capable of improvement. Thus unlike his western counterparts Gandhiji did not see any contradiction between individual and the society. He believed in the inevitable unity of the two. His democratic *Sarvodaya* in rural society is based on the association of village republics. Such a society will be constituted by voluntary cooperation. There will be peaceful coexistence. While living together, all the people will observe non-violence and self-abnegation. They will keep serving the society with simplicity and sacrifice. It will be a decentralised society, which shall voluntarily opt for equality. He aimed to establish a society where nobody will be poor or a beggar. Nobody will be high or low, nobody will be the master or a half fed servant. Everybody will earn his or her own bread with dignity and they will do bread labour with pride and happiness. Men and women will live in equality. Untouchability will be unheard of. All religions will be respected by all.'[9]

Gandhi came to the social stage in India, when the Hindu society was riddled with caste and sub-castes and the bright part of an Indian culture had been forgotten by Indians. So he had to revive and rebuild it. He himself had said 'Indian society has to be rebuilt on the principles of *Swadeshi*, non-violence and non-cooperation.'[10] These are the premises and he based the entire super structure on these foundations. His system is unique, because he saw all problems emanating from the fact that 'Man has lost his manhood.' Unlike Marx, Gandhi saw the individual in his uniqueness. Society is important but individuals are equally relevant.

Human Nature and its Goal

According to Mahatma Gandhi man is not only an organism of flesh and bones, but he is something more than their collection. He has a conscious spirit that guides and monitors this visible, invisible, conscious and unconscious human activity. This spirit is eternal, universal and self-propelling energy. It has been called a Divine particle. In other words this is a part of God and it inheres in human life. Gandhiji had said 'God, man and the lower species of this universe do not have any contradiction. It goes beyond time and space. All living beings are accommodated in this divine plan.'[11] Gandhi wrote 'I believe in the perfect unity of this universe. It leads me to the perfect unity of mankind.[12] There is no duality. All human beings, may all living beings, have an essential unity.'[13] It is true but man must accept this spirit. The Hindu philosophy, Vedas, Puranas and Upanishads establish this glory and greatness of the Atma. *Shvetashvatara* Upanishad mentions that Atman lives in the hearts of men like a thumb.[14] The *Brihadaranyaka* Upanishad believes that this unborn spirit of man is the heart of the sky, which manifests as science in the procreation of man.[15]

This Atman or spirit has a special place in Gandhian speculations. He considered the physical activities of man, but went beyond to discover the real nature or the self of the being. This spiritual realm took him to the power of Atman. His opinion was 'Atman survives after the destruction of the body. Hence a Satyagrahi should not be eager to win in one physical cycle of life. A timely truth may be opposed, but those who die in the pursuit of truth are visualising its triumph after their physical exit.'[16]

Gandhi's concept of Atman, made him believe in rebirth. He wrote 'I believe in rebirth as much as I believe in the existence of my body. Hence no human effort goes waste.[17] If you believe in rebirth then your dreams which may not actualise in few years will ultimately reach fruition in few centuries.[18] Human tendencies evolve. They are neither good nor bad. Human spirit is the symbol of Godly existence. All human beings combine good and evil components of nature. Nothing in this world is exclusive. Human beings are higher than lower species because of their rationality. This rationality enables man to make his self-evolution. People make wrong choices because evil is presented before them in glamorous contexts and contents. Man is endowed with this faculty to identify virtues for his or her self-development. Hence the effort to attain the ideal.'

The goal of human life in Gandhi's judgment was to strive for perfection. Life is inspiration and those who try to attain the self take it to its perfection.[19] He had on record said, 'whatever I want to achieve and for which I have been striving for last 30 years is self-development. It is an interaction with God. This salvation is the perfection and my existence is to accomplish it in my own way. All my articles and activities have this goal.[20] I am a humble researcher of truth. I wish to achieve *moksha* (liberation) in this life through self-development. My national service is my effort to get liberated. It is a part of my training.'[21]

He prescribed this to everybody because 'Atman' had a commonality among all. Its potentialities and probabilities are somewhat similar.[22] Thus Gandhi followed the line of Hindu fundamentalists, but there is one difference and contradiction. The Hindu thinkers want salvation and wish to be neutral. They want personal Moksha in their personal interest. Gandhi did not accept this. He had written, 'I cannot go to the cave to fulfill my goal. A cave dweller sage can make castles in the air. He may hover over the world but cannot attain peace. While a king Janak can do social good inside a palace.[23] So Gandhi is not a *Sanyasi* or a recluse. He is very much an activist searching his political and social truths. Those who search the truth in totality cannot isolate or alienate themselves from realities. My devotion to truth dragged me into this arena.'[24] In fact he saw politics as a natural and wicked reality. Its evils are to be combated, you cannot escape or flee.[25]

Concept of an Ideal Man

Gandhi's view about human nature and its goals can be discerned from various articles he authored and reactions he gave to events and incidents. From this his worldview or a concept of an ideal man can be pieced together for a clearer picture. It is repeatedly said that he was a researcher of truth and he regarded God as synonymous with truth. Hence an ideal human being has to be a Satyagarhi which implies that he or she should insist on truth. But Satyagrah is a hard way to live. It is difficult in practice. A Satyagrahi has to impose self-discipline, which is not mere mechanical. But self-discipline again has to be imbibed as a mechanical process. To love all, to avoid anger and shun prejudices as a matter of habit is not easy. Prayer, mediation and rigorous exercises can rebuild new human values. It is a foundational education in new outlook towards life.[26] Gandhi's ideal man can be called a non-violent Satyagrahi. Huxley calls him a detached person. Huxley says that such a man will be unattached to his bodily desires and cravings for power and pleasures. He will have to abandon lust for domination and ambitions. He will have to be careful about desires, anger, hatred and solitary virtues of his inner being. Money, name, fame and social prestige will have no meaning for him. He may even be uninterested in arts, science, speculations and public welfare.[27] His ideal individual is a *Vaishanav* (a tradition or a group of followers of lord Vishnu in Indian society) who recognises the pain of others and keeps serving others even while his self is in pain. While serving he does not feel arrogant. He who bows to everybody and does not detest anyone. His ideas, words and actions have to be pious. He views everybody without predilections. He has relinquished desire. Other women are like mothers for him. He never lies, does not beg, borrow or steal. Keeps himself away from lust and worldly pleasures. He has to be a committed *Varaigyi*. Rama is always on his tongue. His body is the abode of pious pilgrimage. He has conquered greed, lives a life without deceit. Sex and anger do not invade his physical being. Such a Vaishanav person is an ideal man of Gandhi's vision and conception.[28] The Satyagrahis of Gandhi's Ashram used to take seven vows. They would observe: (i) truth, (ii) non-violence, (iii) non- stealing, (iv) renunciation, (v) celibacy, (vi) fearlessness and (vii) tongue control in their daily life. This is quite difficult, but such people can be created by training. Gandhi himself struggled and tried to become this kind of an ideal individual. He was somewhat successful and that is why the entire country could wake up to a clarion call of this Mahatma.

Gandhiji accepted life in its totality. His belief was that unless people try, social reconstruction would seem like an impossibility. Keeping this configuration in mind he tried to build a social system with out the deficiencies of the old. A new code of conduct was a condition precedent.

Ethical Principles

Commenting on Gandhian Social Philosophy Romain Rolland has written 'To understand Gandhian activities one should start with the fact that it is like a huge mansion of two storeys. The lower storey has a base of religion and on this stands the edifice of political and social movements.'[29] He further adds 'The main part of this building is the basement which is well built and strong. The upper structure is different and constitutes the base of the temple.'[30]

But this religion of Gandhi has nothing to do with sectarian communalism. It implies a belief in the universal ethical order.[31] He did not follow the rituals of his religion, but practised them in a broad sense to get a glimpse of the Divinity that helps humans. It is impossible without a moral awareness. Hence religion and morality were synonyms for Gandhi.[32] True religion and ethics are inseparable. Religion is to ethics what a seed is to the soil.[33] Religion represents the best form of ethical life. Hence Gandhiji called his religion an ethical bunch of precepts. He further clarified it, 'As soon as we lose the ethical base, we cease to be religious. There is no religion that violates morality. For instance no cruel, false or unsocial man can ever claim that God was with him.'[34]

The moral discipline is a means of social reconstruction. These ethical principles determine the contours of non-violent social system. Man will have to follow these moral principles to be called as 'Human'. Those who do not want to discipline themselves ungrudgingly according to these principles, they are not the right kind of individuals.[35] Here this has to be remembered that Gandhi is in the company of illustrious international thinkers, who have trailed the civilisational process of humanism.

Dr Radhakrishnan has exhorted that the entire generation of human beings needs training in the ideals of love, peace and fraternity.[36] Gandhiji believed that by accepting ethics as a base of life one can attain the kingdom of God which is within. Man is born with Divine virtues of temperance, self-control, abnegation, truth searching and more so he is capable to rise and maximise his growth. To win one self, one does not require any high ideal. Man can do it by reconciling his ethical and physical development. Coordination of individual interests with social good is an inspiration, which makes human beings divine. Man feels at home in this divinity. It is the urge in human nature and it seeks to merge with divinity.[37]

Ethics is based on internal consent. According to Gandhiji people who are inspired by ethical values perform their duty willfully and spontaneously. External incentives are irrelevant. The inner being impels and compels. When physical allurements take over man degenerates into barbaric vulgarity. Even to work for family welfare ennobles the truth. When he extends this family to entire society and man of humanity, he marches ahead and develops. This process, if heightened or strengthened man can include animals or barbaric people in his family. Thus a person when inspired by morality, keeps expanding his moral and social universe almost in the same proportion.[38] His ethical principles do not need elaboration but should be examined in the context.

Non-violence

Non-violence has a special place in Gandhi's ethics. He called it the highest kind of religion and morality. It is not a creed of saints and sages. An ordinary person can be non-violent.[39] Non-violence is the creed of humans as violence is the way of functioning of the animals.[40] Gandhi viewed it as a spiritual principle of unity of exchange. What is good for an individual has to be useful for the entire humankind all over.[41] Explaining non-violence he calls it a way of the brave. The cowards cannot tread this path. These brave people can face death. He who opts for death with a sword in his hand is definitely a brave but he is decisively braver who embraces death without raising a finger.[42] Love is the only source by which a man attains God and truth. It can be called as an abstract form of non-violence. Love in human heart in a divine presence a godly quality without which man remains engaged in his petty and mortal deeds and does not realise his social responsibilities. Love and non-violence are superb and incomparable. Hence whatever is unattainable by power and reason, can easily be accomplished by love and non-violence.

Knowledge

Gandhiji accepted the discriminatory role of knowledge in his pursuit for morality. Ethics without knowledge may degenerate into blind imitation. Knowledge sharpens rationality and man can distinguish between selfishness and otherliness. Knowledge is needed for self-purification. But here too mere self-analysis cannot purify the soul. Man should think about himself in the way as others think about him. Thus an enlightened mind makes him moral. Actions compelled by external inevitabilities without knowledge are not moral. A moral act has to be a well thought out act which we perform as a duty. Actions which result from fear and force can never be ethical or moral.

Freedom of Conscience

Gandhiji strived to distinguish between destiny and freedom of conscience. He was of the view that free conscience is a human trait and human beings always strive to be free. He may succeed in this effort but mere rational effort does not explain the divine revelation. Fate and destiny have a role here in making man realise the limits of the unknowable. Indian philosophy believes in this fatalism and explains life in terms of collected actions (*sanchit karma*). So Gandhiji said that man can add his own capability to the *sanchit karma* and proceed towards Divinity. In this sense man can make his own destiny and revise the fate sealed by collected action of previous lives.

Power of Self

Power or will of the individual also gives a moral base to life. Gandhiji believed that power of the self could liberate human beings from the bonds of the body. If man starts behaving as per his soul force, he gets extra enthusiasm to serve humanity. The power of self motivates man to serve others. This self-force, when based on love and humility, transforms itself into a human force, which is more than the animal force. It represents humility, honesty without any ego. Gandhiji had called this true humility a continuous *Karmyog* (man of action), because it emanates from genuine social good. God works all the time, hence his devotees have to be one with Him. For this they will have to do continuous action or *Karma Sadhana*. It is hard but relaxing. Gandhiji found it as the key to perpetual peace and named it as *Aviram Karmayog*.[43]

Ideal Social System or *Sarvodaya*

The concept of *Sarvodaya* is an integral part of Gandhian Philosophy. His ideas centre around the emergence and evolution of society, which should focus on the emergence of all. Gandhiji has called it 'a life philosophy, a new way of life and an effort to build a new society.' It is an admirable human effort.[44] Because he believed in the unity and purity of ends and means, so his Sarvodaya presents an end as well as a means both to reach to the end. In his view this is the ultimate goal of every human society. It is everybody's duty to strive towards this end. He has written 'Sarvodaya might confront mountains, and rivers may obstruct the path. There can be petty irritants and obstacles but nobody can obstruct us to achieve this ultimate goal. Undaunted human will is quite capable to hit this target.'[45] When Gandhiji was contemplating about his concept of Sarvodaya the western world had a sway of utilitarian philosophy. The western thinkers argued that physical pleasure is the goal of life and man must strive to attain 'the greatest good of the greatest number.' The utilitarians believed that if minority suffers in the process of achieving the greatest good of the majority, then it is condonable. Gandhiji found it atrocious. He condemned the majority rule and advocated good of all, i.e. Sarvodaya in an ideal society. Some thinkers believe that Gandhiji mainly revised the Ruskinian concept of 'Unto this last' into his 'Sarvodaya'. But several Indian writers feel that he was modernising the ancient concept of village republics. The truth is close, but can be seen in the daily prayers of Indian sages and saints. The prayer is:

> सर्वे भवन्ति सुखिनः, सर्वे सन्तु निरामयाः।
> सर्वे भद्राणि पश्यन्तु, मा कश्चित् दुख भागभवेत्।।
>
> May all become happy; May all be free from illness; May all see what is auspicious; May no one suffer.

It was the seed, which sprouted in Gandhiji's mind after having read Ruskin. He condemned the utilitarian principle of the west and wrote, 'The Western civilisation is only one hundred years old. The western people have come to anarchy in such a small span of growth.' Gandhiji wanted that India should learn a lesson from the decline of the west. The westerners are power hungry and their colonialism proves that this lust and hunger has rendered their society hypocritical. The huge industrial complexes have devalued the moral life of the west. Gandhiji wanted to prevent this utilitarian wave in India because he knew that this philosophy of majoritarian good will enhance the suppression of the weak. The Englishmen justified Jalianwala Bagh massacre on utilitarian grounds. A Sarvodaya thinker can never justify it in the name of 'greatest good of the greatest number.' Gandhiji wrote 'A protagonist of non-violence can never agree with a majority principle. The good ceases to be good even if one person suffers violence. It is better to die for the ideal of 'good of all' rather than to save the majority to suffer violence. To die for the good of a minority is also desirable. It is good to die if some or even a tiny minority can live in peace. A Sarvodayi will like to die, so that others can live. One can do one's good by eliminating himself. The good of all is inclusive of majority good. Hence the paths of utilitarian and non-violent Sarvodayis may crisscross at various points. But then, there shall come a time, when their paths will depart for good and may take opposite directions. To stay within the bounds of reason, a rationalist will not sacrifice his own interest, while a non-violent Satyagrahi shall always be prepared to die for the good of others.'[46]

In Gandhiji's view 'no service is possible unless the self is not rooted in love and non-violence. True love is limitless like an ocean. It rises from the inner core of the heart like a tide and then spreads out, while ebbing to touch the worldly shores.'[47] Gandhiji stood for *Swarajya* based on truth and non-violence. He was opposed to huge machines and industries, so that good of all can be accomplished in a non-violent manner.[48] Sarvodaya wants to substitute 'Lokneeti' in place of 'Rajneeti'. Therefore discipline has to be accorded priority. Sarvodaya system can be called a march from government to self-discipline, from authority to liberty, from control to regulation and from rights to duties. Thus Sarvodaya is the root of all human development. Being an idealist thinker, Gandhiji talked of a social system which is moral, spiritual, political and economic in its renaissance. The Sarvodaya system will primarily be spiritual in nature and religion was going to be a decisive element to show the way. All people will respect moral and spiritual values. Truth and non-violence will determine the higher law of the land. It will control the social activities, shun discriminations and inequality of caste, religions, gender and race, etc. It will totally obliterate destructions. No group or clan will exploit the other and every individual will get due opportunities for his personal and social development. One of the characteristic features of this system will be the doctrine of non-stealing and non-possession, Aasteya and Aprigrah which spring from abnegation and hence austerity should rule the society and human behaviour.

Sarvodaya doctrine can be called a natural climax of Gandhian argument. The principle behind Sarvodaya is non-duality. It does not accept contradiction in the interests of groups, nations, individuals and seats. Whatever contradictions are apparent they are because of false presumptions and perverted values. If these assumptions can be changed a Sarvodaya society will emerge. It is not a rigid doctrine of finality. In fact it is an ideology of coordination and inclusiveness. Gandhiji believed that truth and non-violence can create a social order desirous to change the present set-up. When he had put a title to Ruskin's *Unto This Last* as Sarvodaya he was thinking that change can come if people become contented and satisfied. Commenting upon this the Hindi novelist Jainendra Kumar has said that calling 'Lastman's wish as Sarvodaya, Gandhiji made Ruskin's desire more comprehensive.' It no longer denotes a tendency but has become an abstract principle[49] – a society based on truth and non-violence and seeking welfare of all. If non-violence becomes the law of life then contradictions will dissolve and die out. Cooperation will follow. Gandhiji deduced three conclusions from this:

(i) Good of the individual is an integral part of social good.

(ii) A barber and an advocate should get somewhat equal remuneration for their works, because both have a right to livelihood.

(iii) A true life is the simple life of a farmer or a labourer.[50]

Gandhiji had confessed that the first principle was known to him earlier. About the second he was not clear while the third one he had never considered before. Ruskin's book made him realise that the first principle includes the remaining two. He dedicated himself for the realisation of all the three.[51]

The term Sarvodaya implies the emergence, the development and the progress of all. The welfare of all will follow because all will be tied by a bond of love without discrimination. Everybody irrespective of the fact whether he was a ruler or ruled, a Hindu or Muslim, touchable or untouchable, white or black, criminal or a saint, they will all be at par. The people and parties will not be allowed to exploit. All members of a Sarvodaya society will be equal. Everybody will be remunerated adequately for his labour security and guardianship of the weak will be the responsibility of the strong. Thus all will help all and do collective welfare.[52]

Sarvodaya is not only a philosophy or an outlook towards life, it is in fact a policy of human behaviour.[53] Dada Dharmadhikari has clarified it as 'a lifestyle of living together'. Life has to be lived with growth, progress and development. All are eligible and everybody is capable, hence Sarvodaya stands for 'developing together'.[54] But unlike the traditional concept of Udaya; Gandhi did not limit to economic affluence. It is the absence of discrimination, exploitation and partisan politics of sectarianism. Shrimannarayan corroborates this view. Gandhiji rejected the utilitarian ethics of larger members and the greatest good as the good of the best. He could never ignore the minority of ideas, interests and followers. Hence the doctrine has to be 'greatest good of everybody'.

Bhave, a dedicated disciple of Gandhi writes 'Integrity is the foundation of Sarvodaya. The term implies a revolution. After Gandhiji's assassination people wanted a Sarvodaya Samaj but they could not agree about its form and organisation. The term evoked debates but it could not get translated into any specific kind of social structure. The battle of words destroyed the concept. The debate eulogised it and simultaneously killed it as a practical way of life'. Vinoba Bhave regrets that it is a sublime philosophy of words which ultimately becomes loud sounding nothing. Everybody has to be developed. We will develop the weak, the strong, the small and the big. Some selected people have to be dethroned from the seats of money, power and honour. Naturally, it is an ideal, a big dream for petty human mortals.[55]

Bhave calls Sarvodaya an ideal of non-duality. Its watch word is coordination. The discriminatory human practices have to go or be minimised. Then alone, will all emerge and will become resurgent to usher in a Sarvodaya society. It can be called a religion, a pilgrimage, the followers can swim and sink in this pond. One can swim and teach others how to swim. It is not a new kind of religion, but has been designed as a religion of religions, wherein the good practices of all good religions can be collectivised and sublimated. This kind of life idea can never die because it is based on the unity of spirit. This *atmekya* (unity of spirit) is an Indian principle which our sages discovered and practised. It is a typical and fundamentally Indian thought and the edifice of Sarvodaya stands on this spiritual idea of human soul.[56] Social good, based on human love is the basis of Sarvodaya.[57] The bond of love, mutual trust and social unity provides the ecology for this human development.

According to Gandhiji this way of life is closer to rural people than people in the cities.[58] Hence he emphasised on smaller units. Sarvodaya society has no place for violence, competition and huge industrial complexes. The society has to have its roots in mutual love, non-violence and goodwill. Military activities, industrial intercourse and mass communication will have to be minimum. Foreign trade being a low priority industrial development shall not be encouraged. More production of medicines and pharmaceuticals will not be needed. Naturopathy will take care of diseases. It will end the greed of the medical community and wasteful expenditure on health. This system being ideal and human, will not need police, courts, doctors, military and inhuman means of production. Thus Sarvodaya society will create participation of all for the development of everybody.[59]

Thus most tenets of Sarvodaya are self-explanatory. They reject the basic assumption that human society is cooperation crossed by conflict. Individuals may have narrow ideas and goals but human collectivity must not envisage conflicts of interests.

Vinoba Bhave expanded the dimensions of Sarvodaya on a practical basis. He said, 'The *Nishkam* Karma of the Geeta, yoga and temperance can be inculcated through education. Joint family is Sarvodaya in practice. The rural communities can instill these virtues through socialisation.' He was of the view that family, village and group life can deepen social allegiance, strengthen feelings of abnegation, and sharing of ones income and profits with others. Accepting discipline is possible and cooperation is also a matter of human volition. If the group can assure a life of minimum wants, people will feel secure and cooperative. In early societies people had equality and belonging to society like family. Gandhiji took this clue from life in ancient India. He was sure that without love and high ethical ideals no society can be benefited by mere rhetorics.

So, Gandhiji asserted that if we are serious about the establishment of an ideal society then a transformation of man and his groups is a precondition. The Sarvodaya Samaj is a step in that direction.

Varnashram Dharma (Varna Vyavastha of Functional Equality)

Individual and society are organically linked like ocean and the drops of water. Both are made of similar components. Gandhiji struggled for the freedom of the individual but he never ignored the duties of the individual towards society. He has said 'I value freedom but I know for sure that man is a social animal. He has come to the present position only after having reconciled his individuality to social self. Individualism is an animal law of anarchy. We have learnt to walk on the middle path, which passes between social control and individual freedom.'[60] He found that 'Varnashram System' of India combines these two concepts of liberty and social duty. Notwithstanding some modifications, he found it as an ideal social system for human beings.

He has said, 'I believe that every individual comes to this world with particular characteristics unique to him or her. They have their limitations also which they may not overcome. The study of these limits has given us the doctrine of specialisation. These functional specialisations can avoid over competitions. The "varna" implies that people are different and have a variety of potentialities and limitation but they are not unequal. Discriminations are abominable. Everybody is entitled to the fruits of his or her own labour. Man should not be a burden on any other living being. Mankind has perverted this natural law of equality into a variety. My belief is that an ideal human society can be conceived or constituted when human beings can understand these mysteries of nature and enforce the law of equality in diversity.'[61]

Gandhiji has called *Varna Vyavastha* a scientific system of dividing the duties as per potentialities of the members of society. It should not create or establish inferiority and superiority among human being and groups.[62] The division of duties into four *Varnas* is not a mere formal principle but it represents a universal tendency among human beings in all cultures. He opined that when human beings live in groups they have to classify these social functions as:

1. Creation and extension of knowledge.
2. Use of force for collection, security.
3. Distribution of wealth and property.
4. Management of social services to keep the society moving.[63]

Gandhiji was a conservative thinker and stood up for this Varnashram Dharm. But then he never accepted the perverted situations of Hinduism. His Varna Vyavastha is basically Vedic[64] and is based on professional division of society. He defined Varnaashram as a duty, which is not mere hereditary. It has to be ethical. Man needs a livelihood but they are not hierarchical. If money comes in a profession additionally, then it should be dedicated for social welfare.[65]

Varnashram dharm indicates what should be the aim and mission of life. Man is not a mere economic creature, discovering new methods of livelihood and collecting more and more money. The mission of his life is to explore the secret of his birth. The traditional way was to follow the traditional path of professions available in the family. But there is no compulsion, no mandate and no helplessness.[66] Gandhiji never accepted that people cannot change their family vocations. To quote him 'There was a time when Brahmins were teachers but a Brahmin who refuses to do physical labour is a fool. Similarly a Rajput without intellectual equipment cannot lead a meaningful life. Sword warfare is not a vocation. A Vaish without moral consciousness will become a demon and his activities will be suicidal. The ethical side of Varna Vyavastha demands that a person should use his natural faculties for the social good of society. Individual excellence may be enhanced by heredity and experience but this excellence belongs to the society as a whole.

Varna Vyavastha does not disintegrate society, but can ensure love, cordiality and equality among varied professionals. It offers a scientific basis to organise the society. It can create an environment, conducive for the maximum development of all human beings. The Hindu Varna System makes 'birth' decisive, but varna is more of a karma. It is an oriented system rather than mere birth. A Brahmin's son if he does not display the virtues of an educated person, then mere birth does not earn Brahminhood. Such a person will fall from his varna and people born in a family of different varna will be regarded functionally members of that Varna, though they may not claim to be so by Birth.[67]

Thus Varna system in Gandhiji's judgment is a discipline which maintains social equilibrium and harmony. This force should be strengthened as advocated by Plato or Greek philosophers. It can reduce bitterness which an avoidable competition generates in society.[68] Materialism and ambitious living in social system need restraints. Gandhiji accepted it as a Hindu system of living. It was a religious way because a continuous search for truth brought Hindu society to this conclusion. He never liked to exclude any section, nor did he accept the wedge between Brahmins and Untouchables. While advocating Varna system

Gandhiji never tolerated any inequality in the varnas of caste hierarchy. He condemned quite vigorously the so called low position of Sudras. In his own words,

'Varna and Ashram are a great gift of Hinduism to our world. But then the Varna and Ashram of my dreams do not exist. Ashrams have finally been liquidated and Varnas have been perverted into privileged groups. Today Brahmins Kshtriyas and Vaishes take pride in being higher. This kind of Varna glory is anti religion. If Sudras are believed as low born and it is regarded as a part of religion, then it is not true to call a Varna as low. It is the negation of religion.'[69]

Gandhiji stood for the revival of Varna system. He had said that 'Today the Brahmins, Kshatriyas and Vaishes are surviving as names. Varna of my definition has become a crossword, a shankar creed. I will prefer that all Hindus willingly call themselves as "Sudras". To expose the truth of Brahmanical religion and to rehabilitate the varna system, it is the only way.'[70] All Sudras should discover their Varna as per their changing vocations. Gandhiji violently opposed the traditional Varna system of birth. In his words,

> It is the opposite of ethical principle that people can be low born or high born. It Brahmins feel that they are superior, then they are denying the very existence of God. There cannot be classes or castes, if all people are the children of one God.

In Vedas the various organs of the body have been compared with each other. The head, the arms, the feet are not comparable or superior. If comparisons are made the body will cease to exist. The Varna doctrine is based on perfect equality of human beings. All religions of the world accept this basic fact that all human beings are the children of God. The *Smritis* create the discrimination and hence their comments about Sudras should be discarded.[71]

Thus Gandhiji linked Varna Vyavastha with the Ashram Vyavastha. The Varna division is for specialisation and commitment to duty of the individual towards society as a whole. The four-fold division of four stages of life, vis-á-vis. *Brahmcharya* (student), *Grahasth* (house holder), *Vanprasth* (retired) and *Sanyas* (renunciation) is the essence of Ashram System. If Varna and Ashram can be combined then life can be meaningful. Gandhiji believed that the two systems of Varna and Ashram are mutually inter dependent and supplementary.[72]

System and Removal of Untouchability as a Caste

Gandhiji aimed to eliminate all those evils which afflicted Hindu society. He dedicated himself for the reconstruction of the nation through social reforms. He accepted society as an organic whole and refused to talk of particle reforms. Hence his reform movement became the part of independence campaigns. This struggle for self-governance was a process of self-purification and hence all social reforms against social evils was a part of freedom struggle. It looks paradoxical that Gandhiji was a bitter critic of Castism, wile he stood for the Varna Vyavastha, so notoriously linked with caste. He wrote, 'I have repeatedly said that I do not believe in the caste system, as it is practised today. It is a surplus organ of Hindu society and has been obstructing its societal progress. I do not accept discriminations among men and women. They are absolutely equal in every respect. Do not push this spiritual equality to physical equality. It is a mental state and requires some assertion to get recognised. Apparently, one finds people as high and low in the world. We have to create parity so that external discriminations do not pervert our view. It is a gross sin, if somebody regards himself superior to others. Castism is an evil to the extent it creates distinction of human worth. But I accept Varna Vyavastha because it is based on traditional patterns of vocations.' The four kinds of vocations are universally found all over the world. These vocations are (1) to educate society, (2) to protect the weak, (3) to produce from the land and do business and, (4) to serve through physical labour and skills. People all over have been working in these fields. The Hindus made it a part of their religion, while in other parts of the world these vocations and professions are practised by social regulations. We may not know the law of gravitation, but it affects us all. The scientists may interpret the law as they like. Similarly, Hinduism searched a law of social equilibrium and this Varna was an experiment. When Hinduism declined then the Varna got perverted into innumerable castes. This further polluted the society into relationships, forbidding marriages and social intercourse. It is called *roti beti vyavhari* (a marriage system in Indian society) which imposed restrictions. In fact religion has nothing to do with these prohibitions. Varna does not affect *roti beti* relations. Some of these prohibitions may be desirable in terms of health and character but a Brahmin and Shudra marriage does not interfere in the operation of Varna Dharma.[73] Caste system also had an economic justification in the early stage because traditional vocations added to skill and put a check on cut throat competitions. It was an insurance against poverty and pauperism. In fact, the advantages of trade unionism could be seen in the caste system of poor sections. Yet, it obstructed adventure and innovation. Some may argue that caste does not necessarily harm the skills and job excellence of the Varnas.

Historically speaking caste system in India can be called an experiment in the laboratory of society, which sought to test mutuality and adjustments in society. If we can rectify and reform it in the cruel competition and disintegrating society of our times it can prove to be a remedial gift of India to the world.[74] But its perverted form which creates high and low makes it a shame. It is a blot on the fair name of our culture. The Varna system makes us conscious about our duties and aims at universal good of the society as a whole. It landed dignity to every job and made all jobs available to all. A Brahmin and a scavenger are absolutely equal and when they discharge their functions with honest commitments they are fulfilling their spiritual duties and are socially eligible to earn a livelihood on equality basis.[75] That is why he was opposed to untouchability in Hindu society. It was a shame and it was abolished in the Ashrams which he established. It was one of the vows for the inmates that they will never practise untouchability in any form. Gandhiji believed that 'All human beings are animated by the same divine spark, hence nobody can be a born Untouchable. It is wrong and crime to believe that people are born in low status or are not worthy of being touchable.[76] It has nothing to do with Hindu religion. It is a disease and every Hindu should guard himself to prove his human character.[77] The Untouchables are brethren.' He proclaimed that 'removal of untouchability implies universal love and service to humanity. So it is inseparable from non-violence.[78] Without removal of untouchability, attainment of Swaraj is not only possible, but it is not worth it.[79] It is a sin, it manifests in false ego and in an abominable selfishness in its social form.[80] It kills human soul and make man low and animal like. It is not any kind of favour by the Savarnas towards Harijans, but it can be called a penance of purification, a kind of repentance of social sins committed by their forefathers.[81]

Gandhiji regarded untouchability an indelible blot on the fair name of Hinduism. He opposed the concept of dynastic continuity and preached tolerance and change of heart. Untouchability disintegrates society, demotivates national consciousness and hampers the evolution of a social order.

Gandhiji being sensitive, felt the pangs of discrimination in his early years. He has condemned it in harsh words. At places he compares its consequences with Ravan and even General Dyer. He renamed the Sudras as Harijan, which literally means the man of God. He called the practitioners of untouchability as 'Durjan'. He said '*Aachoot* (untouchables) in my view are the real men of God. We are the wicked Durjans because the Untouchables have made our clean living possible. He removed the excreta so that we enjoy the cleanliness. We should be grateful to them. Whatever evils or deficiencies these poor Untouchables have been made to suffer, it is our wickedness. We are responsible. We can be Harijans and this is possible only when we sincerely repent for the injustice that we have done to these pious people of God.'[82]

A high level of enlightenment can dispel this scourge of untouchability. Common man should be told and taught that the children of God cannot be unequal. He wished that the results of untouchability removal should be demonstrated in such a way that God cannot do this kind of naked injustice.[83] It is a terrible sin against God and our fellow men which has weakened the vitality of Hindu religion.[84] It has to be ended. Untouchability seen at birth is the denial of non-violence and negates the concept of *Sarvabhutatmabhav*. It renders millions of human beings as mere slaves. Hence Gandhi said publicly that if his rebirth comes at all he should be born in the house of an Untouchable, so that he may comprehend their predicaments and partake in their woes.

Gandhiji did not envisage anybody as low or high in the Varna Vyavastha. This division is based on duties, hence is functional. The two should not be mixed up. All human beings are equal and no caste and Varna can be called an Untouchable. The children of God have to have one common base. Gandhiji wanted to make the Savarnas (upper castes) understand that untouchability has neither any justification nor any proof of lowliness in birth. He wanted to arouse consciousness in Hindu society so that they feel like repenting for the injustice that they have been perpetrating upon the poor Harijans.

Gandhiji opposed to put a ban on temple entry of the untouchables. He organised the symbolic protests which deeply moved the millions. He sat on a fast unto death to open the gates of Gurujur temple for Harijans in Kerala. It included the Harijans into the fold of Hindu society and the temple entry programmes filled the Harijans with self-respect and self-confidence. Although the Harijans were not very enthusiastic to enter into temples, but Gandhiji believed that temples do play a role in the lives of common men in society.

The Vaikom Satyagraha in Travancore by Gandhiji was an epoch making event of South Indian history. Earlier a conference of Saitan Dharmis took a decision that if untouchables live in cleanliness and take a daily bath, then they can have a right to view the deity. Madan Mohan Malviya was the president of the conference. In 1924–25 Gandhiji asked Narayan Guru to lead the Vaikom Satyagraha which opened the prohibited gates for the untouchables.

On 10 August 1932 the English government proclaimed that there will be a separate electorate for the untouchable in the Act of 1935. Gandhiji resolved to sit on a fast unto death against this decision. Gandhiji declared that termination of untouchability is the mission of his life and if he has to terminate it for this end, he will feel privileged. The fast left a deep impression on both the communities. It pressured the government, but more so it gave a message to the Hindus, who took oaths to give up their evil practices.

In brief the leadership of Gandhi could bring the varied groups of Hindus together into one fold. He was a tremendous success and his movement bore fruits. He was a social reformer par excellence. He kept the basic unity of Indian society and arrested its sectarian tendencies. His success was incredible.

Place of Women in Society

Gandhi had a special consideration for all those groups which have been downtrodden and exploited and who were regarded as a second class citizen in society. Today the Indian constitution accords an equal status to women and all sorts of policies are being framed for the upliftment of women. They owe their origin to Gandhiji's basic assumption, 'Woman is a life consort of man and her intellectual prowess is in no way inferior to that of man. She has a right to participate in all activities which a man undertakes. Liberty and independence both belong to both the sexes. The man has a right to scale the heights of his masculine tendencies so has the woman the right to touch the heights of her domain. Women should be educated and then they should be given their rights. It is a wrong notion. The social system should accord parity to women, no matter whatever is their educational status. We suffer from a perverted mode whereby the most stupid and unworthy males are regarded as superior to women. They do not deserve to be respected. Our social movements do not attain spontaneous results because the women are backward. Naturally, our work does not reach to natural conclusions. Our situation is comparable to a miser businessman, who does not invest and prefers to suffer the loss.'[85]

At another place Gandhiji has written, 'Woman is such a partner of man who has equal potentialities and faculties. She has a right to be an equal participant even in the smallest activities of the male world. It implies equal amount of freedom also. In fact, in the areas of abnegation and courage she is superior to man. Physical power of animalism may be more in male personality but in ethical or moral prowess, she is several times stronger and superior to her male counterpart. She is more tolerant and she exhibits stronger traits of courage. No man can have his life or existence without her. If non-violence is the law of human existence, then woman alone will determine the future of mankind.'[86]

Gandhiji learnt from experience that women have played a more dynamic and decisive role in the development of human society and civilisation. She has been more active than man in improving and beautifying human life. It is no exaggeration to say that our Indian society has been unfair to women since early times. Vedic age may be an exception, but the later history did injustice to the gender as a whole. Consequently, evils like child marriage, veil over the face, illiteracy and numerous social atrocities took them over. Gandhiji compared it with untouchability and resolved to improve their lot with a series of social reforms. He even attacked Manu and did not agree with him, when he declared that woman should be protected by father, husband and son. The Indian society in ancient times called them life consort (*Sahdhamini*) and better half (*Ardhangini*) which indicates the cultural respect but the later history made them dependent on man.

Gandhiji opposed child marriage tooth and nail. He accepted the biological maturity of females at 15 years. He has said, 'If I had power or I would have been a law giver then I would have prohibited child marriage without any excuse. In fact the parents who arrange these child marriages are the enemies of their offspring. Such alliances make the children weak and dependent.[87] He held the Hindu widows in high esteem. They were the symbol of sacrifice and piousness. They should be venerable to all. Calling them inauspicious is a crime. They should be respectfully invited on auspicious occasions and bless the youngsters. The parents should make every effort to promote widow remarriage and make these women settled in their lives.

To call woman *abla* (अबला) or weak is a false ego of males. She is stronger as a wife and as a mother. The children are shaped by her and even husbands function the way she makes them work.[88] The unfathomable power woman has, has little to do with her physical and intellectual power. She is uniquely endowed with devotion, emotion and sacrifices. She is tender by nature and has religious orientations. Man loses his commitments and gets involved in frauds and falsehood. A female is always patient, tolerant and stable in treading the path of truth.[89] Hence women should work with men in public life. Prohibition, prostitute rehabilitation and several allied areas can be better managed by women.[90] Gandhiji trained female volunteers for Satyagrah because Satyagrahi required the qualities of temperance, sacrifice, tolerance and penance which women posses much more than their male counterparts.

While opposing *Sati* in highly condemnable terms Gandhiji maintained 'to teach a woman to burn herself on the pyre of the dead husband is an abominable barbarity. It denies human dignity. This social ritual takes the concepts of fidelity and loyalty to inhuman limits. A devoted wife should continue and complete the life mission of her husband. She can imbibe the virtues of her deceased husband and she can exhibit this while alive. Loyalty to husband and dignity of one's person can both be nurtured by loving the society and its creator – the Almighty.'[91]

Thus Gandhiji was a great advocate of female liberty, women's education and their equal status in society. He said 'Education, spirit of sacrifice and faith in one's identity are the factors that ensure female liberty.[92] It is an incontrovertible fact that millions of women participated in the freedom struggle. It was a moral phenomenon, unique in Indian history. This new innovation gave confidence to women folk and they became worthy of the new role, which freedom struggle assigned to them. Gandhiji's efforts brought a social change and women became equal to men although the legal recognition came much later in the constitution.

In fact Gandhiji, like Plato wanted an ideal social system which can be established in a living society. For this he conceived of a Ram Rajya, based on truth and non-violence. He cherished fraternity (*Sadbhav*) of human kind. Followers of all faiths can accept it, without reservations. That is why the great historian Toynbee called him 'The greatest living legend of 20th century'. It was a time when the world was disintegrating, Gandhiji suggested a social system, which is capable to resolve the conflicts by taking all human beings together in the transitional times of growth of our civilisation. Truth, non-violence, love and high ethical ideals can be practised and through this experiment liberty, equality and justice can also be attained and maximised. The Gandhian message is that 'The future of humanity lies in non-violence only.'

Notes

1. Aristotle, introductory passage in *Politics*.
2. Hobhouse L.T., *Social Evolution and Political Theory*, The Columbia University Press, New York, 1911, p. 30.
3. *Sarvodaya Samaj* in Sanskrit language means a 'society that aims for the welfare of all'.
4. *Collected Works* of *Mahatma Gandhi*, Vol. 36, Publication Division, Government of India, New Delhi, p. 102.
5. Ibid., Vol. 6, p. 109.
6. Ibid., Vol. 34, p. 505.
7. *Harijan*, 1 February 1942.
8. *Harijan*, 28 September 1947.
9. *Harijan Sevak*, 18 January 1948, p. 466.
10. *Young India*, 14 October 1921.
11. G.N. Dhawan, *The Political Philosophy of Mahatma Gandhi*, Popular Book Depot, Bombay, 1946, p. 40.
12. *Young India*, Vol. 2, p. 79.
13. *Young India*, Vol. 2, p. 421.
14. *Shvetashvatar* Upanishad, p. 3, 7, 13.
15. *Brihadaranyako* Upanishad, p. 4, 22.
16. *Speeches & Writings of M.K. Gandhi*, Madras, 1934, p. 504.
17. *Young India*, Vol. 2, p. 1204.
18. Romain Rolland, *Gandhi*, p. 45.

19. *Harijan,* 22 June 1935.
20. M.K. Gandhi, *An Autobiography: The Story of My Experiments With Truth,* Navajivan, Ahmedabad, 1940, p. 4.
21. *Young India,* 3 April 1924.
22. *Harijan,* 18 May 1940, p. 254.
23. *Young India,* 3 April 1924.
24. M.K. Gandhi, *An Autobiography: The Story of My Experiments With Truth,* Navajivan, Ahmedabad, 1940, op. cit., Vol. 2, p. 591.
25. *Harijan,* 24 December 1938, p. 393.
26. See Huxley, A., *Ends and Means,* Chatto & Windus, London, 1938, p. 4.
27. Ibid., pp. 4–5.
28. Bhajan of Narsi Mehta.
29. Romain Rolland, *Gandhi,* op. cit., pp. 24–45.
30. Ibid.
31. *Harijan,* 10 February 1940.
32. *Young India,* 14 October 1926.
33. Mahatma Gandhi, *Ethical Religion,* p. 51.
34. *Young India,* 24 November 1921, p. 385.
35. Mahatma Gandhi, *Ethical Religion* op. cit., p. 36.
36. Dr Radhakrishanan, *Religion and Society,* Allen & Unwin Ltd., London, 1947, p. 17.
37. M.K. Gandhi, *Geeta the Mother,* p. 65.
38. Gandhi, *Ethical Religion,* op. cit., p. 58.
39. *Young India,* 11 August 1920.
40. Ibid.
41. *Harijan,* 12 November 1938, p. 329.
42. *Young India,* 11 August 1928.
43. D.M. Dutta, *M. Gandhi Ka Darshan,* p. 64.
44. Ramji Singh, *Gandhi Darshan Ki Meemansa,* Patna, 1973, p. 41.
45. M.K. Gandhi, *Autobiography,* op. cit., 1987.
46. Hindi Navjeevan, 9 December 1926.
47. *Young India,* 20 September 1928.
48. M.K. Gandhi, *The Collected Works,* Vol. 8, pp. 239 and 375.
49. Jainendra Kumar, *Sarvodaya Arthashastra,* p. 58.
50. Gandhi, *An Autobiography: The Story of My Experiments With Truth,* Navajivan, Ahmedabad, 1940, op. cit.
51. Ibid., p. 207.
52. B. Kumarrappa, *Sarvodaya,* Navajivan, Ahmedabad, 1956, p. 1.
53. Ibid., pp. 5–9.
54. Dada Dharmadhikari, *Sarvodaya Sarvasevasangha,* Varanasi, p. 16.
55. Vinoba Bhave, *Sarvodaya Vichar aur Samaj Shastra,* p. 57.
56. Vinoba Bhave, *Bhoodan Ganga,* Varanasi, p. 174.

57. J.P. Narayan, *A. Picture of Sarvodaya Social Order*, Seva Sangh, Tanjor, 1955, p. 43.
58. V.P. Varma, *The Political Philosophy of Mahatma Gandhi and Sarvodaya*, L.N. Agrawal, Agra, 1965, p. 370.
59. V.P. Varma, *Adhunik Bhartiya Rajneetic Chintan*, L.N. Agrawal, Agra, 1989, pp. 573–582.
60. *Harijan*, 27 May 1939, p. 144.
61. *The Modern Review*, October, 1935, p. 413.
62. *Narjeevan*, 4 April 1925.
63. *Dakshin*, 4 March 1923.
64. *Young India*, 6 October 1921.
65. *Harijan*, 28 September 1934, p. 260.
66. *Young India*, 27 October 1927.
67. *Harijan*, 28 September 1934, p. 260.
68. Gandhi, *Mere Sapanon Ka Bharat*, Sarve Seva Sangha Prakashan, Varanasi, 1989, pp. 118–21.
69. *Collected Works of M. Gandhi*, Vol. 80, pp. 222–24.
70. *Harijan*, 25 March 1933.
71. *Harijan*, 29 September 1934.
72. *Harijan*, 28 September 1934.
73. Gandhi, *Mere Sapenon Ka Bharat*, Navajivan Prakashan Mandir, Ahmedabad, 1999, p. 263.
74. *Young India*, 5 January 1921.
75. *Harijan*, 18 July 1936.
76. Mahatma Gandhi, From Yarvada Prison, Ahmadabad, 1945, p. 31.
77. Ibid., p. 32.
78. Ibid., p. 33.
79. *Amrit Bazar Patrika*, 2 May 1955.
80. *Collected works of M. Gandhi*, op. cit., p. 508.
81. *Harijan*, 18 August 1940.
82. *Young India*, 6 August 1931.
83. Ibid.
84. *Harijan*, 11 February 1933.
85. *Speeches and Writings of M. Gandhi*, p. 425.
86. Ibid.
87. *Navjeevan*, 25 March 1928.
88. K.G. Mashroowala, *Gandhi Vichar Dohan*, Navajivan Prakashan, Ahmedabad, 1964.
89. Ibid., p. 43.
90. Ibid., p. 43.
91. A Letter to Prema Ben Kantak, 23 June 1926.
92. *Navjeevan*, 21 April 1921.

4

The Economic Philosophy of Gandhi

All human activities in recent human history have relatively been more economic, as compared to earlier years. The economic forces have been the most potential pressures changing the course of history. Marshal explaining this fact writes, 'Religious reasons apart, the physical means or forces constitute the character of man. The world history is a product of two major agencies, namely religion and economic system. In between there may be military situations or emergence of art and culture, but religious and economic factors have never been secondary. In fact, other factors have also cumulatively contributed to the primacy of religion and/or economics.'[1]

Comparatively speaking religious urges have been more intense than economic compulsions. They touch the very core of every human enterprise.[2]

All human beings need money to fulfill their physical wants. The spiritual needs may be fulfilled by religion, but his or her survival needs are basic and primary. If these physical needs remain unfulfilled, then it does not portend a good social life. History testifies the fact that whenever the wrong economic policies adversely affected the physical well-being of the people, the people have risen in revolt against the state. Hence it is desirable that the economic system should be conducive to fulfill the minimum primary needs and then an over all development of society as a whole. It shall result in search of socio-economic equality which all philosophers and thinkers seek to conceive and envisage. When Gandhiji arrived on the national scene, the economic situation in India was a matter of grave concern and shame. Poverty, unemployment, hunger and illiteracy were the order of the day. The economic system was absolutely incapable to size up the problems of the country. Naturally, Gandhiji had to present a total economic philosophy in all its manifestations and nuances. It had to be based on humanistic and spiritual ideas as in other fields.

According to Gandhiji the economic system in India albeit in the world should be such in which no human being should sleep without food and raiment. His philosophy was that all walks of life should be free from fear, injustice and absolutist arbitrariness. Gandhiji had his doubts about the efficacy of materialistic bases of Western philosophy in economic and industrial fields. So he examined his religious principles in terms of their application in economic realm. But then, this is to be remembered that modern state cannot be divided or viewed segmentally. The varied facts interact and economic ideas cannot be advanced in isolation.[3] So his economic thought became comprehensive and integrative.

The Gandhian economics starts from the promise that man, not money is the centre of economic universe. The ancient Indian thought believed that money is a means to human growth. Hence economics or money has to be linked with ethics and religion.

He believed that economic affairs which harm the individual cannot be beneficial for the society. Economic activities that harm the moral development of individual are sinful and unworthy of human pursuits. Similarly, any economics which allows a country to exploit and plunder other countries is equally immoral. People who have produced goods with hard labour should not be exploited by the market system of industrial powers.[4] An economics, which ignores human feelings is like a puppet of wax, which looks alive, but lacks life itself. A deeper analysis will prove that the new economic laws are wasteful and unworkable. Those who accept them as axiomatic truths are bound to perish.[5]

While expanding his economic ideas in greater details, Gandhiji wrote as early as 1937:

> True economics cannot be in contrast to high ethical principles. Similarly, true ethics should ensure a good economics also. The economic system which worships at the altar of money and earns money by exploiting the weak, is absolutely false and is dangerous and risky. It shall destroy people. True economics must stand for social justice. It must strive for the welfare of all including the weaker sections. Such an economics is essential to ensure a good life.

Unlike modern economists, Gandhiji did not like the professional solutions of the social problems in life. His purpose was the total and complete development of man in all respects. N.K. Bose while commenting upon Gandhian economic way writes 'The evaluation of Gandhian economics will depend upon how does it influence the quality of life of the individual. If the law of non-violence is taken to the economic field then ethics enters ipso facto. Even international trade has to be ethical.'[6] Gandhiji openly advocated the rehabilitation of religious and ethical values so that economic justice may be ensured to all. While replying to a question of Rabindranath Thakur, Gandhi wrote 'Even if God has to confront the hungry then bread alone will be his morality.[7] All poets look to the sky when their belly is full. People do, think and work better when their economic survival is assured or they have finished their daily meal.'[8]

Gandhiji was opposed to the capitalistic monopoly of production, system of distribution, profit motto and competitive economy. He wanted to solve the economic problems by non-economic moral means. He did not want the farmers to give up mechanised farming and its profit. He did not oppose large scale production but he maintained that what can be produced in the villages should not be imported from the cities. The rural centres for urban sales should vitalise village economy rather than the vice verse.[9] He wanted to respect ethical values of society. He preferred an economy which was not based on the principles of profit and competition. The economy should aim at ethical development of men and society. That is why he advocated a Varnashrama economy, an economic system without exploitation and competition. Economic reconstruction needs a base. Here too truth and non-violence can be accepted along with non-stealing, renunciation, love for the poor and emphasis on physical labour and trusteeship. Stressing upon swadeshi he talked of Charkha or spinning wheel which could change the picture of seven lakh villages. He made it a part of his constructive programme and thereby inaugurated a silent revolution by taking the wheel to all the rural hutments. His aim was to establish an economic system which could ensure welfare for all.

Gandhiji had written, 'The Swarajya of my dreams will be the self-government of the poor. Whatever facilities the rich and the rulers enjoy should also be accessible to the common poor. Distinctions have to be minimised and poor people should not aspire to possess palaces. Happiness does not need riches. In fact to live in palaces is highly frightening. But the common minimum needs have to be satisfied. In this respect they are absolutely equal. I am convinced that our Swarajya shall never be complete unless this basic minimum is guaranteed to all.'[10] Complete independence implies that it shall be the same for farmers, feudal lords, Hindus, Muslims, Jews and the Sikhs. No discriminations can be acceptable. Religion, caste and class will have no relevance.[11] Thus Gandhian economic system stands for economic equality with minimum disparities. Minimum need is the criteria and a consensus can be created around wealth and income. So his economic ideas deserve a special mention.

The Doctrine of Trusteeship

To establish social and economic justice all human beings should be regarded as 'equal'. Professionally there should be no hierarchy. Untouchability should be banned and minimum human needs should be fulfilled without much struggle. Keeping this in mind Gandhiji propounded his doctrine of trusteeship in contrast to ownership while he was a student of law in UK. He hit against this idea and the Geeta strengthened him to develop it in detail. He has written in his autobiography:

> The Geeta has become my teacher and a guide. It is like a religious encyclopaedia to me. Non-possessiveness and equanimity have impressed me as concepts and the term 'trusteeship' became the area of exploration. When I had respect for law then I started seeing ethics in jury's prudence. A trustee might have million rupees but he does not own a single penny. The Geeta taught me to act like a trustee in matters of ownership of property.

While explaining the doctrine of trusteeship Gandhiji on record said 'I feel that all of us are a sort of thieves. If I have or I borrow something which I do not need for immediate use, then I am stealing something which does not belong to me. The fundamental law of nature is that it produces only as much as humans need. If people take only as much as they need, not as much as they greed, then nobody will be hungry. I am not a socialist and I do not want to snatch the property of those who have accumulated wealth over generations. If I do this I will cease to be non-violent. If people have more wealth than what I have, then let them have it. I must shape my life on the principle that I should own nothing which I do not need. In India there are millions of people who do not have two square meals. They eat only once and that too the bare bread. These people have a right over all that which is surplus. Unless these people have enough to fulfil their bare needs, we have no moral right to enjoy whatever is in excess. We have a higher level of understanding. So we should follow the law of need and accept the law of voluntary renunciation. It shall facilitate the operation of law of need for the deprived.[12]

For this a trusteeship doctrine has to be adopted by the society. Explaining this Gandhiji said that all land belongs to God. 'सबै भूमि गोपाल की' (Gopal is the owner of the land).[13] If someone has surplus land it is the Divine trust which he is looking after. He cannot spend this wealth for his personal pleasure. He can spend it for the welfare of society as a divine representative of the trust. Exploitation is a product of concentration of surplus property or wealth. People abuse this wealth for personal luxuries. Trusteeship as a theory suggests how to use this surplus wealth for social good. Those who do not accept this, use this wealth for human exploitation in society. Gandhiji propagated trusteeship as a basic principle for the organisation of economic order in society. It is based on non-violence, self-control and equity. Gandhiji regarded 'non-violence' as the key for economic equality because it establishes autonomy of units, engaged in production, self-reliance and social service. Trusteeship implies equal distribution and non-violence which are interdependent. It is not exclusive or one sided. The mutuality is the base and it asks for mutual confidence. Each for all implies that everybody should protect each others interest and have faith in mutual help and dependence.[14]

Gandhian trusteeship starts from the assumption that all members of society are not equal. Some are more able and richer than others. Most of the people are weak and have less ability. The former use their skills and reason to amass wealth. No society can stop it. If private property is not allowed the society will be deprived of their talent and contribution. But if the state uses forces to equalise wealth it will lead to violence. A violent state is a contradiction in terms hence Gandhiji talked about trusteeship which can equalise the distribution of property or wealth without using violence.

Gandhiji unhesitatingly said 'I am of the opinion that not only the rich, but all human beings rarely care how do they earn wealth. This question of means is not irrelevant. However low or immoral a man or woman might be he has to be improved non-violently and with utmost sympathy. We should employ the divine element and make him or her divinely. If everybody uses one's potential for total good in place of personal selfishness, it will positively benefit the society. That society, where people do not use their facilities at all is a dead one and its stagnant groups will destroy themselves by mutual warfare.

So in my opinion the rich people who honestly earn millions, they should surrender their entire wealth voluntarily for the total good of the entire society. 'तेन तक्तेन भूंजीया' (enjoy with a sense of tyaga or renunciation) is a simple mantra which has extra ordinary meaning in life. In the present system nobody bothers about the neighbour and he or she lives for self only. Goodness of all requires a collective approach and it is the only way to welfare.'[15]

Naturally, the question arises how do you proceed to practise this trusteeship. Gandhiji believed that man is an improvable being. He owns the property with responsibility. By nature human beings are good and have ennobling tendencies. He has a divine spark which can be activised or energised. People start realising that human energy can be diverted from selfishness to otherliness. Then it will add to popular good and social welfare. Naturally nothing can be more tragic than the fact that positive human energy is not canalised appropriately, the societies tend to develop suicidal tendencies. Rich people should think that by spending the surplus wealth and energy for social good they are not doing any favour to society. But then, it is a duty which they should fulfil as a compelling obligation. Transfership principle is that mutual service and reciprocity of sacrifice can enable all human beings to scale the impossible. This is the message of the Geeta which states that keep the deities happy by serving them. 'If you serve, you will be a deity or a God by your noble action. You serve the society and society will serve you in return.' Gandhiji propounded this doctrine as trusteeship in 1903 in South Africa. The doctrine has its origin in Ishopanishad. The first couplet says 'Whatever you see in this life is a gift of God. So you enjoy or renounce in the name of God and do not covet other's riches.'

ईशावास्यमिदंसं यत्किंचित् जगत्यां जगत्।
तेन त्वतेन भुज्जीथा मा गृध: स्वधनम्।।

Everything belongs to God. Man has no right on this divine property. He may manage this estate on behalf of God as his representative. This principle explains the equitable distribution of divine wealth, capital and labour. It is ethical. It controls the wealth and property of the rich and simultaneously it decentralises economic power in a more equitable way.[16]

If a capitalist does not accept trusteeship then public opinion should be used to pressurise him. But this will require an organisation. Non-violent non-cooperation is the only power of society. If people become conscious and educated in non-violence and non-cooperation, then trusteeship will automatically follow.[17] To establish trusteeship system, Gandhiji suggested a six point program:

1. Trusteeship transforms the present capitalist system into a social system. It provides an opportunity to reform capitalism by way of voluntary change.
2. It envisages the termination of the personal right to property.
3. It does not separate the rights to ownership and use of property from its regulation.
4. It does not permit the individual to accumulate private property for personal ends against the collective good of society.
5. It delimits the minimum income or remuneration for labour and the maximum income or remuneration for labour along with maximum amount for his earning.
6. Social control over production in the economy will depend upon social needs rather than on personal gains or desires.[18] Trusteeship according to Gandhiji was not mere opportunism. It was a doctrine of ethical non-violence. Gandhiji was frequently asked about its meaningfulness. Answering to their queries he said 'You may say that trusteeship is a theoretical jurisprudence. It will be difficult to practise in social order. Still if people keep practising it and give continuous thought to the idea then love will emerge as a regulating power in human society. It shall become more and more decisive. Yes, I know a complete trusteeship is a pure myth, like a point in Euclid's geometry. Naturally it is

> unattainable. But then if we try then we can go quite far to attain it. It will be a relative achievement and very satisfying in an incremental sense.'
>
> I am certain that if violence is taken resort to suppress capitalism then state will be a victim of violence. Non-violence will be lost for good and lost forever. State in organised violence is a concentrated form. Man has a living spirit, but the state is an inanimate structure of power. State originates in violence and it can never be disassociated from crude force. Therefore I prefer trusteeship. It is permanent and restrains violence which state may use against all those who dissent. I will be very happy if people willingly and voluntarily take to trusteeship. If they do not do so then we should use minimal violence of state to take away their property. It is the reason I told the round table conference that property of implied interests should be inquired into and the state should forfeit this property with some compensation or without any compensation. Personally I would like that state should not centralise. Rather trusteeship should expand and thrive. In my opinion individual ownership is less harmful than the violence of the state. But if ownership of state becomes inevitable, then I will advocate minimum ownership of the state.[19]

In a nutshell what Gandhiji envisaged through trusteeship was an attempt to establish a moral and non-violent economy which was to be based on cooperation rather than on conflicts among various groups of the state. It was to believe in non-violence and restore human dignity. Trusteeship can transform such an economic system to yield social justice.

The communists argue that Gandhiji was striving to protect capitalists. But it is not true. In fact he knew that state intervention will generate violence and Sarvodaya ideal will be inaccessible in an activist state. Every model of the state has to have some intellectual beliefs and commitments. The ideal behind trusteeship is that unwanted and superfluous property should be avoided. Property beyond wants is harmful and should be surrendered in social interest. Some communists may argue that Gandhiji was an agent of capitalists, but the entire world knows that Gandhiji's trusteeship doctrine has the potentiality to change the world system without any bloodshed or force.

Gandhiji's Outlook towards Socialism

The two ideologies were competing when Gandhiji came on the scene. Capitalism was there since 18th century and socialism started spreading during the 19th century. He believed that socialism was not a reaction to capitalism, but it was born because the reformers of capitalism lost their faith in change of heart. The scientific socialism of Marx claims that property can be equalised by revolutionary fights. To Gandhiji socialism was a legacy of our ancestors who believed that all land belongs to God or Gopal and boundaries are manmade. In modern parlance this Gopal or God implies the state or people.[20] But today land does not belong to people. The capitalist control a major part of it. The Soviet Union achieved this ideal by violence. India wants to attain it by non-violence. The spinning wheel is a forceful weapon to take the place of violence. Land and all other forms of property belong to those who work for it. The peasant and workers either do not know this truth or they are not allowed to explore it.[21] Gandhiji maintained that social justice does not require force or violence by the weaker sections. Contrary to this if they are properly educated they can confront all injustices by non-cooperation. Violence can never achieve this. But non-violence is capable to accomplish it. Even the perpetrators of evil can be transformed by change of heart techniques.

Elaborating socialism Gandhiji has written:

> 'Socialism is a beautiful word. So far as I know it stands for equality. Neither high nor low. The physiology of the body and the anatomy of human beings do not make them equal or similar. But then, all the organs of the body are equally important. In a society, its human members are like parts and they should be somewhat equal. Rhetorically the king, the people, rich and poor, employees and employees all are equal. Thus socialism implies absence of discriminations. It is a natural way and distinctions should not be encouraged. Hence

> ends and means should be in congruence. If the means are not holy then the end also gets polluted.
>
> One king can be murdered but one subject cannot become an emperor. By killing the employer the employees cannot become employers. Hence only non-violent socialists can practise socialism. We want to establish it in India. But to the best of my knowledge there is no country which has or can practise pure socialism.'[22]

Comparing socialism with Sarvodaya, Gandhiji found that these are apparent or false similarities. Both believe that wealth and property should be equitably distributed. All should have control over means of production. Both want a new kind of economic order which shall come into existence after the destruction of capitalism. Both advocate the welfare of the lowliest and the lost. But this does not mean that the two systems are synonymous. There is a fundamental difference between the two. Socialism believes that man can develop to his fullest stature only in society, but Gandhiji advocated a stateless society. He believed that individual is capable to resolve his own problems. He should develop his individual self. Socialism regards state and its coercive power as necessary and useful. People in socialism will never give up property without force while Gandhiji believed and advocated that property can be voluntarily renounced or given up. Socialism needs political party which has a major role in reshaping the society. But Gandhiji called the political system an evil and the individual should not fall in this trap to change human nature.

Gandhi's View about Communism

Gandhi had his reservations in adopting communism in the Indian society. The root cause was his belief in *Satya* and *Ahimsa*. Marx openly accepts violence and civil war to build a new economic order. Gandhi never gave up non-violence to operationalise his ideals. Marx permits nationalisation and socialisation of private property through violent intervention of state. Quite contrary to this Gandhi will call it a plunder and say that all these violent transformations are short-lived and will not endure. Marxism starts from the premise that man is selfish, but to Gandhi man is superior to animals because he can be selfless and abnegating. Man listens to his conscience which does not restrain an animal. Man, if he so likes, he can sublimate himself and rise above selfishness and violence. He can abandon everything for the welfare of society and the world. Animals are violent by nature. They cannot give up greed. Gandhi accepted socialism as an adorable ideal but the means to achieve this ideal have to be human, i.e. non-violent. Gandhi disagreed with his Marxist friends that inequality and differences can be levelled down by forceful methods of civil war and mass violence.

Gandhiji rejected the Soviet communist world for India. He explained the violent nature of the Bolshevik state. In his opinion India has a culture rooted in non-violence and people here cannot accept loot of the property no matter how one amassed it. He wanted capital for social good and the capitalists should not be forced or killed but should come forward to serve the society on their owns.

Thus Gandhiji was not opposed to socialism or communism. Rather he advocated for a classless society. His opposition to communism is the 'means' which they adopt to attain a noble ideal. He felt that we should prefer to live in poverty as an independent nation, rather than coveting the wealth of others by immoral means. We should accept alien ideologies to the extent we can assimilate them in our culture. We should know the difference and resist in getting swayed by their tempting slogans.[23]

Opposition to Machine and Advocacy of Cottage Industries

The Gandhian economics is comprehensive enough to cover all the fields of social life. Its base is strong and adequate. On return from Africa when he studied Indian conditions he concluded that it required a robust thought that was novel and daring. He observed that there was widespread poverty and the western way of mechanisation and industrialisation was worsening it. To fight against these two evils he accepted the spinning wheel economy and opposed mechanisation. He envisaged an economy based on non-violence. He advocated decentralisation to combat centralised exploitation and inequality. He concluded that centralised economy makes life complicated and the individual loses his initiative. It reduces opportunities of self-help and inhibits moral life of the individual.

The versatile development of society requires decentralisation. It ensures moral and spiritual development by offering democratic political base to social life. Decentralised economy and politics multiplies opportunities and decentralised groups explore new and competing areas of growth and production. It facilitates distribution and consumption also.

Gandhiji believed that decentralisation as a policy can end monopoly and market can be made free from black deals, speculations and evils of a competitive economy. He stood for decentralised means of production because machine brings centralisation. He was opposed to industrialisation and mechanisation as evils of western economy.

USA might need a machine economy in its under populated society. But India with a huge population of crores will require hand based economy. Machine will render men unemployed, hence it is harmful and destructive to meaningful production. We have more hands and less machines will offer them more and more work.[24] He knew this fact that for a long time our surplus population will need jobs which mechanisation tends to diminish. He foresaw the future and predicted:

> I wish to make it clear that large scale collective production is responsible for the present day crisis of the world. For arguments sake suppose we accept that machine can fulfil all our wants. Still we will need decentralised production to send them to the consumer. We cannot afford centralisation of distribution and consumption. So production of a centralised machine system will go ill with the methods of distribution

and consumption. Centralised production enables the stronger nations of Europe and America to exploit the weaker nations of the world. It is a fraud which increases speculation and non-work. If poorer nations organise themselves and resolve to consume less within the framework of their production, the capitalist nations will die a natural death. If production and consumption can be balanced then economy acts as a check on production. The capitalistic profits decline and large scale production becomes counter-productive. Decentralised production ipso facto counteracts capitalistic system and its natural evils.[25]

Gandhiji realised that unemployment in India was an offshoot of decline of college industries. The machine economy of the West had ruined the Indian markets. These Western machine made goods have glutted Indian markets and the cottage industries stand devastated. The harm which Manchester alone has caused to Indian goods is enormous. The Indian handicrafts have literally disappeared because of Manchester machines. We started wearing clothes manufactured by mills of Manchester. We are guilty, but they provoked us and robbed the employment of our weavers.[26] These machines have devastated European economy and now they are coming to Bombay and Ahmedabad. Our labourers have become slaves and womenfolk are in a terrible state. These women were earning well before the advent of machines. It is better if we purchase all Manchester textiles rather than permitting British machines to invade India.[27] These machines are weakening our moral character and economic dependence has hardened the political bondage.

Gandhiji knew for sure that mechanisation and opening of mills cannot be arrested in India. Hence people should request the mill owners not to expand their mills. They should not set up new factories and withdraw their commerce. They should repair their spinning wheels and sell and purchase home spun Swadeshi clothes. If the businessmen do not do so then consumers should come forward and refuse to purchase mill made goods. It may not be possible to replace manufactured goods by handmade goods. Gandhi asked 'how people lived in the past when these machines were not there. We should learn to work without superfluous goods. Oil of earthen lamps can save our eyes and our money. We can win Swarajya with *deepak* and *charkha*.'[28]

Gandhiji believed that rich people were responsible for maintaining British rule in India. Actually, it enabled them to fulfil their interests. He maintained that large scale industrialisation encouraged competition, raised market problems and made villages the victim of their exploitation. So we should concentrate on the fact that our villages become self-sufficient and consume products of their own making. If this production technique is accepted and our villages start manufacturing their own implements, then we should accept it with pleasure. But we should not abuse machine for exploitation of others.[29] 'I do not think industrialisation is inevitable in our country in all conditions. India needs it the least. In my judgment India will be doing her duty by leading a simple and friendly life with other countries. Worshipping wealth burdens our lives with complexities and it does not fit in our way of "simple living and high thinking". We should learn and lead the life of virtue.'[30]

This explains that Gandhi took a middle position. He was neither totally opposed to it nor he was a blind supporter of industrialisation. He wanted small machines as labour saving devises and millions of people in villages should welcome it so long it saves, physical hard labour. But then these inanimate machines should not compete with animate human beings. The machine should make life easier. It should help men to fulfil their tasks. But if machines lead to concentration of wealth in fewer hands, then they will add to unemployment in a country like India. In my view if machine can reduce unemployment then I am all for it. The tragic fact is that mechanisation makes rich richer and poor poorer.

Spinning wheel of Gandhi was also a sort of a machine. He called 'Charkha' as the second lung of Indian nation. All those petty machines which can reduce common man's burden without weakening the human clay were more than welcome.[31] Sewing machine was one such implement, but he knew that sewing machines have also to be manufactured in huge plants. So he was opposed to big industries in private sector. Here he advocated nationalisation and government control without profit making. It generates class conflict. Gandhiji never accepted that social conflicts can ever lead to social good. His Sarvodaya aimed to arrest selfish, arbitrary and uncontrolled desire for wealth. Gandhiji opposed the notion of class conflict on the ground that it leads to revenge, violence and selfish class interests. Class conflicts disintegrate society and hence it is ruinous for social development. He advocated a coordinational cooperative approach in place of conflict, struggle and civil violence.

Khadi and Charkha

The Swadeshi movements of Gandhi had the purpose of reviving the Indian economy. It was supposed to prepare the Indian industry to compete against British power as a weapon of strength. Gandhiji took away radicalism and violence from this movement and gave it a moral and spiritual twist. He proposed home spun cotton Khadi to generate a total revolution. It pulled out the movement from the elite group and gave entry to the cottages of the masses. It was a constructive program. He advised the boycott of foreign clothes and appealed to accept Khadi and Charkha. In his words Khadi was the symbol of people's unity, economic liberty and equality. In Jawaharlal Nehru's phrase 'it was the livery of India's freedom.' It means maximum economic sufficiency. Goods can be produced and distributed in a decentralised manner. The principle is rural people should be self-sufficient and if possible, they should export handmade goods to the urban areas. Some cities may have large producing centres, but if the rural areas have their own rural centres of production, the cities will not harm them.[32] In Gandhi's philosophy Khadi (home spun cloth) had three meanings:

1. It will instil patriotism and love for the goods made in India. So every Indian should resolve to use village made goods. It will make the seven million villages self-sufficient and

independent. The enrichment of the English rich will suffer a setback.

2. We will realise our lost potentials. If we change our way of life, life will not be miserable.
3. We will produce all goods needed and will distribute them among ourselves equitably.

In Gandhi's view political freedom is the obverse side of economic coin, so when freedom comes India should be economically self-sufficient. Pt Nehru used to say 'Mahatma Gandhi has pre-post programmes of revolution, simultaneously running. He demolishes the walls of slavery and constructs the ramparts of freedom with the same bricks.'[33] Andrew Freeman asked Gandhiji about the message of Charkha to America; his question was 'how will spinning wheel counteract the atom bomb.' Gandhi's reply being 'the message of Charkha is for the entire world including USA. It requires a living example and India should prove it by reconstructing a hand spun economy. Till date India has not accepted Charkha. There is no fault with the wheel. I have no doubt that this symbol of manual labour and self-help can revolutionise world economy.'[34] His contention was that it is very cheap. It requires no huge investment, but it can alleviate poverty in a natural way without any ostentious exhibitionalism. Hence it should be in every home. It is the symbol of freedom and affluence. It does not wage a commercial war but negotiates a commercial peace. It gives a message of goodwill, self-sufficiency and harmony. It will never need defence preparedness or maritime protection. It will ask people to spin cotton threads as they cook their daily meals. Only a resolve will do. It sees peace, love and goodwill in every thread of Khadi. In fact India was enslaved because we gave up Swadeshi production or Charkhas. The deeper meaning of 'back to the wheel' will be 'let us go to freedom from this enslavement of machines and that of the aliens.'[35]

Inter Relations and Interactions between Industrial Capitalists and Working Class

Gandhiji was a thinker, saint and a political activist who had deep roots in Indian culture. 'Good of all' was the credo of this intellectual. He adopted 'Non-violence' as his religion. He stressed upon human cooperation. Unlike Marx he believed that social groups and classes should not quarrel but the capitalists and workers should coexist in peace and harmony. He openly said that class war is against the very nature of Indian society. India can build a new society on the basis of liberal communism.[36] He said 'I do not want to eliminate landlords, but I know feudal lords are not inevitable. I wish to change the hearts of these rich friends. So I do not accept class war as a doctrine. Minimum conflict in my judgment is the fact of non-violent experiment. The movement of the workers will realise their strength, and the evils of zamindari will get dissolved. If their children are not ensured food and raiment and the parents are not paid fair wages, how can you ensure justice. The truth is that the tiller of the soil is the real owner. If labourers unite they can produce an unprecedented force which will render class war irrelevant. If I would have not believed in it I would have preached differently.' In fact he was opposed to the notion of class conflict. He knew the power of a working class and felt that when workers will realise their strength, the capitalists will abandon mischief and behave properly.

'Conflict is a system of crises and should be avoided at every cost. It represents weakness and inferiority.[37] So the workers should recognise their prowess and glory of work. In contracts the capitalists do not have any power or self-respect.[38] An honest and non-violent organisation of labourers can drain out capital like a magnet and the capital owner will get reduced to a trustee. The distinction between the capitalist and the labour will disappear on that auspicious day for which I am working. In this ideal situation labourer will get food, live in neat houses and their children will get education and medical care.'[39] But this requires the spirit of unity among workers. Gandhiji felt that labourers lack unity and capitalists are past masters in manipulation. The drops do make an ocean. If workers unite non-violently, they will be capable to achieve the impossible.

Gandhi was of the opinion that labourers are more dutiful as compared to masters. The two have their duties towards each other. The labourers should know how to get their demands accepted and to what extent. Which demands are right? They should know how to respect the limits and stay within the field of justice. If they take resort to force of numbers it will be suicidal. They should wage non-violent struggles on the basis of pure justice. It will change the heart of mill owners. The owners depend upon workers for their profit and naturally labourers can put them in immense loss also. But this does not mean that labourers should take undue gain of their key position. Naturally it is equally immoral to pressurise for unreasonable demands. The labourers should know and realise that taking advantages of emergent situations is gross selfishness. It can jeopardise economic balance.

In 1920, the Ahmedabad mill workers took to agitation. They did not get Deepawali bonus. There were no laws in existence. The mills were earning profits during the World War. The workers agitated for bonus and threatened to close the mills. But it was wrong to sabotage production and the owners were made to surrender. Gandhiji was unhappy about this. He said 'If mills are earning they should pay bonus in a systematic manner. But the workers need not put situational pressures and the mill owners have a right to resist'. The situation had become critical. Surrender by the owners would have proved ruinous. Gandhiji argued with them and when they did not listen, he along with Ansuyaben resigned from their posts. The employees realised their mistake. They requested Gandhiji to mediate and one month bonus was agreed upon on the eve of Deepawali every year. The labourers have rights but they also have a responsibility towards the society for their actions.[40] The mill owners agreed to include the following for the amelioration of conditions of the workers as a part of law:

1. Labourers should get adequate time to rest and leisure.
2. They should get training facilities.
3. Their children should enjoy facilities like free education and subsidised food.
4. Their houses should be neat and clean.

5. Their package should yield savings for their old age and emergencies.

Most of these conditions are not met by both the parties. The owners want to take maximum work and do not care about their working conditions. The workers also struggle to work less and get more and more. The net result of all this is that wages increase but the production remains stagnant. This leads to bitterness. The labourers have a right to strike but they should maintain a discipline for peace. For this his conditions were:

1. The cause for strike should be just.
2. The strikers should have consensus in their decision.
3. No violence should be resorted to against those who refuse to go on strike.
4. The strikers should be in a position to manage their family expenses without help from union funds.
5. If the strike fails, the workers should quietly accept failure and rejoin their posts.
6. Still strikes take place. If the strike succeeds it means that employers were in the wrong and their conscience was guilty.

Gandhi may be called a protagonist of strike methods but he insisted on a genuine moral cause for its occurrence. Wrong strikes should neither succeed nor people should sympathise with the strikers. It is the last resort and other peaceful methods should always be explored and experimented upon.[41]

Doctrine of Economic Equality

This doctrine of Gandhi is again based upon non-violence. He believed that inequality of income deprives the poor from getting their due. Property and wealth get concentrated in fewer hands. In consequence, the majority had to suffer pain, deprivation and violence of a low variety. Hence Gandhi wanted to abolish harrowing economic inequality from India, not the whole world. He opined that economic system should be such that every individual is assured the basic minimum. Each and every person should have some job which can guarantee food, clothes and a roof. This ideal can be attained only when primary needs are controlled by common people. They should fulfil these primary needs without hindrance. Food should be like air or water. No body should run exploitative trades for personal profit. No one country should monopolise these resources. Poverty not only in India but also in other parts of the world is a result of this monopolisation of resources by individuals, societies and countries.[42]

The Gandhian plan of society ensures economic equality. It implies that the struggle between property, wealth, capital and wages should eventually be ended. The share of wealth of the rich should diminish and poor commoner should have a bigger share of the cake. The society should be so reconstituted that everybody gets two square meals and fulfils the minimal primary needs of life. For this kind of economic equality each individual can strive and make others work to do their duty. The rich can cut down their wants by comparing their living with that of the poor. Man can curb his instinct of self-seeking and spend his legal wealth with honesty and ethical scruples. One can avoid luxuries and each household should take care of bare necessities. He should start from self and then propagate it among neighbours to adopt the same. Gandhiji did not accept criticism by calling this approach unrealistic. He advocated non-violence to the extent that rich people should not do violence, but should avoid to become the victims of violence. The rich have to undergo change of heart. They should accept trusteeship and show the way to society.

Swadeshi: A Way to Reconstruction and Resurgence

Gandhiji was not an economist, nor was he interested in making India a super economic power. He was an activist, a thinker whose prime mission was to liberate the motherland from foreign yoke. But he pondered over a variety of issues and concluded that British rule was the root cause of Indian poverty. The Golden Bird has lost its economic glamour. The draining of the Indian capital had broken the backbone of our economy. So he started working for economic emancipation for political liberation of India. Khadi and Charkha were added to the constructive programs. They became symbols of national unity and economic progress. Swadeshi to Mahatmaji had a special meaning. He wrote 'Swadeshi means a feeling which teaches us to serve the people nearer rather than those stationed remote. It applies on religion also. We serve people who are close to our ancestors.

If it is faulty, the faults can be eradicated. In political fields also the locals should be helped first. I should use only those goods which are made by our neighbours. It is real service because it improves our capabilities. So Gandhi called Swadeshi a step to revive the golden age of mankind.[43]

He included these characteristics in his concept of Swadeshi:

1. Role of Swadeshi in religious field.
2. Role of Swadeshi in political realm.
3. Role of Swadeshi in economic development.

1. Gandhiji took a very comprehensive view of Swadeshi. From economic field it can extend to politics and religion. Swadeshi is Swaraj – rather its pre-condition. Gandhi will call Hinduism a Swadeshi way of living. Hinduism never cared to expand or convert people of other faiths. That is why Hinduism is more liberal and tolerant. Hindus should not be aggressive. They do not need missionaries to expand their Swadeshi dharma. But they resist and fight conversions. The Christians who carry out their missionary activities of conversion should give up their efforts of proselytisation. The mission of service in Christianity is great, but converting others into Christianity is abominable.
2. In political field Gandhi was an advocate of local institutions. He wrote 'India is a real democratic country. It has suffered a lot because of these values of liberalism. The rulers who came from outside collected taxes and never cared about peoples' welfare. The Hindus obeyed them but did not give up their freedom of religion. The Varna and

caste system fulfilled the social spiritual needs of society. Even political system went on functioning when rulers were waging wars against Hindu rulers. The rural folk were undisturbed by alien rule or alien ways. The socio-cultural system of religion stood in good stead. The political crises blew over but the Hindu system rooted in Swadeshi was immutable.[44] Unfortunately the panchayat system lost its vitality. If we can revive this 'Swadeshi Spirit' – we can take over the country.

3. The economic poverty of India can be explained by breaking away with the law of Swadeshi. The foreign goods have brought this misfortune and misery. It ruined our cottage industries and the Indian capital was drained out to England. So India should avoid competition and fulfil her economic needs by her own resources. Swadeshi doctrine implies that every Indian should search one unemployed neighbour and the two should mutually fulfill their needs or wants. These unemployed people should learn and manufacture desired goods. By this every village will become self-sufficient and stop importing articles from outside. The villages should interact and produce what is Swadeshi. The Geeta says, 'महाजनों येन गतः सः पन्थ', i.e. common man treads the foot-steps of leaders. If villagers follow their rural leaders the Swadeshi products will get a boost. The critics may ridicule it. But they should know that 'our property is a gift of God. It should be so used that neighbours bet benefited. It is not a question of law. It is a moral principle. It can be called the key to non-violent living.'[45]

In brief Gandhiji wanted to restructure Indian economy, but not on European principles. He kept Indian Swadeshi as his 'moral mantra'. Charkha and Khadi were his economic weapons in political battles against the British. He succeeded to some extent. In fact Gandhiji could visualise a future. The entire world is a family. Society has to be decentralised and the lowest rural unit, i.e. village must be autonomous and self-sufficient.

This links Gandhian moral system of economy to the international economy of minimum machines and absolutely free from atomic violence.

Notes

1. Mahadev Prasad, *Mahatama Gandhi Ka Samaj Darshan*, Haryana Sahitya Academy, Chandigarh, 1989, p. 201.
2. Ibid.
3. *Young India*, Vol. 3, p. 350.
4. Ibid., 13 October 1921.
5. Ibid., 27 October 1921.
6. Ibid., 26 December 1924.
7. *Harijan*, 24 December 1938, p. 393.
8. *Young India*, 13 October 1921.
9. S. Radhakrishanan, *Gandhiji Ka Dharam Aur Rajniti*, Sasta Sahitya Mandal, 1971, p. 12.
10. M.K. Gandhi, *Mere Sapanon Ka Bharat*, Navajivan Prakashan, Ahmedabad, 1999, p. 10, *Young India*, 26 March 1931.
11. *Young India*, 5 March 1931.
12. *Speeches and Writings of M. Gandhi*, op. cit., p. 384.
13. Sabe Bhumi Gopal Ki.
14. *Harijan*, 12 April 1942.
15. Ibid., 1 February 1942.
16. S.L. Verma and B.M. Sharma, *Bhartiya Rajnitik Vicharak*, Panchseel Prakashan, Jaipur, 1997, pp. 271–272.
17. *Harijan*, 31 March 1946.
18. S.L. Verma and B.M. Sharma, op. cit., p. 272.
19. *The Modern Review*, 1935, p. 412, M.K. Gandhi *Mere Sapanonon Ka Bharat*, op. cit., pp. 72–73.
20. *Harijan*, 2 January 1937.
21. Ibid.
22. *Harijan Sevak*, 13 July 1947.
23. *Harijan*, 6 October 1946.
24. J.L. Dwivedi, *Bhartiya Rajneetik Chintan*, Delhi, 1999, p. 162.
25. *Harijan*, 2 November 1934.
26. M.K. Gandhi, *Hind Swarjya*, Sasta Sahitya Prakashan, Delhi, 1958, p. 102.
27. Ibid., pp. 102–103.
28. Ibid., pp. 102–104.
29. *Harijan*, 29 August 1936.

30. *Harijan,* 1 September 1946.
31. *Young India,* 5 November 1925.
32. Gandhi, *Rachnatamak Karyakram,* Navajivan, Ahmedabad, 1989, p. 20.
33. B.N. Pandey, Gandhi, *Samagra Chintan,* op. cit., p. (iii).
34. Ibid., pp. 152–153.
35. *Young India,* 8 December 1921.
36. *Amrit Bazar Patrika* 21 August 1934.
37. *Harijan,* 18 October 1935.
38. *Harijan,* 7 September 1947.
39. *Harijan,* 7 September 1947.
40. Vishnu Prabhakar, *Yah to Sarvjanik Paisa Hai,* Delhi, 1996, pp. 14–16.
41. *Harijan,* 11 October 1946.
42. *Young India,* 15 November 1928.
43. M.K. Gandhi, *Mere Sapanon Ka Bharat,* op. cit., pp. 128–129.
44. Ibid.
45. *Speches and Writings of Mahatama Gandhi*, pp. 336–344.

5

The Political Philosophy of Gandhi

Mahatma Gandhi was not essentially a political thinker. He cannot be ranked with philosophers like Plato and Aristotle. He was a political saint who had faith in God, truth and non-violence. In his political career spanning four decades he threw enough light on all aspects of his public life.

He started as a patriot agitator, whose prime aim was to liberate India. He never sat down in any library to contemplate upon the political system and unlike other thinkers, he never had the urge to define or preach politics. He worked in three continents in one lifetime. India and South Africa were his workplaces and laboratories. Like a natural scientist he experimented upon social problems in his Ashrams and prison cells and invented new techniques of struggles. He won several political battles and crystallised his ideas. He has been called a political activist or a *Karamyogi* (man of action). He had profound commitment to higher values of life but kept his words flexible to make practical experiments.

His political contribution to theory and practice of politics is enormous. His ideas gave a new twist to Indian politics. He never propounded theories by writing books, but he was more concerned with the ups and downs of practical politics. He kept total development of the entire country as his motto and presented the plan of action. The political subjection, coupled with social injustice, economic disintegration and diversities made life miserable in India. So leaders like him had to keep track of the changes and develop new strategies. So he rose above. His times and his ideas became relevant for the whole world. His political speculation emerged on a moral canvas, which was wide and neat.

Gandhiji examined the circumstances and the problems of his times and his political philosophy offers a total solution of vexed problems of his age. As most of these problems were similar and somewhat uniform, so his philosophy became a live answer to human problems. Gandhiji's uniqueness lies in being practical. He did not borrow but only redefined his borrowings. When these techniques succeeded he advised others to adopt. He did not care to develop a grand Gandhian Philosophy of his own. He did not even systematise the stray ideas borrowed from East or West. His writings on Africa and later on Indian experiences remain separate and distinct. He was a journalist as well. So he published papers and presented ideas in *Indian Opinion*, *Young India* and *Harijan*. His important books include *Hind Swarajya* and *Satyagrah in South Africa*.

The total writings and ideas of Gandhi have been published by Government of India in 90 volumes under the caption *Gandhi Vangmaya*. A serious study of this colossal exercise gives the conclusion that the philosophy has a sound intellectual base. Opinions or shallow evaluations cannot uproot this gigantic tree. The British rulers had made bridges to contain tides of Indian nationalism. The tidal waves of nationalism demolished them. These waves were intense and human and Mahatma Gandhi was the illustrious and unparalleled force behind them. Mahatma Gandhi generated this tide and when it was at its height the entire world of poor people took inspiration from it. Several people influenced and made Gandhi but the two women who chiselled his ideas about God, truth and non-violence were his mother and nurse. Their ideas in the unconscious solidified the ground on which rested the pillars of saint.

He was a spiritualist and he built his political philosophy on the edifice of ethics. Politics is only a branch of this huge tree. While discussing questions like Swarajya, democracy, parliamentary system, human rights, justice, end, means and synthesis he developed ethical criteria of truth and non-violence. This makes the philosophy weightier as compared to the idealist philosophers of the west. He is regarded as an idealist, a liberal, and a non-violent revolutionary, etc. His Sarvodaya goes beyond socialism and touches the fringe areas of philosophical anarchism. But Gandhi said that all states should struggle to attain it. He believed in human dignity but it was more than a liberal creed. Man alone has consciousness, so he needs liberty. This makes him somewhat similar to T.H. Green who says that liberty means being willing for things worth living. He had faith in rule of law and representative institutions but he did not believe in imitating the West. He has been called a non-violent revolutionary. Like other revolutionaries he aimed to change the system, but without bloodshed. His means were change oriented, but non-violence was more important than the change aspired for. He asked people in Africa to burn their identity cards. Thousands of patriots like Sapru and Nehru burnt their foreign clothes. He refused to pay unjust taxes. Civil disobedience and non-cooperation were his methods, which he very continually kept in the limits of non-violence.

Thus Gandhi is the first political agitator, who changed the contours of Indian struggle and infused energy and vigour in the freedom movement. He taught people to suffer and develop non-violent defence. Let us discuss some of his ideas and techniques.

Truth

Integrity is the basic foundation of Gandhian thought. He was an ardent theist and God was a synonym for the term truth. So it is a pillar on which rests the scaffold. He said God is truth and then later concluded truth is God. Through truth one can feel the existence of God. Whenever truth reveals or truth is stated in conversation, one feels a communion with God.[1] Truth is truth because it is divine. Divinity reveals itself in integral character of man. The other aspects of divinity like beauty (सौंदर्य) and welfare (शिव) reflect in truthfulness (सत्य)[2]. Moreover man being mortal, his transitional body cannot experience the eternalness of truth. Love and truth have no limit and men with limited perspectives cannot visualise the eternalness of God or truth.[3] Truth is all comprehensive omnipresent and omnipotent. God has many names, choose any, it will be truthful. So truth is God.[4] It is the element we can perceive in every living being. Truth is not dependent upon other factors. It exists in its own right. Everything else is transitory but truth is eternal and permanent.[5]

Truth in Gandhi's philosophy is situational and complete. But man has to be satisfied with its partial perception. To confront truth one has to introspect and thereby develop the technique of Satyagraha. Just as God can be perceived through non-violent ways, similarly truth is also unattainable without non-violence. Truth and non-violence are mutually inclusive and the two cannot be separated. They can be called the two sides of the same coin. Hence nobody knows which side is the head and which side represents the tail.[6] God is invisible. It is as close to the flesh as is the nail. God dwells in all of us and we should establish communion with him. In daily language we call it 'Love'.[7] Love implies that man should drain out his arrogance and accept the state of zero or emptiness.[8] Hence human beings should rise and conquer greed, sex, anger and pride. They should realise their power of self. It gives enthusiasm, because the Almighty God directs his own force.

In Gandhiji's view God is not a human being. It is an idea. It is a way to live.[9] The purpose of life is to meet God and the best way to see him is to see him manifested in his creation. To be one with God means to serve the man God has created. Man is divine to the extent he accepts serving other men.[10]

The human life has its roots in ethics. Religion is close to ethical norms. Gandhiji called a religious person ethical or vice versa. The ethical rules require an inner sanction. Ethical people abide by the moral rules of religion. External rewards are secondary. The inner sprit compels man to do noble things. Hence the individual good and social good become inseparable. Those who live for personal pleasures are animals and even worse than animals. So all human beings should strive to advance towards family, village, society and country.[11]

It was the search of truth which took Gandhiji to non-violence. 'I want to see God, but I know truth alone is God and the only way to detect this truth in my judgement is non-violence.[12] Non-violence is the light which shows you the path of truth. Non-violence is the spirit of truth. It is not an individual virtue. Millions and millions of individuals need Ahimsa. It is the highest moral virtue.' This definition of God varies with atheists and several white men became his followers.[13]

Non-violence

The concept of non-violence in political realm is a valuable contribution of Gandhiji to political science. Non-violence is the law of humans, almost the same way as violence is the law of animal world. The animals have a dormant spirit, so they do not know any other way except violence. Human dignity demands that man obeys a higher order. He should accept the soul force. Non-violence is a perfect state. Even when it is unconscious, human nature advances towards non-violent activities.[14]

He believed that non-violence can solve every human problem. It is not a superficial law of conscience, but it explains the disposition of human nature. It does not smell jealousy.[15] It gives insights to understand other people. It is superior to violence because it can conquer hatred. Non-violence is a means to attain the truth. One cannot be truthful without the power of Ahimsa. This non-violence is the essence of all religions. It is truth by itself and represents its mature fruitation. Human beings search the truth and hence there is no possibility of exercising coercion or violent force. When you do not inflict pain on others, you yourself suffer the pain. Truth and non-violence were the pain. Truth and non-violence were the two weapons which Gandhi wielded to fight Apartheid in South Africa and slavery of British Raj in India. He came out with flying colours.[16]

Love and morality are decisively more powerful than weapons and brutal force. India had to rely upon this.[17] He wrote 'I thought of truth and researched into it.[18] Complete truth is impossible for this moral coil. So the original researchers were encouraged to consider about non-violence. The question before the searcher was those who disintegrate this creation in my presence, should I live with them or destroy them. The searcher realised that those who destroy, do no progress. But those who coexisted and suffered obstacles, they kept advancing and ultimately others started appreciating them.'[19]

Non-violence was regarded as the absence of violence. Gandhiji examined the source. He came to the conclusion that evil ideas, jealousy, envy, falsehood and harm to others ultimately result in violence. So man will have to rise above negativism and his positive duty, will is Ahimsa. This positive meaning of non-violence directs the individual to perform things which are morally righteous. It is love, pity, popular welfare and a self-denying discipline of purifying nature. One can search and reach to truth only through non-violence. Gandhiji classified non-violence into three distinct categories.

1. *Enlightened non-violence:* The voice of conscience gives birth to this kind of sublimity. It is the best form of Ahimsa. It has the capacity to make the impossible possible. It appeals to the inner spirit of man in a spontaneous manner.
2. *Non-violence of expediency of practical people:* Like an opportunist such people keep shifting their positions and justify violence and non-violence as per their rational thinking. It is a lower variety of non-violence but can be practised with honesty and sincerity.
3. *Non-violence of cowards:* It is a passive variety of non-violence. In fact it is the opposite. Like fire and water non-violence and cowardice cannot go together.[20] He openly said that if there is a choice between cowardice and violence I will elect violence, because I cannot direct a non-violent coward in

the same way as I cannot ask a blind person to enjoy beautiful objects.

Non-violence can be compared with radium. If a small particle of radium is attached to the malignant part of the body, it starts working silently and continuously. It does not stop working unless the malignancy is finally cured or healed. Similarly a belief in non-violent change cures the society at its basic grassroots.[21] Non-violence is a great force in the hands of human race. The weapons of mass destruction which mankind has made, non-violence stands out as a mightier weapon of power. Destruction and death are not the law of nature. Human beings may prefer death to live in liberty rather than to kill others for pleasure. Every murder or harm done to others (whatever may be the purpose) is a downright crime against humanity.[22]

So Gandhiji called non-violence an active force which illuminates the soul.[23] It is the divine light that never dies. Ahimsa works in the midst of bloodshed or murders just as scientists research violence with dexterity so should non-violence be researched into.[24] It is a philosophy of duty and Gandhiji converted it into a principle.

Satyagrah

Gandhiji knew for sure that violence has extended to dangerous proportions and mankind has no way out but to take resort to truth and non-violence. Violence cannot be combated with violence. Non-violence alone can counteract violence. To develop this kind of non-violent power has been called Satyagrah.

It literally means to stay firm on truth. The term was used for the first time in South Africa. Gandhiji published a paper on techniques against injustices. This style came to be known as 'Satyagrah'. He wrote 'We want to conquer hatred by love in South Africa. We do not wish to punish people but wish to suffer at the hands of those who punish us.' He used the term passive resistance and then later on revised it to Satyagrah. He sought the proper word in his paper *Indian Opinion*. Magan Lal Gandhi suggested 'Sada – Grah' which Gandhiji reformed into

'Satyagrah'.[25] In English it means 'Force of Truth'. Tolstoy has called it 'Force of Love' or 'Self-Force'. It is close to it.[26]

Satyagrah is a political tenet of Gandhian principles. By this a person presents his position of truth against the position imposed by vested interests. It may assume varied forms from personal non-cooperation to organised civil disobedience. The Gandhian Satyagrah is more dynamic than mere passive resistance. Vinoba Bhave called 'Bhoo Daan' a Satyagrah. Gandhiji believed in peaceful struggles and compromise was his way of resolution.[27] The Satyagrah ideal originates from truth. Hence a Satyagrahi must protect the piousness of the bases of truth. Naturally, it involves the soul-force against all sorts of injustices, exploitation and torture. To suffer and fight with spiritual force is Satyagrah. It does not endanger but energises the Satyagrahi with its innocence.[28]

Gandhiji wrote, 'If the truth force is accompanied with non-violence, one can subdue the universe. This is the essence of Satyagrah. We are here to allow truth and love in the humdrum of national and political life.'[29]

A Satyagrahi trusts his opponent and he is fearless. Even if the opponent attacks upon him twenty times, he will express faith and repose confidence the twenty-first time. To trust people is the essence of non-violence.[30] It can be used by the individual and the society. Even family can use it in every walk of life. It proves its permanence. Men, women, children – all can be Satyagrahis. It is not the power of the weak. It can be resorted to against the violent and the non-violent.[31]

Gandhi developed this technique in a decade. Several thinkers shaped the idea. He called Jesus the divine ambassador of love[32] and saw Satyagrah philosophy in the life of Saint Paul.[33] He got this training from Christian missionaries, who maintained that no problem can be resolved by vengeance.[34] It was Tolstoy who impressed upon him the dictum 'Hate the evil, but not the evil doer.' So in his Satyagrah struggles he never hated his adversaries but kept fighting their evil ways.

Satyagrah and Passive Resistance

Some people do not see any distinction and accept them as synonyms. But they differ fundamentally. Passive resistance is a political weapon while Satyagrah symbolises spiritual power. The former is based on the latter. But Gandhiji distinguished the two in his South African experience. Here he said passive resistance is resorted to by the weak. It may slip into violence. Some of his British colleagues pointed out that violent means are permitted in European passive resistance. So Gandhiji has to employ the term Satyagrah. In his view 'Satyagrah is a sword which is sharp on all edges. One can use it as he or she likes. It benefits both the attacker and the attacked. No bloodshed follows. The cut is quite deep. It does not get rusted. Nor can it be stolen by others. It needs no cover. Nobody can snatch it.'[35] It represents humility and does not harm anybody. It is an antonym of coercion and can be called an alternate way of violence.'[36] The reformer who adopts Satyagrah should not raise fingers but should be prepared to face bullets without any care of security.[37]

Explaining the difference in an article in *Harijan* Gandhiji wrote 'Satyagrah symbolises strength, while passive resistance may be called a weakness. The latter had no room for love, while Satyagrah is love in myriad forms. Satyagrah can be employed against the dear ones while passive resistance cannot be resorted to against your own friends. Passive resistance can harm the opponent, while Satyagrah wins the heart even after personal suffering. Jesus was a Satyagrahi. The Christians suffered enormous difficulties in early years. It cannot be called passive resistance.'[38]

Fifteen Points of Constructive Programme

Constructive programme was a part of Gandhian Satyagrah. He included these programmes in his notion of complete independence. He reduced the constructive programme into 15 points, which are as under:

1. Spread of Khadi
2. Promotion to rural development

3. Rural cleanliness and hygiene
4. Basic education
5. Adult education
6. Empowerment of women
7. Village service
8. Spread of national language
9. Love for mother tongue
10. Promotion of economic equality
11. Communal unity
12. Elimination of untouchability
13. Prohibition
14. Tribal service
15. Organisations of farmers and students

These directives led to constructive change. A Satyagrahi is a Nishkam Karmyogi of the Geeta, who strives to harmonise the end with the means.

Foreign Invasion and Satyagrah against War

Gandhiji has advocated about the efficiency of Satyagrah in international affairs. He held that it is an effective weapon to checkmate foreign aggression. No war can establish permanent peace. It is barbaric and brutal. Satyagrah is preferable because of its peaceful approach towards justice. It shows its impact instantly. War invites total destruction while Satyagrah evokes love, compassion and friendship. After the cessation hostilities, bitterness continues and the fire keeps smouldering. Satyagrah can breed love and satisfy warring parties.

So Satyagrah is a technique to change the heart and use love and non-violence to restore cordiality. Satyagrah should be patronised.[39] There are three limitations in Satyagrah approach to peace:

1. Satyagrahis should not keep adding to their demands.
2. Satyagrah should be used to pressure the accomplishments of Satyagrah.

3. Satyagrah never fails, though the achievements can be called modest.[40]

It is a dynamic process. Here the minimum can be called maximum because nothing declines. Satyagrah continues for long and it can achieve the targets in instalments.[41] The numbers do not matter in the fight. The voice of conscience ultimately becomes decisive.

Techniques of Satyagrah

It is an approach towards political conflict. It is not a collective fight. It can resolve a domestic quarrel by self-restraint. Bandurai calls 'it a discovery which combines relative truth, non-violence, humanism and self-injury.'[42] Gandhiji searched his Satyagrah as an alternative to violence and cowardice. He stood for pacific settlement of conflicts and hence his condition was that all constitutional means should be exhausted before launching a Satyagrah.

He experimented with some of the following constitutional means during his Satyagrahs:[43]

1. Gandhiji believed in patience and preferred to wait for nature's solutions. He was a theist and a Satyagrahi should exhibit faith in divine judgment.
2. A Satyagrahi should weigh the pros and cons and should proceed with caution after examining the opposite ideas of his colleagues.
3. Gandhiji contacted people by his 'padyatras'. It raised popular consciousness and participation. People's responses and their cooperation was ascertained before he launched his Satyagrah movements.
4. Gandhiji always strived to develop a dialogue with the opposite party. This enables a Satyagrahi to restrain his prejudices. Dialogue is the best way to resolve conflicts. So no Satyagrah can be launched without knowing or talking to the people.
5. Cooperative efforts require organisation. They are not automatic. The leaders should organise, communicate and

search for a common ground. He organised Natal Indian Congress in 1894 and South African British Union Committee in 1919. His Satyagrah Sabha in India was a step in this direction.

6. Satyagrahis should be trained in advance about the goals and techniques of their activities. The appraisal of situation helps. His Sabarmati and Vradha Ashrams were used as training institutes for Satyagrahis.
7. He believed in oath taking by Satyagrahis. It strengthens them in their resolve. It prepares people for sacrifices. Like a prayer to God, oath taking develops spiritual power and purifies the soul. It changes the atmosphere of hatred or bitterness.

Gandhiji had suggested the following techniques or methods for a successful Satyagrah.

Non-cooperation

It encounters evil and falsehood to generate good and truth. Its purpose is to present a situation wherein love and cooperation can be established. The non-cooperator sees his own fault and there is no ill-will against the opponent. The government exhibits its force but the people are not cooperating. No government can work or still less survive if people do not cooperate and offer a willing support. If a government suppresses peoples' will, they have a right as well as a duty to oppose. In Gandhiji's view nobody should obey an unjust law. It is downright slavery and opposed to law of nature. Non-cooperation cannot be non-violent and all comprehensive, unless people willingly consent to it.

Non-cooperation creates public opinion because coercive non-cooperation will be called violence. The criterion for non-cooperation has to be willingness of people. So non-cooperation can be called a dynamic situation of self-pain of high order.[44] Here non-cooperation does not imply surrender or harming the opponent. It simply means withdrawing all support against injustice. A support for justice will change the oppressor's heart. If both the parties suffer pain then situation changes. Non-cooperation is not against the individuals. It is a fight against injustice. The Satyagrahi must make his opponent feel that he alone is his true friend and well wisher.[45] Gandhiji took resort to non-cooperation against British government to make the rulers feel that they were in the wrong.

Civil Disobedience

It is a means to Satyagrah. Thorne was the first American thinker who applied it in practical politics. He very humbly disobeyed the laws against his conscience. It enables the citizens of a slave country to oppose immoral laws. It is a weapon to fight without violence. Gandhiji's civil disobedience was a way to protest and break immoral laws without any violence. This non-violent protest is a part of Satyagrah. But it is not total Satyagrah. It is a substitute of a bloody revolution and can be called a weapon of bloodless revolution.[46] General Smuts of South Africa opined about civil disobedience as under 'I do not like you people nor do I care a fig about your activities. But I am sorry, I am helpless. You people help me where I need it. How can I beat you, I wish you to do some violence, then I can let you know how to deal with an opponent. But you people do not harm me who is your enemy. You want victory by infliction of pain on yourself and do not violate the self-discipline. This makes us powerless.'[47] Gandhiji attracted the attention of government by opposing immoral laws. The purpose was to correct and rectify the laws. It will improve the laws and people will comply to them more willingly.

Civil disobedience stresses upon civility rather than disobedience. Humility coupled with disobedience makes it pleasant. The non-violent refusal takes away the bitterness. It combines liberty with law. The two look seemingly opposed but their supplementary nature makes the opposition pleasant and acceptable. The self-discipline takes away the non-acceptance part and civility pleases the enemy as his victory. This technique is used against the state or against immoral laws, paraded as sovereign laws. It can alert people, arouse their conscience and make people aware about the consequences which have not been duly anticipated.[48] Thus civil disobedience is the last phase of non-cooperation. It forces the government to talk to Satyagrahis and take their point humanly rather than legally.

Strike

Its literal meaning is to stop one's business activities for a short while. It implies that public life disapproves a government action. When business stops both the government and the citizens are affected adversely. Gandhiji always warned the strikers that they have to be particular about the decision. Non-violence is the first condition. Gandhiji wrote 'The labourers have a birthright to go on strike for gain. But if the employers accept arbitration, strike is a sin. Certain services like electricity, water supply, police, banking, transport are essential services and the right to strike can deprive people from their right to access these essential services'.

Boycott

Gandhiji called boycott a sort of Satyagrah, but his advice was to avoid and minimise it. If some people do not accept the reasonable decisions then boycott call may be given, but the condition is that those who perpetuate and those who suffer both should have sympathy and fraternal feelings for one another. Boycott does not mean one way infliction of pain. Nobody can be or should be unilaterally deprived of any service, any food, clothes or medical care. Gandhiji returned his 'Kaisar-i-Hind' title while launching boycott against Rowlett Act. Such boycotts bring moral force into play. If people boycott elections or return government awards or do not participate in fairs and festivals, such activities do not put people into inconvenience so they are non-violent.

Dharana

Dharana is also a technique to awaken people, build the environment and change the heart of the opponent. Gandhiji used it in 1920–22 and 1930–34 during his civil disobedience and non-cooperation movements. People waited and protested at liquor shops and at counters of foreign goods.

Fasting

It is the last resort of the Satyagrahi. It is the most effective one also. But Gandhiji insisted to avoid it till other methods are available.[49] It should be resorted to only by leaders of moral stature and those skilled in the art. Medical fitness is also a condition precedent. The leader must have deep faith in God. It is not mere imitation. The inspiration should come from within and be used very rarely.[50] Fasting requires patience, total peace and commitment to goal. These virtues do not dawn. It is a way of self-purification. The Satyagrahis should take to fasting only if they think themselves fit enough to endure.[51] Fasting for just causes purifies. If the cause is not just he will give it up or his pain infliction will weaken him and he will change. Gandhiji took to fasting for 138 days in his entire life.

Ashram System: The Training Ground

Gandhiji was highly influenced by this idea of Tolstoy that like warriors in battle fields, the soldiers of peace should also be duly trained. The Satyagrahi should know what are the means available and how should he use them. A violent war is easy because violence is only to destroy. Unlike this army warrior a Satyagrahi has to develop the capacity to suffer without inflicting harm. He has to coordinate the end with the means and stay on the path with firmness. He should not get excited or emotional. The constructive work minimises the possibilities of conflict. For this he made efforts to train Satyagrahis in South Africa and India. This idea came to him from a 'Yanasya Polyyana' of Tolstoy – a farmhouse about which Tolstoy shared his vision with Gandhiji in details.[52]

Gandhiji opened Tolstoy Farm and Phoenix Ashram in South Africa. They were followed by Sabarmati and Navgaon in India. He prescribed 11 vows for the Ashramites in 1930 during training. It was not a mechanical formula, but the directives were to help the Satyagrahis while treading the path of self-sacrifice. These vows were:

1. *Truth:* Avoid falsehood. It should be indeed and thought. He related truth with God and accepted it like worship. It has to be the centre of all social and human activity.
2. *Non-violence:* To Gandhi it was the mightiest weapon in the struggle for truth.[53] He explained that non-violence is not mere non-killing or non-harming. It may be a part, but it touches the minimum. He extends the scope of non-violence to all areas like hatred, falsehood, ill-will, unwanted haste, etc. He equates love with Ahimsa. It means equal application without discriminations. One has to be careful and it is the most difficult kind of human conduct. He goes to the extent that one may be violent while breathing, sleeping and ploughing the fields.
3. *Celibacy:* Elaborating the Ashram system Gandhiji called 'Grahasth Ashram' as the base of life but success comes to those who take the rest of the three Ashrams around Brahamacharya. A Brahamchari is one who can restrain his sensual forces in words and deeds. It is wrong to think that control of mere sex or animal instinct makes one a Brahamchari. He restored female dignity by saying that 'Woman is not the gatekeeper of hell but she can be a caring mother in the management of heaven.'
4. *Control over sensuality:* He delved deep and called it a 'Swadendri' which can canalise sexual instinct to nobler purposes. Food is like medicine. One must not overeat. If you cannot restrain your tongue or desires, you are bound to be ill or diseased.
5. *Non-stealing:* Gandhiji stood for a life of minimum wants. Stealing and loving cannot go together. All grabbing without knowledge is stealing. Similarly picking up things unclaimed is also a theft. Never accept what is not yours. It requires knowledge of what one needs. People unknowingly increase their wants and fall in the trap. God gives enough for the needs. Those who expand their minimum needs as per their greed, are the thieves guilty of violating the law of nature.

6. *Non-possession:* In fact non-stealing has the other side of the coin. It is non-possession. It is a mental state. We should not have or possess things more then we need. So minimum wants can regularise habits of non-possession.
7. *Livelihood:* Labour is a blessing for all those who practise truth, non-violence and celibacy. Those who work by hand or body do not possess more. They cannot be thieves like mental workers. The physical labour keeps the body going and avoids social harm.
8. *Swadeshi:* It is a universal law. Our first obligation is neighbourhood. It does not mean hating others. If neighbourhood duties are fulfilled nobody will be left uncared for. So serving the neighbour is serving the universe. This spirit obliterates otherliness.
9. *Fearlessness:* Without fearlessness, people cannot be truthful. It is the virtue of virtues. We are afraid of consequences, so we resort to falsehood. Those who fear God, they cannot be fearful of other human beings.
10. *Emancipation of Untouchable:* Nobody can be untouchable because all of us have the same divine spark. Birth cannot be discriminated against. Love the so called untouchable. Love every living being almost the way as you love yourself. It implies love and service. So it is a part of non-violence.
11. *Tolerance:* Gandhi believed that all human beings are imperfect and and that the concept of religion is also incomplete. Therefore, he preferred to use due term tolerance. Tolerance implies that those who follow different paths, have something new to contribute. Tolerance teaches learning from others. Tolerant people control their prejudices and can see the truth in opposition.

Thus it is a code of conduct which goes to build character. 'I feel confident that we need this character building, much more than others. Its absence can be explained but cannot be suffered in nation building. My Ashrams are an attempt to build this much needed character.'

State as an Idea

The concept of state in Gandhian thought can be called philosophical anarchism. Like Tolstoy and Thoreau, Gandhiji disbelieved in the state. He called it sheer violence institutionalised. He was prepared to believe that a modern state is an instrument of exploitation of the poor sections of society. It obstructs the moral development of man by his tactics of violence. Truth alone is the way and every individual has to tread it, no matter what the obstacles are. Individuals should not confront impositions. He will not like people who depended upon the support of others.[54] In his own words 'state represents mass violence. Man has a conscience but state is a machine without any qualms of conscience. It can never be shorn of violence because it survives only through violence.'[55] Hence Gandhi did not accept state intervention even for a pious vision like socialisation of property. He viewed the increase of states' power with alarm. Seemingly it has a noble objective for progress but in practice it harms and damages personality. This kind of thought distinguishes him from philosophers like Aristotle, Hegel and Green. State is not natural. His non-violence pushed him to the extent that 'the ideal state is one where there is no state.' Stateless democracy is a Gandhian ideal. This anarchism has been described by Gandhiji as under 'Everybody will be his own sovereign in this enlightened anarchism. It will not harm his neighbour because the violent state will not be there to pollute him.'[56]

Thus Gandhism comes close to Marxian ideal of withering away of state. Human development is from violence to non-violence. Hence as society marches towards non-violence the violent state will become dysfunctional. But the transitional stage will need 'The State'. Moreover so long violence remains a part of human nature, state will be needed in all societies for survival.[57] So he advocated a minimal state and agreed with Thoreau that, 'that government is the best, which governs the least.'

Gandhiji was a practical idealist. He knew the obstacles in abolishing the state. Human being may never succeed to say goodbye to state. In 1940 while replying to a question he said 'no government can be totally non-violent because it represents the imperfect man. The golden age may dawn where state may be more and more non-violent. I am working for this ideal.'[58]

In 1946, he accepted that there may be no state without government, but he hoped that if people constantly endeavour, it may be possible to establish a welfare state of non-violent variety. He affirmed that such a state can or will dawn first in India, because India is a country, where such efforts have been made in the past. To abandon fear of death is a step towards non-violent state.[59]

Thus Gandhi accepted that state is a necessary evil and the disappearance of violence will cause the collapse of the state. Stateless society is unworkable, hence he would work for a society which he depicted in his Hind Swaraj.

Swarajya: An Ideal Political System

Gandhiji believed in doing what he used to dream. White head had said 'An unstable age is a great period of history.' Gandhi was a product of such an era wherein he strived to practise truth, non-violence, Swarajya and Swadharma. India of Gandhi's dreams is possible through Swarajya.

Gandhiji struggled to coordinate end with the means. Hence Swarajya and Sarvodaya became somewhat co-terminus. Swarajya is a total idea – much more than mere political liberation. It includes spiritual, moral, economic, social and political aspects. His book *Hind Swaraj* conceives of a self-system which gives a destination for the polity. Indian and Christian philosophies declare salvation or 'Moksha' as a state of liberation from sin and pain. He advanced this idea of a man free from sin and pain. The nation of Gandhi's Swarajya is something like this liberation of an individual. It is a reign of goodness.[60] Hence his Swarajya includes Sarvodaya. He repeated it several times, but did not change to improve it.

His concept of Swarajya is flexible. He conceived of it in South Africa and there he played himself as a successful Satyagrahi. In 1917 he said 'My idea of Swarajya has evolved over decades.'[61] In 1908 he wrote in his paper *Indian Opinion* 'Swarajya is not what India has been cherishing. The real Swarajya implies self-control. It can be enjoyed only by moral people, i.e. people with self control and self-discipline.'[62]

He called 'Swarajya a pious term from the Vedas.' It means rule of the self. The term independence denotes absence of restraints.[63] He opined that Swarajya in India will be a government of public committees elected by the majority of Indian adults. These people should have served the society by physical labour and should be enrolled in voters list. Real Swarajya does not mean capturing power and abusing it. People should have the capacity to oppose it. Swarajya is a concept of awareness which enables people to regulate and use power.[64] He equates it with Rama Rajya which is known for equality, justice and piety. People will do 'Swa Dharma' and share their joys and sorrows in common. Rulers have to keep the ideals of truth, duty and sacrifice. The rulers will be happy and unhappy in the state of their people. To be a good citizen will give him or her an eligibility to be a responsible ruler,[65] thus Swarajya was a positive ideal of equanimity (*sambhav*). It cannot be a gift. It is a precious treasure for which generations have shed their blood. It needs constant striving and endless series of sacrifices.[66]

In Gandhi's view a country rises only with sacrifice. A mother suffers to serve her progeny. The plant grows when seed gets dissolved. Life is another name of death.[67] A great country has to have citizens prepared to sacrifice their lives. Those who challenge death become fearless.[68] The patriots alone can defend their country. The country's good has to overweigh other petty personal gains. If the majority of people are selfish, then the government has to confront anarchy.[69] So Swarajya requires dutiful citizens. It depends upon peoples' power. People should fight difficulties – individually as well as collectively. The only way to attain Swarajya is that each individual controls his or her own self without external control.[70]

Free individuals ipso facto attain Swarajya. He wrote in *Hind Swaraj* 'Our young man talk about Swarajya because the great grandfather Dadabhai Naoroji did the ground work. Hume wrote ceaselessly and awakened us to do something. He made us awake. Sir William Wederburn sacrificed everything to spread the idea of Swarajya. G.K. Gokhale prepared the nation for 20 years and lived like a beggar. Even today he lives like a poor Indian. Late Justice Badruddin Tayaab ji sowed the seeds of Congress organisation. All these patriots in various parts of the country deserve our reverence.'[71]

Gandhian Swaraj reflects the efforts of moderates and radicals. He regarded Congress as a purposive and creative organisation. He addressed Naoroji and Gokhale as pillars of Indian freedom.[72] In his opinion early Congressmen – British or Indian made the real contribution. All of us who aspire for Swarajya cannot ignore our worthy predecessors. Englishmen in general were not opposed to Congress demands.[73]

He strengthened Congress in his own way. He was a moderate but he did not condemn those who were true patriots. He used the term Ram Rajya but it has nothing to do with the Hindu rule of the son of king Dasrath.[74]

Varied Aspects of Swarajya: Positive and Negative

Gandhiji explained his concept of Swarajya quite comprehensively. Positively he called it a total idea of self-rule. He wrote in *Young India* 'Race and religion have no place in Swarajya of my dreams. It shall not be monopolised by the rich and the educated. It includes peasants and also millions of labourers who are deformed and hungry.'[75] He was keen that once English leave India, then Indians will frame their own constitution and elect their own form of government. They will have the right to change governments. He agreed with Thoreau that the government will govern the least and people will have minimum impediments. Government will promote only those functions which will be morally worth doing.

He spent over 30 years to fight for India's freedom. During these years he not only developed the concepts but made concrete efforts for their realisation. Negatively Swarajya implied absolutely no intervention by any alien power. It was not just England, he did not accept the princely rule of native rulers who were not elected by the people and were imposing their dynastic rule on the basis of sword. They were divine despots and never accepted their accountability to their people. Naturally these monarchies were against the natural inclinations of the people. Similarly Gandhiji was opposed to military despotism and all other sort of aggressors. These dictators have been imposing their rule and suppressing the popular risings. History is full of such dictators who over a we people. Even Genghis Khan falls in this category. To quote Gerald Heard 'Genghis Khan was notorious for his brutalities. A saint condemned him for his inhuman regime. He heard him with patience.'[76] Alexander conquered empires with brutal force. But he felt feeble when a naked fakir stood in front of him. So Gandhiji wanted to fight brutal force with non-violence and his fight was against the evil not against the evil doers.[77]

Gandhiji stood for total independence, so that people may develop their capacities and English rule may not paralyse them.

Theoretical Basis of Swarajya

While elucidating Swarajya he said 'you do not want a tiger but you love his habits and nature. It cannot work. If you keep the English ways in India, then India becomes England. I do not want such a Swarajya.'[78] Self-government underlines self not government.

Swarajya does not mean you own something which you do not accept. If you have tasted Swarajya you can never give it up. Each one has to enjoy it. Those who do not know how to swim cannot save drowning men. We are slaves, how can we liberate others.[79] He propounded some of the following principles for Swarajya:[80]

1. Man is superior to other species. He has the divine spark in him. He is conscious about his process and is capable to improve his society and state.

2. He is rational and logical, he can make right choices. It is a political process which yields self-governance. All human beings are endowed with reason. So everybody should rule over his body and mind. Gandhiji offered a rationale for self-governance or a valid reason to oppose the foreign rule.

Spiritualisation of Politics: A Necessity for Swarajya

He made a spirited plea for spiritualisation of politics. Politics is not factionalism, but has to have truth and justice. He called religion the root of politics but his religion included the best of all religions. He respected all religions. To him religion was a creative way to follow the divine path on the basis of beliefs and experiences. The paths are different but the destination is the same. Hence politics should include truth and human values. He stood for 'Lokneeti' in place of 'Rajneeti' and worked for it in earnest.[81] Religion establishes coordination and so is the purpose of politics also. He felt that Swarajya will evade India unless Hindus, Muslim, Parsis, Bheels, etc. do not get united.[82] Humanism is true religion and a religion which does not coordinate social situations cannot be called a religion. He believed that those who believe in God must accept it as their duty to oppose all injustices and exploitations to the best of their might.

Ram Rajya: An Ideal Swarajya

It literally means rule of justice or rule of love. It can also be called as 'non-violent self-rule of the people.'[83] It endows power to people and originates from the power of self-rule. It is possible only when everybody does his or her duty.[84] People may not know their rights but duties are more important and have to be fulfilled with care. Gandhiji believed that all duties include rights, in fact rights flow from our duties. If we do our duties honestly, nobody can deprive us from any of our rights.[85]

A Swarajya based on non-violence has to have citizens who are dutiful. The true rights are linked with duties and are needed only because duties are to be performed. Duty based rights are used in the service of society. Swarajya includes individual freedom and if duties are carried out in good faith then their aggregation ends up with social Swarajya. People do not think of rights but they have these rights when needed. They help in the fulfilment of duties.[86]

A non-violent self-rule does not envisage enemies of freedom. Everyone cooperates with one another in a willing manner. They improve their knowledge and performance. The number of diseases decline and nobody is poor. Work is available to all and discriminations shrink. It abolishes class conflicts and social evils like drinking, gambling automatically disappear. Rich people do not waste money but use their wealth for social good. The present situation of some living in palaces and many languishing in slums will be unthinkable. Nobody will violate the just rights of other person. Aggression will be abominable. Nobody can forcefully deprive others of their due. If some people still indulge in undesirable activities, the non-violent pressures of the groups should be strong enough to rectify it.[87]

Thus Gandhian Swarajya is a perfect non-violent state. The Indian Swarajya can be conducted by Indians and they are capable to sustain it. The Lok Satta can be generated by truthful means. The differences are not to be suppressed but sorted out with goodwill and open ended discussions. It will preserve individual freedom.[88] Naturally, it will need popular awareness and they should know and preserve their genuine interests. The people should have courage to fight and resist, no matter the entire world stands opposed to the non-violent force of Swarajya.

Freedom from foreign rules and economic independence are the twin pillars of this Gandhian Swarajya. The social and religious ends of this edifice are important. The four corners constitute the parallelogram. No angle can be obtuse. Truth and non-violence will keep the balance. It will aim at the highest moral values of life. The equality of all religions will pervade and each for everybody will be the principle of survival and development.

Swarajya and the End Means Synthesis

Individual in society has been seen from two perspectives. The individualists believe that freedom is more important than equality. The socialists on the contrary contend that social welfare cannot be sacrificed at the altar of freedom.

Gandhiji was an original thinker. He believed in the parity of means to attain noble ends. Non-violence in his philosophy is an end as well as a means. It is an original aspect of his thought. He was an ethicist and an idealist who had deep faith in moral means. Every political doctrine needs a moral grounding. He called ends and means inseparable.[89] He rejected Machiavelli outright who said that end justifies the means. The means build and determine the end. So are the means, so shall follow the end. Noble ends cannot be attained by ignoble means. The proverb has a meaning: 'Whatever you sow so shall you reap'. Mangoes do not grow on Babool trees. In fact end is the ultimate or last name of the series of means.[90]

Comparing the means and end with seed and tree, Gandhiji proved that seeds become trees and yield fruits. Improper means cannot lead to proper results. He wrote 'people say means cannot be the end. But I will say that means include the end. Means are determinants and the end is only a by-product. If violent means are employed then Swarajya will get perverted. Such a Swarajya will bring crisis to all. France is the example, which has been paying the price of French revolution.[91] There is no dividing line although God has endowed mankind to control the means (that too in a limited manner). End is absolutely beyond our control. People succeed in their ends only to the extent they control their means. It is a rule without exception.[92] In my way of thinking the end and means are synonymous and always go together.'[93]

Thus Gandhian Philosophy is a philosophy of purity of means. If people take care of purity of means, they may not care about the end. He also said that God takes care of pure all those who practice fair means to achieve ends. Gandhiji was opposed to Nazism and Fascism which openly supported violence and war as an instrument of politics. Gandhi strongly rejects and condemned those who think that politics can succeed with fraud and manipulations. He believed means, if not controlled, the end will be overwhelmed and ultimately eclipsed.[94]

Synthesis, unity and purity of end and means is Gandhi's contribution to political philosophy. He made politics an instrument of social service. He not only said and wrote his doctrines but practised them to the best of his capacity.

State as a Structure

Gandhiji was opposed to the Western notion of state. He criticised the British system and the parliament in most vehement words. By 1920, he revised some of these ideas. He said, 'Today I see parliamentary form of government in India as my ideal. A democracy should ensure an all round development of people to attain common goals.'[95] But he maintained that violence and democracy cannot coexist. If a state is a democracy only in name it can give up the force.[96] He advocated indirect elections through village panchayats. The seven lakh villages should elect their own representatives and the pyramid may keep on electing the higher bodies indirectly. This pyramid may ultimately elect a president to preside over from the pinnacle. Thus power will be diffused among seven lakh units. It will energise the rural life. People will cooperate and freedom will be a reality.[97]

Organs of Government

A democratic government has these organs, viz. legislature, executive and judiciary. Gandhiji was a votary of unicameral or one chambered legislature. He felt that poor countries like India cannot afford the bicameral legislature. 'I do not bother that one chamber will legislate in a hurry. I firmly maintain that by abolishing bicameralism India will be benefited. One chamber is enough. It is highly economical.'[98] About the president his view was that he should represent various sections of society. In view of the conditions in India he suggested the following qualification for the candidate:[99]

1. He should be a farmer from the village because 70 per cent people are rural.
2. The president may be an illiterate so that the government can work for literacy.
3. A woman should be the president.
4. A Harijan may be a good candidate to check atrocities on Harijans.
5. Muslims should be given a chance to allay feelings of insecurity of the minorities.
6. Youngsters should be encouraged. A young man of 18 years will be the best president of India.

All these qualifications of eligibility cannot be satisfied by one individual. But then a system should be built around the principles. He suggested Gulnar, the daughter of Maulana Mohammad Ali. Gandhi wished that a person for the office of president should be one who can represent the interests all sections of the society. Gandhiji supported an independent judiciary. The judicial system should dispense free and prompt justice, no matter whatever hurdles have to be encountered.

Decentralisation as a Philosophy

Individual freedom and dignity were close to Gandhi's heart. He wanted a social and political system which respected the individual. This is possible only when authority is decentralised. Centralisation hampers the growth of individuality.

The citizenry has to be developed as a whole. Versatile development has to be aimed at. Most of the people live in villages. They have to be liberated and protected against exploitation. So decentralisation can be a good means to achieve the end. The power should flow from centre to villages not vice versa. It will ensure full democracy and shape democratised villages. He advanced his philosophy of 'Oceanic Circles'. It literally means circles within circles. The formation begins at the lowest level and then circles keep widening.

The original circle is the Sarvodaya Samaj, wherein every villager will participate. Then circles will keep widening successively. Gandhiji envisaged these oceanic circles as independent circles without burdening over the lower circles. The oceanic circles do not disturb smaller circles. Rather the smaller circles push the wider circles to be independent.

To quote Gandhiji 'Such an oceanic circle in/of society will include innumerable villages. They will neither crash nor swallow. Life will not be vertical. The summit will not narrow down. Every wave of the oceanic circle will be wider and will encircle the smaller circles one by one. Individual will be in the centre. He will live for his village. The village will work for the community (wider circle) around. It will integrate society and they will never invade over one another. They will all enjoy the oceanic security and glory as an integral part of the sea of humanity.' The outer circle will not suppress the inner circles but keep the inner circles functioning.

It is an operational model of Rural Republics of Gandhi. The belief was that India lives in villages. Hence rural folks have to be empowered. This concept of Gandhi was enshrined in the directive principles of state policy. The scheme says 'State will strive to make village panchayats as instruments of self-government.'[100] Accordingly the Nehru Government launched community development programme on 2 October 1952.[101] Later on Panchayati Raj was given as a three tier network on the recommendations of Balwant Rai Mehta Committee.[102] Gradually these institutions were revitalised and 73rd amendment was an attempt to empower the villages and the villagers. The bread labour theory of Gandhiji can be practised here. The present class division will gradually be obliterated and he who does not labour shall not rule, may be a panchayati democracy of India.[103] It is an effort in Gandhian direction, but enough remains to be done to make Panchayati Raj a rural democracy of Gandhi's dream.

In April 1999 the Chief Minister of Madhya Pradesh Shri Digvijai Singh made a heroic attempt to introduce Zila government in place of Zila administration. The District Planning Committee (DPC) of constitutional provision [243 ya (य) & Gha (घ)] was empowered to function as district cabinet responsible to Zila Parishad. The establishment of district government in a three tier federatism of India seems like a rational evolution of Panchayati Raj. It was seriously and sincerely experimented in Madhya Pradesh. It was called 'Zila Sarkar' in place of 'Zila Prashashan'.[104] It was a new chapter in Indian politics and it linked district level politics with district administration of traditional variety. The Madhya Pradesh experiment was to be operationalised in 15 years. Unfortunately the political change at state level could not pursue it and it had to be abandoned. Now several states are struggling to revive this model with notions of Gram Swarajya.

Adult Suffrage

Mahatma Gandhi was a proponent of adult suffrage. Several schools of thought advocate limited suffrage, i.e. right to vote of the educated. The Constituent Assembly debated about it at length and rejected education as a qualification for voting for the candidates. Adult suffrage takes care of minorities and poor workers or farmers. Gandhiji's argument was that money and literacy do not add to character. Nobody should be deprived of franchise just because of so called education. People who toil and live with dignity shall have a right to vote.[105] The founding fathers respected the idea of adult suffrage of the father of the nation and the constitution allows franchise without discrimination of caste, class, creed or gender.

Public Opinion

Public opinion is an instrument to keep the society healthy.[106] Public opinion should not be violent, otherwise it becomes ineffective.[107] Law should follow and respect public opinion. Public welfare, popular good and public opinion are overlapping terms.[108] Governments should understand the differences in their concepts.

Franchise and the Voter

Press plays a decisive role in shaping the opinion of the voters. The media may also be dishonest. The voters keep changing their opinions like pendulum of the clock. The voters can be hypnotised or corrupted. This has made western democracies undemocratic. Parliaments are abused and people are exploited by elected leaders. Elections breed corruption, waste of money, time and energy. Democracy will remain an illusion, unless people stick to truth and non-violence.[109] In 1934, Gandhiji Concluded that Western democracy has passed through a testing phase and has failed quite miserably. 'Today people are losing faith in these institutions and I doubt it will ever succeed in India. Democratic spirit cannot be imposed from outside. It has to be an internal instinct.[110]'

Gandhiji felt that property and educational qualifications cannot be the basis of eligibility. Physical labour or bread labour should be tried. Shram Dan can be prescribed as a qualification. Labourers will prevent the citizens to develop class character. The mental labourers are a tiny minority and they should not exploit the majority of labourers and farmers.[111]

Gandhiji on Westminster Model

Before returning to India Gandhiji launched his first non-violent agitation from Phoenix Ashram in India. He confronted worse situations. He thought and wanted to develop the best system after contemplation and experiment. In Africa he discovered the inadequacies of the parliamentary system. His *Hind Swaraj* bears a testimony of his dissatisfaction. He criticised the British Parliamentary System and industrialisation vehemently. This pushed him to think about Swarajya in a positive manner.

British Parliament and Prime Minister

In his treatise *Hind Swarajya* Gandhiji, while condemning the British Parliament wrote 'The institution which you call mother parliament is a barren woman, comparable with a prostitute. These are harsh words but they are true. She is barren because she does not deliver good laws. It does nothing unless forced. I compare it with a prostitute because the cabinet controls her.'[112]

Gandhiji was criticised for this statement. It was said that it was an elected body and should control policies. Gandhi's reply was that 'a fertile parliament should contain good people only. Its members should be honorary. They should serve the people. People should not petition to parliament. It should work in a simple way and its members should not be selfish and mischievous. Parliamentarians work under fear and change their decisions under pressure. When important matters are discussed the members of parliament either sleep or cry at the top of their voices. A writer has called it a talking shop. Members vote as asked by the party whip. The exceptions are punished. Members waste time, money and energy. It is a toy of the people which costs them dearly. These are not my views, several British thinkers agree with me. One Englishman has said that good religious people have no place in such parliaments. Others have called it a child. It, parliament is a child after 700 years, when shall it be young.'[113]

Gandhiji was an idealist and he was sad when he read about the conduct of British members of parliament. He compared British parliament with a prostitute first because there was no master and the Prime Minister who had to protect it, normally remained engaged with his party politics.[114] The British P.M. is not a patriot. He may be honest, but he is always obsessed with the idea of monopolising power. The Prime Minister does not serve. He does not have a clean conscience and non-partisan behaviour. Still Gandhiji stood for the parliamentary system without its obvious and apparent pitfalls.[115]

Police and its Popular Obligations

Police has a special role in a democratic system. It has to implement the laws enacted by elected representatives. Moreover, it should serve the greatest good of the greatest number.[116] Gandhi revised it as 'the good of all'. At that time the police was regulated by Indian Police Act of 1861.[117] It gave wide ranging power to police and made it the master of the colony.

Gandhiji fought against this concept to make police the servant of the people. He said, 'I admit that even a non-violent state will need police. In fact it represents incomplete non-violence. I cannot dare to say that we can live without police and army. Army we may not need but police we shall always require. But my picture or image of police is quite different. The policemen can also be non-violent. They will serve, not control. People will offer cooperation to police and conflicts will gradually decline. Policemen may keep arms but they will use them rarely. It will convert police into social reformers. Only extreme variety of criminals will fall in the jurisdiction of police forces. The present day conflicts of labourers and capitalists will disappear in a non-violent state. People in large numbers will respect police as their own. The communal riots will also have no place in a non-violent state.'[118]

So Gandhiji's police would reform the society without weapons. It will not use arms against people, but criminals will get their due.

Gandhiji viewed crime as a disease arising out of the society. Free India will treat criminals differently. Society will have to find means like medicine to combat this menace.[119] Believing in reformatory theory of punishment he argued that jails should be hospitals and criminals can be treated or cured as patients.

He wrote 'I strongly hold that criminals should stay in jails very much like patients in the hospitals. Crime is a pathological phenomenon. Criminals suffer from mental ailments. Jail authorities like doctors should do diagnosis and prescribe. Jail authorities should behave like nurses or medical employees. The prisoners should feel like friends with the prison staff. The criminal need not be tortured. The right way is that he is cured and rehabilitated. The people's governments should make laws for it. It is not easy but enough can be accomplished if the philosophy of non-violent prison hospitals is adopted by the state and society.'[120]

Gandhiji had to stay in prison in India and South Africa. His experiences were harrowing and he has written a lot about the jail torture and neglect. He advised the prisoners to be disciplined and obedient. They should improve their skills and behaviours. The prisoners should learn to argue out their case before authorities and avoid bitterness. They should try to be productive and useful citizens when they come out from the prison.[121] They should contribute to the good of society in their second career.

Judiciary and Law

Gandhiji was a lawyer by profession and training. His primary task was to liberate the country from foreign yoke. He got ample opportunities to think, confer and do activities in the areas of law and justice. Swarajya, Sarvodaya, Satyagrah and social system made him write on these public issues. *Young India* was his mouth piece. While in South Africa he thought as a Vakil about his duties and his conclusion was 'A Vakil should integrate various aspects of truth of the case.'[122]

He maintained that life would have been happier if people did not have respect or faith in courts and Vakils. Those who come to courts often complain that courts work in a polluted atmosphere. The witnesses take date from both sides and talk lies without any qualms of conscience. They sell their conscience for money and friendship.[123] Hence Bar should not be a place to make money but to serve the nation. There are very few or rare examples of Vakils serving the society in poverty. This is the story of all countries and all cultures. Lawyers get higher fees in proportion to their work. It is a universal practice that advocates to teach falsehood and train clients in immoral methods. One of the barristers has on record said that it is the duty of the advocate to save his client even when he knows that he is a criminal. Gandhiji was horrified to see this. An advocate should speak the truth and help the judge to see the truth. To prove the client innocent is neither justice nor object of the legal court procedure.[124]

Gandhiji supported the jury system of law and justice. The juries promote the spirit of independence. It requires morally committed individuals in the justice system from bottom to the top.[125]

Over emphasis upon law makes the society negligent and dependent. Law has a limited role in removing evil. Laws are made for certain evil intentioned persons. No reform can be imposed by law. Such reforms are superficial and do not endure.

State Reorganisation

He was a believer in the unity of state and stood for integrity of the nation. Gandhiji wanted diversities to be preserved and reorganise the Indian state in national interest. He supported linguistic[126] state. He was pained to see communalism and regionalism dividing the country. In a prayer meeting Calcutta, he exhorted that 'Bengalis and Biharis should live in peace. They are brethren, not aliens. All rights originate from duties and we are performing duties as always.'[127]

India belongs to all. Assam cannot belong to Assamese. We all are Indians. We can live and move anywhere. But we should not exploit or harm our poor brethren in the name of regionalism. We all are servants of India and we live with this spirit of service for the motherland.[128]

Notes

1. B.C. Roy, *Gandhian Ethics*, pp. 5–9.
2. Ibid., p. 8.
3. Ibid., p. 9.
4. *Collected Works of Mahatama Gandhi*, Vol. 78, p. 390.
5. Ibid., Vol. 50, p. 204.
6. M.K. Gandhi, *Ahinsa and Satya*, Varanasi, pp. 624–630.
7. Ibid. p. 630.
8. *Collected Works of Mahatama Gandhi*, Vol. 33, p. 952.
9. M.K. Gandhi, *My Religion*, Navajivan, Ahmedabad, p. 43.
10. G.N. Sharma and Moin Shakir, *Politics and Society: Rammohan Roy to Nehru*, Parimal Publication, Aurangabad, 1976.
11. M.K. Gandhi, *My Religion*, op. cit.

12. M.K. Gandhi, *Ahinsa and Satya*, op. cit.
13. Thakur Das Bang, *Gandhi Vichar*, Sarva Seva Sangha, Varanasi, 1992, p. 7.
14. *Young India*, 14 August 1920.
15. K. Mashroowala, *Gandhi Vichar Dohan*, Sasta Sahitya, Delhi, 1999, p. 16.
16. S.L. Varma and B.M. Sharma, *Bhartiya Rajneetik Vicharak*, op. cit., p. 249.
17. *Collected Works of Mahatama Gandhi*, Vol. 10, Delhi, 1963. p. 46.
18. S.L. Varma and B.M. Sharma, op. cit., pp. 249–50.
19. Gandhi, From Yarvada Prison, op. cit., p. 8–9.
20. Gopinath Dhawan, Sarvodaya Tatva Darshan, p. 74.
21. *Harijan*, 12 November 1938.
22. *Harijan*, 20 July 1935.
23. *Young India*, 16 June 1927.
24. K.L. Mashroowala, *Gandhi Vichar Dohan*, op. cit., p. 18.
25. Mahadev Prasad, *Mahatama Gandhi Samaj Darshan*, Chandigarh, 1989, p. 124.
26. *Indian Opinion*, Golden Number, p. 9.
27. Gandhian *Concept of State*, Navajivan, Ahmedabad, 1965, p. 9.
28. V.P. Varma, *Adhunik Rajneetik Chintan*, Laxmi Narayan, Agra, 2000, p. 359.
29. *Young India*, 10 March 1920.
30. Mohan Mala, Navajivan Trust, Ahmedabad, 1997, pp. 58.
31. *Young India*, 3 November 1927.
32. G.N. Dhawan, *The Political Philosophy of M. Gandhi*, New Delhi, 1990, pp. 25–37.
33. *Harijan*, 14 March 1936.
34. Adi H. Doctor, *A Probe into the Gandhian Concept of Ahinsa*, Renaissance, Calcutta, 1962, pp. 31–52.
35. *Hind Swarajya*, Delhi, 1958, p. 88.
36. *Harijan*, 15 April 1933.
37. *Harijan*, 6 July 1933.
38. M.K. Gandhi, *Satyagrah in South Africa*, op. cit., pp. 113–115.
39. Vinoba Bhave, *Swarajya Shastra*, Varanasi, 2000, p. 34.
40. *Collected Works*, Vol. 16, pp. 515–17.
41. S.L. Varma and B.M. Sharma, op. cit., pp. 252–53.
42. Ibid., p. 251.
43. Ram Ratan and Sharda Shobhika, *Gandhi Ki Rajneetik Avdharanayen*, Delhi, 1992, pp. 109–14.
44. Pattabhi Sitaramayya, *Gandhivad*, Part I, pp. 102–3.

45. K.L. Kamal, *Gandhi Chintan*, Jaipur, 1996, p. 51.
46. S.L. Varma and B.M. Sharma, op. cit., p. 254.
47. K.L. Kamal, Gandhi Chintan, op. cit., p. 51.
48. S.L. Varma and B.M. Sharma, op. cit., p. 254.
49. *Harijan*, 21 April 1946.
50. *Harijan Sevak*, 18 March 1939.
51. *Harijan*, 13 October 1940.
52. G.N. Dhawan, op. cit., p. 4.
53. Sobhakant Jha, *Champaran: Ahinsa Ki Prayog-Sthali*, Delhi, 19 August 2001, p. 9.
54. S.L. Varma and B.M. Sharma, op. cit., p. 265.
55. *Young India*, 27 March 1930.
56. *Young India*, 2 July 1935, B.R. Purohit, op. cit., p. 247.
57. Ibid., p. 247.
58. Pratap Singh, 'Gandhiji Ka Darshan', Research, Jaipur, 1997, p. 68.
59. Ibid.
60. M.K. Gandhi, *The Collected Works of Mahatama Gandhi*, Vol. XLVI, p. 167.
61. Ibid., Vol., XIV, p. 49.
62. *Young India*, 19 March 1931.
63. *Young India*, 19 March 1931.
64. *Hindi Navjeevan*, 29 January 1925.
65. Magan Bhai Desai, *Swarajya Kya Hai*, Navajivan, Ahmedabad, 1962, p. 5.
66. *Young India*, 5 June 1920.
67. *Young India*, 19 June 1920.
68. *Hind Swaraj*, op. cit., p. 48.
69. *Young India*, 28 July 1925.
70. *Hindi Navjeevan*, 8 December 1927.
71. *Hind Swaraj*, op. cit., p. 10.
72. Sandhya Arya, *Bhartiya Chintan Main Swaraj*, Jaipur, 1996, p. 94.
73. Ibid.
74. Ibid., pp. 94–95.
75. *Young India*, 26 March 1931.
76. A.N. Pandey, *Gandhi Samgra Chintan*, op. cit., p. 114.
77. Pyarelal, *Pilgrimage for Peace*, Navajivan, Ahmedabad, 1950, pp. 157–60.
78. *Hind Swaraj*, op. cit., p. 23.
79. Ibid., p. 67.
80. Ram Ratan and Sharda Shobhika, op. cit., pp. 45–46.

81. Vinobha, *Lokneeti*, Varanasi, 1999, p. 81.
82. Sandlya Arya, *Bhartiya Chinten*, op. cit., p. 101.
83. K.G. Mushroowala, *Gandhi Vichar Dohan*, op. cit., p. 76.
84. Ibid.
85. Mulk Raj Anand, *Gandhi Ke Amar Vichar*, Delhi, 1989, p. 29.
86. *Harijan*, 25 March 1939.
87. *Harijan*, 25 March 1939.
88. *Harijan*, 27 May 1939.
89. B.R. Purohit, 20th *Sadi Ka Rajneetik Chintan*, Bhopal, 1983, p. 233.
90. Ram Ratan and Shobhika, op. cit., p. 130.
91. *Young India*, 17 July 1934.
92. *Young India*, 17 July 1924.
93. *Young India*, 26 December 1924.
94. B.R. Purohit, op. cit., p. 234.
95. *Harijan*, 27 May 1939
96. *Harijan*, 12 November 1938.
97. Louis Fisher, *A Week with Gandhi*, pp. 55–80.
98. Mahadev Prasad, op. cit., p. 189.
99. Ram Ratan and Shobhika, op. cit., pp. 54–55.
100. Bharat Ka Samvidhan, Article 40.
101. B.M. Sharma, Zila Prashan se Zila Sarkar, *Prashasnika No. 2*, Jaipur, July–December 1998, p. 5.
102. Report of ARC on District Adm., Delhi, 1967, p. 19.
103. B.S. Khanna, Development of Panchayati Raj in India, *Madhya Pradesh Journal of Social Sciences*, Vol. 2, No. 1, 1994, pp. 30–31.
104. B.M. Sharma, *Zila Sarkar*, Rawat Publications, Jaipur, 2000, p. 28.
105. *Young India*, 8 October 1935.
106. *Young India*, 18 December 1920.
107. *Young India*, 7 May 1931.
108. *Young India*, 29 January 1931.
109. B.N. Pande op. cit., pp. 115–16.
110. Ibid., p. 117.
111. Ibid., p. 117–18.
112. *Hind Swaraj*, op. cit., pp. 24–25.
113. B.N. Pande, op. cit., p. 115.
114. *Hind Swaraj*, op. cit. p. 23.
115. *Hind Swaraj*, op. cit., p. 115.
116. A.K. Mishra, Loktantra Me Police Ki Bhumika, *UP Journal of Police*, Lucknow, January 1999, p. 11.
117. G.C. Singhvi, To Whom should Police be Responsible, IJPA, (IIPA) Vol. 24, No. 4, 1978, pp. 113–122.

118. *Harijan,* 1 September 1940.
119. *Harijan,* 5 May 1946.
120. *Daily Diary,* pp. 117–118.
121. Ibid., pp. 117–118.
122. K.L. Kamal, op. cit., p. 9.
123. *Young India,* 6 October 1926.
124. *Hindi Navjeevan,* 29 December 1937.
125. *Young India,* 27 August 1931.
126. *Harijan Sevak,* 19 April 1942, p. 118.
127. Ibid., 7 September 1947, p. 264.
128. *Harijan Sevak,* 7 September 1947, p. 259; Gandhiji, *Bharat Ke Naye Rajya,* Navajivan, Ahmedabad, 1961, p. 7.

6

Gandhi and Secularism

Gandhi combined in his personality a prophet, a saint, a super human and a moral politician. He never accepted politics without religion and conducted the freedom struggle through Satyagrah, based on non-violence. He combined the end and means in such a way that the moral and spiritual character of human beings got strengthened.[1] His life was a saga of spiritual force. All of his struggles in varied fields of life had a spiritual goal. His message was 'the spiritual development of India is the only thing that matters.'[2]

Gandhi was a *Karamyogi* (man of action) who believed that self-development can resolve all the social and economic problems of a nation. He had his own definition of religion. His view was that religion has a common foundation and it brings the individual face to face with God.[3] Nothing which is opposed to rationality and morality can ever be religious. It should be practical and offer solutions to day-to-day problems of life. He has said 'whatever I have said or done thus far has a religious consciousness and religious goal behind.[4] The political doctrines are only sub goals or principles of the all pervading religious system.' He elaborated it further by saying 'Politics devoid of religion is like a noose of death, which kills the soul.[5] Without religion and morality life becomes a footpath without destination. Like every other action politics needs to be disciplined by religion. Without moral laws life becomes meaningless and immorality takes over.'[6] Gandhiji subscribed to humanism and did not accept other worldliness. He stressed upon the basic unity of all religions. Every religion explains the fundamental reality of life in its context. Religion is capable to control every aspect of life.[7]

A true religion represents the hub of life and notwithstanding all its evils, religion is necessary for human beings. 'If I participate in politics then the only reason for it is the fact that politics coils around our life like a snake. One cannot get out of its circle. I want to combat with this snake, so I am trying to introduce religion into politics.[8] I cannot abandon politics because it is my religious duty. The goal of life is self-actualisation. This actualisation needs coordination with entire humanity. So I work for the good of all. It is possible only through popular participation. All human activities represent an integrated whole. The political, social and pure religious aspects of life cannot be separated or divorced from one another.[9] He who does not understand patriotism cannot comprehend duty or religion.[10] Religion is service of mankind, good of all and hence a collective version of patriotism.'[11] Gandhiji believed in the creative power of religion because it prescribed a moral discipline. In his own words:

> In my view religion means morality. I cannot accept any such religion which rejects morality or preaches immorality. Religion in its essence is the culmination of moral activities in practical life.[12]

He examined religion in its wider context and redefined it on the basis of his experiences and experiments. To him religion held the world and bereft of religion individual and society will be lifeless and mere vacuum.

Gandhiji brought all activities and all aspects of life to religious fold.[13] He did not accept sects or groups. Religion is a perennial element of human society. It is much beyond Hinduism, Islam and Christianity. His speculation made him conclude that the spiritual force of man is far more superior to his physical power and virtues. The spiritual power comprises of truth, non-violence, love, peace and service of humanity. This moral speculation was spiritualism. He said 'I alone can know my spiritual experiments. In my judgment spiritualism coincides with morality.'

Gopal Krishan Gokhale made earlier attempts to spiritualise Indian politics. He established Bharat Sevak Samaj for this purpose. But Gandhi's contribution to this field is unique and all pervading. He made this spiritual force respectable in politics.

Religion in Gandhian Philosophy

The concepts of truth and God are the starting points of this philosophy .Unlike several other activists, he was not an atheist or a materialist. He believed in duty and hence religion became prominent in his thought.[14] His religion rose above Hinduism. Although he called himself a Sanatani Vaishanav[15] but his belief was that 'my Hindu religion is the religion of humanity and it includes the best of all religions. I have reached to this religion by my experiments with truth and non-violence. Now I say God is not truth, but truth alone is God.' It influences people. Truth can be actualised only when one identifies himself with his whole world. So you cannot escape social service. He urged people to expand and accept the Upanishad dictum 'ब्रह्म सत्यम् जगत मिथ्या!' (God is the only reality and the world is not real). The entire universe is the expansion of divine consciousness. It is mere divine reflection and Braham includes all whatever cannot be included is falsehood.[16] Hence keep the God with you and abandon all that assures safety.

Religion is like a tree. It's branches get nourishment and energy from one source, i.e. God. Religions are paths to take you to the destination, i.e. the super natural.[17] Religions have given varied names to paths and the destinations. But they explain the variety of perceptions of characters of the individuals. At one point all these paths merge. The primary basis is one and it can be called a world religion.

While delivering his prayer sermon he once said 'I am a true Hindu, a Sanatani Hindu. Hence I am a Muslim, a Sikh, a Parasi, a Jew and a Christian. All these religions are the branches of a tree. Which branch I should choose and which I should ignore, where from should I pick my leaves or which ones I should exclude. All religions are one. If all people understand religion as I do, there will be total peace and harmony in India.'[18]

He was a Hindu, but he had love for other religions. He was tolerant and respectful for brethren from other religions. He used to say 'My Hinduism will get insulted if I do not help or save a Muslim or a Christian in distress. I must stake everything I have to save and serve people of other religions. My Hindu religion is all comprehensive. It does not support opposition to other religions. All religions are inter-connected, you can search good principles in all religions. To compare religions and hold one higher than others is petty mindedness. All religions supplement each other. No religion can or should contradict other religions. One must accept and respect all religions as his own.'[19]

Why he accepted Hinduism, he explained it in *Young India* 'Hinduism is extremely tolerant of all the religions which I know. It lacks extremity. I like its liberalism. One can express himself and Hinduism gives ample opportunity to all. Hindus can appreciate and own good practices of other religions. Non-violence all religion talk about, but Hindus give a special place and respect for non-violent traditions. In my view Jains and Buddhists are also Hindus. Hinduism regards human beings as one entity or children of God. Cow worship has helped in developing love and pity towards all living beings. Accepting and respecting all living beings is an experiment of respecting the creations of God. Rebirth can be seen in this perspective. Similarly Varna System is a result of continuous research in social experimentations of truth.'[20]

Service to human beings is the highest religion. This is what Vaishnav virtues are. While addressing a rally of RSS workers in 1947, Gandhiji expressed his religious tolerance in the following manner, 'While I am proud of being a Hindu, my Hindu religion is neither narrow nor intolerant. It is unique. A Hindu must internalise and include all good qualities of other religions. If non-Hindus cannot live with equality in India, or Muslims in Pakistan will keep the Hindus in subordination, then it will imply the end of both the religions.'[21] This warning of Gandhiji holds good in present day parlance. India is struggling with its religious tolerance and Pakistan has ruined its very identity with this hate campaign.

Place of Religion in History

It is true that religion has a creative role in history. Religion means a faith that accepts the divine discipline which governs the universe. He condemned Bolshivism and atheistic doctrine of communism.[22] He always maintained his faith in Hinduism but rejected communalism, factionalism and narrow sectarionism in social life. In his view the essence of Hinduism was precious but what goes on as ritualisation or propaganda in all religions, including Hinduism has to be dropped. He practised it with rigour and said in bold words that all religions say what Hindus have been upholding since times immemorial. Search for truth is Hinduism. Moral values are spiritual. Human religion is perfection in human values. If ethical values are damaged, religious values are obliterated. All religions came into existence to preserve moral values of their times which have internal import. My religion unites all these permanent values of human societies, no matter yesterday, today or tomorrow. When Dr Radhakrishnan asked the following questions to Gandhiji about his religious point of view, his answers were self-explanatory:

1. What is your religion?
2. Why did you get attracted towards it?
3. What is the impact of religion on social life?

Gandhiji's answers were spontaneous. He spoke securely and boldly to give clarity to his ideas.

1. My religion is Hinduism. To me it is a religion of humanity and humanism. It includes all the noble principles of all religions which I know of.
2. I was attracted to Hinduism because it permits me to search for truth and non-violence. It is the expression of human love in its widest form.
3. Social life is a reflection of religious values in all societies. Religious people serve others and surrender before God, the Divine creator. One can face truth only when he establishes contact with all living beings. No religion permits escapism. My religion teaches me to be the first servant of people. It is a pleasant job, a life of detachment and non-involvement as

> preached in the Geeta. You can attain Moksha or liberation. Once duties and responsibilities can be discharged with अनाशक्त कर्म योग. It needs global and spiritual awareness. All sorts of forces of good and evil keep fighting within human soul. Their triumph is *Karma Yog*. The victory of Ram over Ravan personifies or exemplifies this struggle. Buddha and Jesus were dutiful and highly inspired by universal love. He upholds the Biblical truth that 'abandon this world if it forces you to destroy your own soul.'

Religion can never be abolished from this world. If efforts are made to destroy religion, society will disintegrate. The world survives and functions because of love, truth, non-violence, otherliness, tolerance and justice. They regulate the social order. The very fact that so many human beings are alive and functioning, it is because they live on the basis of love and truth. People have been fighting wars, but the world goes on.[23]

Gandhi's Ram

His Ram has been a butt of social debates. He believed in God and did 'Ram prayers' in his congregations. He used to sing a song about Ramcharit Manas.[24] It has evoked confusions and misunderstandings. He clarified it that Ram is not the son of Dasrath, the ruler of Ayodhaya. He has written 'Ram of my prayers is not the historical personage – a descendent of king Dasrath. I worship a Ram who is unborn, omnipresent and omnipotent.'[25] The Ramayan is not only a wonderful epic but it is the best book on devotional thought.[26] Even Tulsidas who was a devotee of Saguna (सगुण) Rama uses Ram symbolically in abstract form.[27] Similarly Gandhi's Rama has nothing to do with history. He is a symbolic representative of God, the lord of this universe. He has clarified 'God is a useful idea. I can see truth in the midst of darkness. So my conclusion is that there is a God who is the truth, the light, and something all noble.'[28]

Spiritualisation of Politics

Mahatma Gandhi came on political horizon like a prophet. He propounded hard principles during his struggle and then experimented with them in political life. He was not a saint, but he lived like a saint in public view. He hated Machiavellian politics. He could not conceive politics as a game of fraud and selfishness. Politics is and should be a neat moral game of human goodness. So he tried to inject truth, non-violence and ethical values in political transactions and struggles. Satyagraha is one such technique which shook the foundations of British Raj in India. His biggest contribution to politics is its moralisation or spiritualisation in the literal sense of the term. Religion in his judgment was not sectarianism, but he redefined it as moral values of collective good. It should be remembered that he was not the first philosopher to ethicise politics. G.K. Gokhale had started it much earlier. Gandhiji has openly acknowledged his debt and he called him 'his political guru and a teacher'. Gokhale was the first to advise him to comprehend multidimensional politics of India and then decide his course of action.

Gokhale left a legacy of spiritualised politics of the liberals. He believed that politics is a means of social service, provided it keeps religion as its base. Without religion it will not be prescriptive or curative. Following Gokhale, Gandhiji evolved his religious perspective on Indian politics. Jainendra Kumar has pertinently commented:

'Gandhi's realism can be examined through religion and not through political activities. Politics is true from the glasses of religion. Otherwise it is all falsehood and chicanery. Politics is always changing and timely. Politicians do not care about their promise or oaths. But at some point they have to be fixed and rigid. This explains the key to politics. Gandhi could not accept the utilitarian logic that religion is a personal affair and cannot be related to political affairs of the society.'[29]

Gandhiji raised the stature of politics and made it an instrument of human improvement. He strived and struggled quite hard to induct religion in politics. In his own words 'to me the only way to win salvation is that I labour hard to serve the society and humanity. I wish to establish my communion with every living being. In the Geeta's language I wish to live with my friends and enemies in peace. Hence patriotism to me is a voyage of peace and a destination of liberty. To induct religion in politics means taking justice and truth forward. A religious person can do it because he cannot suffer exploitation and unwanted human torture.'

He declared that all human activities of politics should be inspired by religion. They may be social or economic overtones but should be treated as spiritual.[30]

A true religion is eternal. It is beyond scriptures. It seeks conformity to all beliefs. The moral and spiritual dimensions make human concerns alive and poignant.[31] Taking religion in philosophical sense, Gandhi argued that religion cannot be separated from politics. 'Those who know religion cannot be neutral to public affairs. He lives with his values and evil has to be resisted. Fighting evil is good religion. Politics without religion emits bad smell and religion minus politics is a waste of time. Politics means popular good. If you wish to serve God you cannot be apathetic to good or evil. To me truth is God. So I wish to reinforce truth like God in every temple of power.[32] Spiritualisation means you shun the riches and pleasures of physical world. If you want a moral order in the world then follow this way of truth and love and respect the moral laws of life.'[33]

Gandhiji used to say that no part of life can be excluded from religion. There is no politics without religion. Rather politics should be subjected to the supremacy of religion. Most of the religious leaders are political activists. Similarly several political leaders are essentially religious persons at heart.[34] They may be called religious idealists. Their lives have been inspired by divine spirit. 'I will regard morality, character and religion as synonyms. Without religion moral life becomes a house, standing on a sand dune.'[35] Gandhiji was keen to change the present day civilisational values. The Indian tradition accepts this relationship between the two. Everything in this world has a divine spark. God rules this universe. He is our master and we owe everything to him. Let us surrender all we have and accept only what he gives as his grace. There is nothing that can be called ours, because everything visible or invisible belongs to him.

This politics becomes a branch of religion or morality. It can never be an instrument of power. Bal Gangadhar Tilak once said 'Politics is not a game of saints.' To this Gandhi's reply was 'Politics is the place of saints and saints only.' Here saints mean noble people. Rabindranath Tagore also differed with Gandhiji. He asserted 'religion is a great legacy to mankind. Do not put it in a boat which has to steer through party politics.' To all this Gandhi's response was 'Politics is a dead corpse without religion. Burn it on a funeral pyre if it is devoid of life.'[36] Dr Radhakrishnan endorsed Gandhi's ideas and maintained that politics has succeeded, where it could separate and dominate religion.[37]

Induction of religion to politics does not mean state should have its own religion or seers and theologists should control political activities. For Gandhiji it was an ideal model of governance and it could yield a secular state by politico-religious discipline.

He maintained, 'every citizen should have right to observe his religion without any obstacle. State should offer no special protection to any religion, nor regulate a particular religion. In a nutshell, state should divorce itself from its particular religious character. But this does not mean a religionless or anti-religious state. State should patronise moral principles like truth, non-violence, service, love, etc. Similarly politicians should respect all religions, persuasions. Politics should be firmly based on universal human values. All religions agree on this. So a secular state is viable and workable.'[38]

Mahatama Gandhi's effort was to spiritualise politics. He practised it in his life and behaviour. As a saint-like politician he struggled to uproot rebellion, disintegration, fraud and cruelty from polities. Love, sacrifice, non-violence, good will need to be induced in politics which religion can conveniently lend to political behaviour.

Sarve Dharma Sambhav

This concept is better than secularism. All religions have a common vision and a common perspective, so *Sarva Dharma Sam bhav* indicates the correct meaning of a secular outlook. The religious differences are not doctrinaire, but they are seen in the observance of rituals or practices. These rituals are time bound and the variations are geographical or historical.[39] Gandhiji studied all the scriptures of Hinduism vis-á-vis Vedas, Upnishads, Purans and the Geeta along with the Bible, the Quran and the Granth Sahib. His conclusion was that they are all searching and experimenting with eternal truth.

In Gandhi's own words 'there has to be a fraternal relationship among all religions. If followers of all religions honestly pursue their faith, they will agree on fundamentals and differences of interpretations will narrow down.[40] Sarva Dharma Sambhav can integrate religions in their basic search of truth or God.

He gave elaborate details on how religions developed the so called differences. The situations of history were different in different countries and therefore religion's externals became different. If roots are traced and believed, no communal riot can take place.[41] Trust in God is the common source, but I do not envisage a period or society when there will be one religion. Variety is the law of life. Two human beings cannot be identical, still lesser will be their visions of creation and the creator. Hence a variety of religions will coexist. Let them be so. Even with differences there can be unity and efforts should not be made to obliterate diversities of religions. Uniform religion of similar people will be a false ideal unattainable in the world.[42]

As a saintly thinker Gandhiji did his prayer studies and concluded that all religions are truthful. Even if they have evil practices, I should respect them and love them as my own. It leads to the conclusion that all human beings need to be loved as our own kin and no discriminations should be accepted or encouraged.[43] This idea was clear to Gandhiji because he had studied and discovered the essence of all religions. When he liked 'Tolerance' or Hinduism about Islam he said 'It is a religion of peace like that of Hindus, Buddhists and Jains. There may be a difference of degrees, but the objective is the same.[44] Islam's contribution to our national culture is that it believes in one and only one *Allaha*. Within this frame it practises fraternity which is truth. It is a special and useful contribution because Hinduism has become too philosophical. Hindus have discovered deities which Islam does not accept. But the Hindus are relatively more liberal and flexible than the followers of Islam.'[45]

In fact Gandhi developed his faith in religious unity from Islam. He has written, 'When I was in Yerwada prison, then I read the biography of Prophet Muhammad by Maulana Shibli. This book captioned as *Uswa-e-Sahaba,* I can claim, that I have read it with honesty and I objectively conclude that Quran regards non-violence superior to violence. Non-violence is a duty but violence may be permitted if need be. What the Prophet did or did not do is not my concern. I follow his preaching and try to put them into practice. It is a truth that sword did not make him a prophet. He prayed to *Allaha* with sacrifices and it was a search for truth. If these prayers and sacrifices are withdrawn, he ceases to be a prophet. His hardships and sufferings elevated him to the position of a prophet. Once accepted as a prophet, the followers followed him as a model. Prophets cannot be evaluated by followers.'[46] Thus to Gandhiji Islam notwithstanding its rigidities was a religion of non-violence and service to *Allaha,* the creator. All religions cannot be explained in words. Their meanings are imperfect. Human explanations of people are mere perspectives. They all may be truthful or wrong. Even partial truths are called religions. Therefore extreme tolerance is needed in religious interpretations. No religion can be ignored, still less condemned. One should have extra faith in his religion, but this should make us more respectful to other religions.[47] He developed this concept like a huge tree with hundreds of branches offering similar flowers and fruits. True religion is the trunk and trunk alone is not the tree.[48]

He has reiterated quite vehemently that 'Jesus alone had the divine spark. He was divinely like Ram, Krishan, Mohammed and Zoroaster. I cannot say that every sentence of scriptures is divine. The inspiration may be godly, but there are million of things and ideas which have nothing to do with the scriptures and the God. I respect all[49] and people should read all these scriptures.'

Conversions and the Philosophy of Gandhi

According to Gandhiji all religions are true, yet they are also incomplete.[50] The paths are varied, so people should have a right to choose their own path.[51] If people have chosen the path, let them walk or march, where is the need to ask them to change. Service to God can be attained by one or the only path of a particular religion.

Once Mirabehn expressed her desire to be a Hindu. His reply was that she should keep her faith in her own religion because conversion will not make her a better or a more moral human being. So in place of changing a religion why not change your ownself to attain the truth. He advised her in these words 'My Hindu religion teaches me that all religion are partially right. All religions originate from God, but all are incomplete. It is because we human beings are imperfect. The real reform will come when we strive to perfect ourselves by living in our religious fold. The human character is the only criterion for a good religion. By changing homes or sects you cannot improve your moral self. The real joy is the service of God. Those who commit sin deny the existence of God. The adage 'physician heal thyself" applies more pertinently to religions than to other philosophies of life.'[52]

He opposed religious conversions vehemently, because it has nothing to do with character building and moral development of society. Addressing the students of Gujarat Vidyapeeth, Gandhiji once said 'I do not want high walls around my house. Shutting the windows causes casternation. I wish the fresh wind of all cultures should flow all around. But no gust of wind is capable to blow off my feet.' He further added 'Gujarat Vidyapeeth should not keep repeating what she believes is the ancient culture of India. The Vidyapeeth should build a new culture – comprising our new experiences. It should get richer everyday. All those cultures which have settled down here are a part of our culture. They have influenced and shaped the life spiritually and culturally. Naturally we should coordinate them in our own way. All cultures will integrate and weave the web of Indian culture. We do not want to imitate United States of America where the dominant cultures have swallowed the smaller groups and have digested their own native ways of life. Such an imposed unity is artificial and does not produce an integrated culture of the masses.'[53]

He compared a culture with an orchestra where every instrument produces the note of music but the synthesis is called the music itself. Hence to love India every Hindu and each Muslim should be a real Hindu and a real Musalman of faithful variety. There is no conflict between national interests and religious interests. If one sees a conflict, he should rectify his religious perspective. A true religion believes in moral values. Naturally it supplements patriotism and social good. Adding two synonyms yields no result.[54]

Religion is a personal affair. It pertains to matters of heart.[55] To invoke pity for conversion is harmful to society. To quote his own words 'if a Christian doctor cures me, it does not imply that I change my religion. While curing why does he expect that I should be grateful to him. The medical service is a satisfying job in itself. If somebody teaches, why should he teach from the Bible only. Education should not be imposed, otherwise it leads to bitterness. People may doubt your intentions. Like Caesar's wife religious teaching should be above suspicion. Religion can be taught like other mundane things. It has to be in the language of the heart. If the religion is alive then its fragrance automatically spreads like a rose flower. Smell is invisible. The flower petals make it poignant. I may not be against conversion, but I am certainly opposed to its present techniques and the propaganda. It has assumed the form of a trade. I read a report which describes how much money was spent per conversion. It sounds like a product per capita. Our religions are quite capable to take care of this kind of propaganda. Indian religions are live and vibrant. People love their religions dearly. So we should spread harmony and fraternity. What has harmed is the competition or proving one superior to the other. Only a friendly relationship can eradicate the evils or deficiency. Unwanted criticism harms the collective good of society.

The need of the day is self-purification. It is not conversion. The purpose of converters is exterior, mundane and selfish.'[56]

Gandhiji was a humanist. He believed in action. He kept respecting all and nurtured a Banyan tree of national patriotism which offered solace to millions for decades in his shadow as a saint.

Places of Worship

Gandhiji knew for sure that Gods do not live in temples or mosques. Satans can also dwell in these holy places of worship. If the worshippers do not have deep faith in God, worship can be a fraud. The priests determine the nature of worship and the institution.[57] Temple going is good or irrelevant depends upon the faith of the worshipper. We should go to these places of worship with humility and spirit or repentance. God lives everywhere. We, imperfect humans impose our ignorance and believe that temple is purer than the impure world.'[58] We should purify our soul and beliefs. To pray to God with humility makes the prayer pure and effective. We should become more aware of our duties as man or woman. This old man can advise you that physical liberation of the untouchables will positively make your soul more sensitive to human conditions.[59]

Gandhiji used to go on fast to cleanse his soul. So he had all sorts of mystical experiences. He wrote about his 21 days long fast as under 'I was in deep sleep. Something woke me up at midnight. Some whispering noise was heard in the ears, you should go on fast. For how many days, I asked. There came the reply – 21 days. When should I commence?, I asked. The reply was from tomorrow itself.[60] Such an experience I had only once in life – never earlier nor later than this particular dream.'[61]

He wrote in details – 'I never saw any person or image. But I did hear a voice from a distance, it was a human voice, sweet and soberising. It was not a dream, but I did hear the voice. I was struggling within me and this voice decisively solved my dilemma. I thought over it and I got a clear-cut answer. I was quiet for sometime. I resolved accordingly and the fast date and days were finalised.'[62]

Such mystical experiences may not be acceptable to a psychoanalyst. Pandit Nehru called it para psychological. According to him 'Gandhi used to follow his inner conscience, which was much beyond human reason and logic. His religious teachings were called out from the essence of all religions in their wide ramifications.'

Gandhiji's life and struggles in South Africa and India were manifestations of his religious beliefs and faith. He attracted the attention of the world to prove that politics is not a trade for rascals. It is for those who cherish social good and surrender before God with humility, truth and non-violence. He stressed over and over again to prove that all principles and premises are secondary. Humanism and good of the lowliest and the lost is Gandhiji's religion. Sarvodaya is what he cherished. Swarajya is incomplete so long people have their eyes filled with tears.

Gandhiji had a comprehensive canvas. He dived deep into details. He was open, flexible and accessible to all who wished to search the truth. He spoke common man's language in an intelligent way. People loved him because they respected him from the very core of their hearts.

Thus religion and politics intermingle and merge in Gandhiji's speculations. He confessed that all his words and deeds have a religious consciousness. His actions demonstrated what he actually believed. He did not talk of rituals, days or festivals. His religion is a religion of living species. It is not to be preached but to be practised in daily life by all.

Notes

1. Valmiki Choudhari, 'Gandhiji Paigamber bhi the aur Rajnitigya bhi', *Hindustan*, 2 October 1971.

2. U.N. Dhebar, 'Samaj Kalyan Ke Sutradhar', *Hindustan,* 2 October 1969.
3. M.K. Gandhi, *My Religion,* Navajivan, Ahmedabad, 1955, p. 3.
4. Ibid.
5. Ibid.
6. P. Mani Mahajan and K.S. Bharati, *Foundations of Gandhian Thought,* Detance Publishers, Delhi, 1987, pp. 1–20.
7. *Hind Swaraj,* op. cit., pp. 47–53.
8. M.K. Gandhi, *My Religion,* op. cit., pp. 123–158.
9. Romain Rolland, *Mahatma Gandhi,* op. cit., pp. 98.
10. *Harijan,* 24 December 1938, p. 393.
11. *Young India,* Pt. II and III, pp. 296 and 184.
12. *Navjeevan,* 21 July 1929.
13. S.R. Tripathi, *Gandhi Dharam aur Samaj,* p. 22.
14. M.K. Gandhi, *My Religion,* op. cit.
15. Ibid., p. 152.
16. *Harijan,* 17 April 1937.
17. *Hind Swaraj*. Ch. 10.
18. Prayer Speech, 19 October 1947.
19. *Harijan Bandhu,* 19 March 1933.
20. *Young India,* 20 October 1927.
21. Pyare Lal, *M.K. Gandhi: The Last Phase,* Part I, Navajivan, Ahmedabad, pp. 440–45.
22. M.K. Gandhi, *Non-Violence in Peace and War,* Vol. I, p. 38.
23. N.K. Bose, *Selections from Gandhi,* (ed.) Navajivan, Ahmedabad, 1948, p. 22.
24. Epics authored by Tulsidas.
25. *Harijan,* 28 April 1946.
26. Ramcharitmanas, Geeta Press, Gorakhpur.
27. Ibid., Balkand 7.
28. Yound India, 11 October 1928.
29. Romain Rolland, op. cit., p. 98.
30. *Navjeevan,* 30 January 1921.
31. *Harijan,* 10 February 1940.
32. *Navjeevan,* 21 June 1925.
33. *Yound India,* 11 October 1928.
34. M.K. Gandhi, *An Autobiography: The Story of My Experiments With Truth,* Navajivan, Ahmedabad, 1940, op. cit., pp. 540–557.
35. Ibid.
36. S.R. Tripathi, op. cit., p. 140
37. Ibid.

38. Ibid.
39. B.N. Pandey, *Samagra Chintan*, op. cit., p. 123.
40. *Harijan*, 16 February 1934.
41. *Harijan*, 16 February 1934.
42. *Young India*, 19 January 1928.
43. *Young India*, 19 January 1928.
44. *Young India*, 21 March 1929.
45. *Young India*, 10 March 1927.
46. *Harijan*, 12 July 1940.
47. Gandhi, From Yarvada Prison, op. cit., p. 10.
48. Ibid.
49. *Harijan*, 6 March 1937.
50. Gandhi, From Yarvada Prison, op. cit.
51. Hind Swaraj, p. 65.
52. *Young India*, 29 May 1924.
53. *Young India*, 1 June 1921.
54. *Young India*, 9 January 1930.
55. *Young India*, 23 April 1931
56. *Young India*, 23 April 1931.
57. *Young India*, 19 May 1927.
58. *Harijan*, 10 December 1938.
59. Ibid.
60. *Harijan*, 10 December 1938.
61. *Harijan*, 14 May 1938.
62. *Harijan*, 6 May 1933.

7

The Concept of Village Swarajya in Gandhian Thought

The State System and its evolution is a part of human civilisation and it keeps revising and improving with its growth process. Adult suffrage is the latest link in the political experiments of democracy. Although democratic values are getting stronger everywhere but there are contradictions in the systems in their operations. It makes Gandhian philosophy relevant and effective in the present day context.

It is a paradox that political systems have been shaped in history more by thinkers rather by political activists. Gandhi and Marx are the two outstanding examples in history. The technological revolution has reduced the world into a global village. This makes Gandhi's village self-rule useful and workable. By this 'construct' Gandhiji attempted to make world family a practical ideal. This *vasudhev kutumbkam* (the world is one family) is an ancient one which our *rishis* and thinkers conceived as a human ideal. The terms सर्वे भवन्तु सुखिन: (may all become happy) and सर्व भूत हिताय (may welfare of all) were given to the local bodies to practise it in ancient India. This made village the primary unit of government. A British Governor, Sir Charles Metcalf explained this rural unit in the following words:

> 'These rural units are small democracies. They are self-sufficient and are literally free in external affairs. They

> survive and endure against odds in history. The rural unit being independent enjoyed autonomy and offered self-sufficiency to village life on the farm.[1]
>
> Nehru admired this rural life of India and has presented it as an ideal rural way of living. It offered local freedom and autonomy. There were several other good features. India has to rebuild these rural local units.'[2]

The village republics of ancient India declined and disappeared with the advancement of history. The medieval India witnessed the decline and modern India rendered them dysfunctional. The British rule suppressed them and our villages lost vigour because of famines, drought, heavy taxation and unemployment. Gandhiji prepared a comprehensive plan to fight out and his village Swarajya is a concept that comes out as a remedy. It is not mere revivalism of the past. Rather it is an idea of reorganisation in the changed conditions of Indian villages. It seeks to rebuild rural India in such a way that they become self-sufficient and stay dynamic. The rural republics of Gandhiji's dream as described by him in an article in *Harijan* are as under:

> In my view it will be a democratic system which will be economically autonomous. It may seek mutual cooperation but most of the things needed will be produced by the village units. All villages will produce their own goods like food grains and clothes. They will have surplus land to graze their cattle and provide playgrounds for children. If the land permits they may grow additional food for others. Tobacco and other drugs like opium, etc. will be prohibited for cultivation. Every village will have a village theatre, a school and a conference hall for meetings. The water supply system will be locally managed. Wells and tanks will be under public control of the village. *Buniyadi Talim* will be compulsory for all school going children. Untouchability and caste discrimination will be abolished. Rural people will cooperate for self-development.

Satyagrah and non-violence will keep peace through Gram Samitis. It will be a voluntary force and all villagers will serve as *sainiks* by rotation. A panchayat of five elected *panchas* will regulate the rural system. Adult suffrage will be the basis and the panchayats will be self-sufficient and autonomous. There will be no power of punishment and every panchayat will perform legislative, executive and judicial function with elected functionaries.

'Even today the Panchayats can function autonomously. They are not mere revenue collection agencies. Here I am not thinking about external relations or international contexts. I am presenting an outline and the details can be filled up by the elected leaders of the village. The villagers will respect their institutions and protect their dignity in every respect. It will not be easy to work out full rural autonomy. Everybody can decide his or her role and spend a lifetime in fulfilling the rural mission. The good result will follow when village teachers, doctors, *choukidars*, sweepers and business persons will sit in one panchayat and take decision about their jobs.'[3]

This points out that Gandhiji did not have an expert plan or final blueprint of Panchayats. People will vote and think freely and disagree in a creative way. The village unit being small will interact and sort out differences like a family. It is not possible in big units where people have only formal relations. Decentralisation was Gandhiji's principle and a self-government based on sharing was his concept of rural self-help. Power will flow from below and top will be amenable to the dictates of the bottom. Non-violence and truth can link them to the noble ideal of collective good. People will run their own affairs. The basic unit will be strong and subsidiary units will work in a spontaneous manner.

Every rural person will participate in village government in one capacity or the other. The villagers may plan their development for five years or in any manner acceptable to all. The participation will improve the quality of governance. Cooperative approach to rural problems will resolve conflicts and multiply silent benefits of public life.

Fundamental Principles of Village Self-government

On return from South Africa, Gandhiji toured all over India and the pitiable conditions of India made him speak 'Our villages stand ruined. We do not know sociology and economics.'[4] In 1918, Curtis who was helping to prepare Mont-Ford Reforms made a comment 'the Indian villages give an impression as if they have been established on toilets.'[5]

This bitter truth can be verified even after independence. Gandhiji resolved to change this truth. So he thought of principles for this change. He conceived of rural self-government which was something like as follows:

Highest Place to the Individual

Any rural system should start around the individual and he should be valued the most. Human good alone should be the consideration. Explaining his concept of moral and mental good he wrote, 'The happy world should have an economy where people have food and clothes without hardships. Everybody should have work to earn his or her bread. This fulfillment of primary needs requires that means of production are controlled by people themselves. Like air and water food and clothes should be free. Using them for trade and profit is exploitation. In no part of the world such a situation should exist which breeds poverty and hunger.

That economy is false which disrespects the moral principles. Non-violence implies that international trade should conform to the law of morality.'[6]

A person, born in the world has a right to live. For this he or she needs food and clothes and they should be ensured. Hence primary needs have to be guaranteed with human birth. All religious scriptures repeat it. Do not accumulate. Affluence cannot be a criterion to success. The real criterion is that nobody should be hungry or a bigger right to livelihood is a fundamental right. All plans and schemes should use human resources for human good and collective welfare.

Physical Labour

Gandhiji propounded his original concept of bread labour. He who does not earn bread by physical labour, cannot have the freedom to consume world resources. Every healthy person must earn. Human faculties are not meant to accumulate wealth beyond needs. People should serve and never exploit. If accepted, hunger will vanish and people will be somewhat equal. Those who follow this law, their own lives transform and miracles follow. His health improves and happiness expands. Gandhiji saw this law in the third chapter of the Geeta. In *shlok* 13 it is said that whatever remains after *yagya* is the result of physical labour. *Yagya* in the Geeta corresponds to physical labour.[7] It is necessary for survival. Millions of people in India do not get a two square meal. They work extra and starve. Like all beings humans should labour and get food. Those who eat and do not earn their bread are thieves.[8] Tolstoy revealed this, which Gandhiji found repeated in the Geeta. In the Bible he found a clear direction, 'you earn your bread by perspiration.' From this Gandhi deduced that truth and non-violence demand physical labour. If people earn by labour there will be plenty to eat and time for leisure also. This will reduce birth, disease and pain.

Gandhiji confessed that it is a difficult idea but it can be achieved. If people strive to achieve this ideal their needs will be less and they will avoid unwanted luxury.[9] It is wrong to earn livelihood only by mental labour. The physical labour adds an element of silent revolution in social configurations. Human struggle can be replaced by human service. The animal law of life has to be replaced by a human law to establish justice and reign of duty.[10] Physical labour with intelligence is the highest social service. Hence it can be included in physical labour made society.[11]

Equality

Equality of opportunities for development is a human right. If all get it the collective growth will follow.[12] There is contradiction between true economics, high ethics and a welfare state. Economics should strengthen the weak and arrest accumulation of wealth. It should enhance social justice and ensure the good of each and welfare of all. Equal distribution is difficult but it can be made equitable as a practical ideal.[13] Swarajya requires economic equality. The yawning gulf between capitalists and labourers has to be narrowed down. Superfluous wealth of the rich should be reduced and wealth of poor physical worker has to increase. A non-violent state is an impossibility in the present state of economic disparity. If this state is dragged for long, a violent revolution is in the offing.[14]

Trusteeship

Economic equality can be practised by the concept of trusteeship. The rich people should not have more wealth than what they need. But if surplus wealth is snatched then violence will follow. Violence will not solve the problem and the rich person's capacity to add to national wealth will be weakened. Hence non-violent trusteeship will be feasible and collectively useful. One can become a trustee of surplus wealth and spend it for social good. It will be a silent change and economic equality will become a realisable ideal.

Decentralisation

Non-violent reconstruction requires a decentralised society. Centralisation cannot be sustained without use of violent force. If all villages become powerful, the dangers of over centralisation will diminish. Urban India will be powerful and the dangers of foreign invasions will increase.[15] So a new India cannot rely on industrialisation, it should be self-sufficient and free from exploitation. So decentralisation is a panacea.

Swadeshi or Homemade

Gandhiji worked for the spread and promotion of Swadeshi. Lokmanaya Tilak was the pioneer of Swadeshi with his concept of Swarajya. But Gandhiji made it a tool of freedom struggle. He used it against the imperial power. His concept of Swadeshi was 'Swadeshi is a universal religion. Individuals owe a duty to their neighbours. It does not imply envy to others. It is not favouritism. The body has its limits. It is quite difficult to fulfill good neighbourly obligations. If people do this faithfully, several evils of the world will disappear. Hence it has been said that serving the neighbour is service to society. Swadeshi duty obliterates the duty to *pardeshis* (non-native). The entire world is a family and all can be served if people serve their neighbours. It is natural and its scope can be expanded.'

Tolstoy goes further. According to him 'people are riding on neighbour's shoulders. We should get down.' In other words nobody serves anybody without selfishness. Those who do self-seeking in the name of social service are harming the society. Whatever one does in this world has social repercussions. It may not be visible. But the impact is natural and cannot be helped. We should realise our duty and responsibility. Hence Swadeshi cannot be called anti-*pardeshi* or *videshi* (alien). Still Swadeshi is not *Sarvdesi*. When you want to include all, you may lose whatever you have or whatever is you own. If you do your neighbour's good the collective good automatically follows. One can love all only when he loves his neighbour. All people are equal, it ignores the neighbour who is more than equal. One cannot live for his ownself. Hence the nearest second is my neighbour or Swadeshi.[16]

Self-help

The villagers should develop a spirit of self-support and self-sufficiency. The small unit will be sufficient in the sense that it does not depend on others.[17] A village should fulfill its needs, run its own business and project its own existence.[18] A self-sufficient village should produce its own foodstuff and cotton for clothes. Khadi clothes should be spun. Cotton production should be decentralised. After this self-sufficiency in food and clothes the village should build its own defense. These needs when fulfilled, self-sufficiency can be conceived.

Cooperation

As far as possible the villagers should develop cooperative services.[19] The farmer's cooperatives can be developed on government land. It will increase production and yield more profit to the farmers. But this cooperative movement has to be organised on the principles of non-violence and mutual cooperation.[20]

Satyagrah

It is a technique by which Gandhiji waged the national struggle for freedom. This technique will make the villagers powerful and promote non-violent solutions of their problems.[21]

Equality of All Religions

All religions like the leaves of a tree are similar but look different. The trunk is more important than the branches and leaves. Attached to the root, they do not quarrel but jump and flutter in glee and produce cool air.[22] All religions express the final truth by the incomplete men. They have been mixed up. So one should respect every religion no matter whether he understands it or not in its entirety.[23]

Religion has a deep root in human life. No one can pull out this tree root and branch. So respect it and give equality to all.

Panchayat Raj

Gandhiji had outlined his vision of Panchyat Raj. Each Panchayat will have elected five panchas according to specified rules. There will be no provision to punish people. The Panchayat in its tenure of one year shall act as a legislative, executive and judicial body.[24] This system has to be for the entire country. The adult people without any discriminations of caste, class or gender will elect these local leaders. More than one panchayat can have a mandal and the pyramidal structure will elect the higher bodies which will direct the lower bodies. He gave details of 200 panchayats and local leaders were to be elected at each level. These panchayat leaders would then elect state and national leaders. This Gram Sabha to Lok Sabha model as envisaged by Jayaprakash Narayan was Gandhi's original plan whereby he sought to filter and strengthen local leadership.

New Educational System

Literacy is necessary but it is not education. Education needs varied efforts at all ages. Earning while learning is a necessary principle, so that students do not feel dependent on parents. Art, craft, physical labour should be a part of curricula. School should be self-sufficient. State should promote Khadi and school industries in rural areas.

Gram Swarajya of Gandhi

While Gandhiji was engaged in Quit India Movement a foreign journalist asked 'why are you opposed to British?' Gandhiji's reply was 'I am not opposed to British people. They may stay here as friends, but English rule has to go and English way of life should end.' The English rule has ended but English mentality continues. By English mentality he implied the style of alienation. Some people are enjoying luxuries unmindful of common man's miseries. He was opposed to elitist English style of living. On 15 August 1947, Englishmen left our country but the Swarajya of Gandhi's dreams is yet to dawn in India. Modern India has a bunch of privileged elites of politicians, civilians and rich people who have nothing to do with the masses and their problems. Gandhiji could foresee this. So he thought and gave a concept of village self-rule. It was based on the following fundamental principles:

1. Villages are the basic unit of government. It accepts the small farm as the rural unit of governance. The village panchayat has maximum powers and the higher units will have declining powers and functions. There will be coordination between village, district, state and national units, but the power will ascend not descend. Each level will decide its functions and roles. The national issues will be decided at the top. Overlap will be avoided and coordination will not result into control.
2. Popular participation: It will be enhanced to generate consensus because majority decisions will be avoided in the panchayats. Unanimity will be encouraged and every panchayat will have a right to veto, the so called majority decisions. This principle of Sarvodaya negates majority rule and one man can be right adds a new dimension to democracy. 'Let you be the lonely' (एकला चालो रे) is also a

democratic principle. According to Gandhiji a lonely individual if he is truthful and non-violent has a right to go against the course of a crowd or majority.

3. National security: It was often asked how these autonomous village republics can guard their national freedom against foreign invasions. Gandhiji's reply was that the world will gradually accept the power of moral force as is the case with United Nations. It was just a club to begin with. Today it has the propensity of playing a world government. The Security Council will become the representative and national security will become a part of international obligation. If people are united, the world public opinion will have to accept their verdict. Only a very strong spirit of village autonomy can protect such villages. Armies may be there but their abuse shall not be acceptable to the people with high patriotism or nationalism.

Ideal Indian village

Gandhiji has given the picture of an ideal Indian village in the following words, 'The village unit will be extremely strong. Each village will have one thousand residents. If organised well it can accomplish the impossible.[25] The village will be clean and the cottages will be well maintained. All things required will be available in a radius of five miles. The house will have open space for gardens and animals. Streets and roads will be washable. There will be wells and worship places. The village Sabha Bhawan will be close to the village school. Dairy, industrial training centres and Panchayat house will be around. People will do all jobs at different points of time.[26]

Gandhi planned the ideal village like an Ashram. It will have amenities but will be autonomous. He did not accept the established rural settlements of India. The new villages will encourage rural handicrafts and educated people will guide the villages in religion, science and technologies. The basic amenities will be cheap and accessible to all.

Economics of Self-rule

The two leading systems of economy called as capitalist and socialist have their limitations. Market and state have been the dominant factors in USA and USSR. Gandhiji rejected both the models as they too European and one sided. Unhealthy competition is the bone of its economy in USA and state control over individual life is what makes Marxism unacceptable. Cottage industries of India can play a middle role in the two systems and Swadeshi will be a new component of Indian economy which will be farm based and labour oriented.

Village self-government is a simplistic economy for India. It will be decentralised and exploitation free. It ensures work guarantee to all. It strives to make citizens independent and autonomous with regard to primary needs. If village industries die, seven lakh Indian villages will be ruined. India without villages will cease to be India. Indian message should not be lost.[27]

The Gandhian plan stresses upon village made goods to be used in every household. Whatever villagers can produce in rural areas they should produce on cooperative basis. Machines are needed when there are no hands. We have surplus people. Naturally machine economy and machine cultures should be shunned. Mechanisation on western pattern will add to numbers of unemployed workers. So village industries should be revived. Khadi can be the sun of Indian solar system. Khadi can energise a variety of cottage industries but ancillary cottage industries should keep Khadi industry surviving. The villagers should get work in all fields. It can energise the stagnant rural economy.[28] He appealed to all to accept Khadi and encourage village industries pertaining to dairy products, bee-keeping, leather goods, soap-making, paper-making, etc. in the cottage industry sector of our villages. It will give impetus to village Swarajya.

Rural Hygiene

Rural reconstruction is a multifaceted revolution. He concluded that rural India is stagnating and languishing in dirt and disease. Children are vulnerable to infections. Dirtiness is widespread and causes diseases. People cannot afford medical treatment and malnutrition is a mass killer of the poor. He suggested natural cure which is inexpensive and simple. This kind of natural cure can be possible locally. Natural food, exercises and natural cleanliness are the guarantee of good health. It is not a matter of cheap medicine. Free medicine makes patients beggars. Natural cure is self-managing. It eliminates poison; food and exercises make patients healthy for a long time.

Like us our villages are extremely poor. Vegetables, fruits, milk are the part of a natural diet. The natural cure is an investment in nature's growth. It is ultimately beneficial for the country.[29] The natural cure comprises of five elements of nature, viz. soil, water, hollow space, air and energy. They can cure all diseases because human body is composed of five elements. A booklet *Arogya ki Kunji* by M.K. Gandhi explains this philosophy and suggests ways and means to cure human body without external intervention. It is very instructive.[30]

Village Worker

Gram sevak is a powerful instrument of social change. He will teach, train and improve the villagers. Ideals have to be taught. Moreover situations and circumstances need to be clean, healthy and conducive to development. Gandhiji prescribed the following qualifications for his Gram sevak:

1. He should be a god fearing theist whose moral virtues are critical.
2. A follower of truth and non-violence, a pious person of virtues.
3. A man of character with a spirit of sacrifice.
4. A spinner by habit, who dons Khadi with pride.
5. A person without vices to stay in reason and cleanliness.
6. A strict and strong disciplinarian.

These qualities are not educational. He should be a moral man of character. His functions have been enumerated as under:

1. He should use his homemade goods, avoid tobacco, alcohol and avoid ostentatious living. A Hindu should fight against

untouchability and castism. He should respect all religions and believe in equality of status and opportunity to all.

2. He should keep a live contact with every villager in the field.
3. He will choose his team, train them and keep all records.
4. The daily activities and accounts will be specially and neatly maintained.
5. He will organise his village in a manner that it becomes self-sufficient and autonomous.
6. He will teach public hygiene to rural folks. Cleanliness and petty medicines may be administered by him to prevent epidemic and mass infections.
7. Nai Taleem Scheme will be implemented by him. It will extend to people of all age groups.
8. He will revise and update electoral rolls for Panchayat elections and developmental activities.
9. Voting right will be compulsory and Gram sevak will register villages and keep the records up to date.[31]

So the Gandhian Plan is total and well laid out. Spinning wheel is the hub around which will rotate the rural life. Khadi industries will expand, improve and make people prosperous and bread winning. Gram sevak will advise about economic activities. Cleanliness will be his major concern. Harijan colonies will be improved by living with the Harijans. Village children will get oral lessons from their teachers. Rich classes will not be encouraged but primary needs of every household will be satisfied. Gandhi gave the total picture as under:

> The 18 point programme can cover total village services. For example identifying all the villagers, their needs, availability of resources, training others and enabling others to stay in productive works. The Gram sevak will influence villagers and they will ask for physical labour. Each will help all. Suppose I run an oil thani. I will do all jobs pertaining to my vocation, but I shall not be an ordinary oil man to earn my livelihood. I will become a Mahatma Gandhi (I am just joking). I will be a *teli* who will teach Geeta and Quran to children in neighbourhood. If people will complain that as a *teli* I am a poor teacher, I will

ask villagers to give me money to hire an educated teacher. I will teach them to weave. As demand will grow I will have specialist professionals. I will teach to remain clean. When they will ask for a scavenger, my suggestion will be why cannot you be a scavenger and a janitor yourself. I will teach them scavenging. This is my concept of a total village service.

The government will have vital role in materialising Gram Swarajya. The government will inform the villages, what is expected of them. They will manufacture or weave Khadi in prescribed time. Then no cloth will be supplied or made available. If need be, cotton will be supplied by the state. The extra Khadi will be purchased by the government. Cottage industry revival will be the duty of government. Sooner than later, so much Khadi will be available in the village that import of clothes will come to a stop.

Gandhian philosophy believes that political power is only a means to an end. This end is the versatile development of man. On 29 January 1948 a few hours before his assassination he wrote 'Political freedom has been achieved but a social and economic liberation of 7 lakh villages from cities is yet it be accomplished'.

His Rural Swarajya is an ideal though it is not easy to implement. It requires millions of volunteers who can work for a simple, honest and disciplined life. Difficult it is, but can be achieved even in modern times.

Notes

1. Pt. J.L. Nehru, *Vishwa Itihas Ki Jhalak.*
2. Ibid.
3. *Harijan,* 2 August 1942.
4. Thakur Das Bang, *Asali Swarajya,* a Sarva Seva Sangha, Varanasi, 1995, p. 8.
5. M.K. Gandhi, *Gram Seva,* Sasta Sahitya, Delhi, 1967, p. 11.
6. *Hindi Navjeevan,* 26 December 1924, p. 155.
7. *Satyagrh Ashram Ka Itihas,* 1959, pp. 40–44.
8. *Young India,* 13 October 1921, p. 325.
9. *Harijan,* 5 July 1935, p. 160.

10. *Harijan,* 22 June 1935, p. 156.
11. *Harijan,* 1 June 1935, p. 125.
12. *Harijan,* 10 November 1946, p. 387.
13. *Young India,* 17 March 1927, p. 83.
14. M.K. Gandhi, *Rachnatamak Karyakram,* Navajivan, Ahmedabad, 1989, p. 40–41.
15. *Harijan,* 30 December 1939, p. 391.
16. *Satyagrah Ashram Ka Itihas,* pp. 44–46.
17. Pyarelal, *Towards New Horizons,* Navajivan, Ahmedabad, 1959, p. 8.
18. *Harijan,* 28 July 1946, p. 236.
19. *Harijan,* 2 August 1942, p. 243.
20. *Harijan,* 9 March 1947, p. 46.
21. *Harijan,* 2 August 1942, p. 423.
22. *Harijan,* 22 February 1948, p. 43.
23. *Satyagrah Ashram Ka Itihas,* p. 77.
24. *Harijan Sevak,* 2 August 1942, p. 244.
25. *Harijan Sevak,* 4 August 1946.
26. M.K. Gandhi, *Mere Sapanon Ka Bharat,* op. cit., p. 105.
27. *Harijan,* 29 August 1946, p. 226.
28. *Harijan,* 23 November 1934, p. 381.
29. Ibid., 2 June 1946, p. 165.
30. Gandhi, *Aarogya Ki Kunji,* Navajivan Prakashan, Ahmedabad, 2000, p. 34.
31. *Harijan,* 22 February 1948, pp. 49–50.

8

The World View of Gandhi and Challenges of the New Millennium

Gandhi was an apostle of love, peace and non-violence. His message talks of high ideals of humanity. This life philosophy reflects peace, self-sufficiency and tolerance. Gandhiji dominated the Indian political scenario from 1920 to 1948. He remained firm, committed and clear to his ideology till end. He was a pioneer who led a unique struggle of masses against a mighty alien power, i.e. the British Empire. His ideas in varied fields have the solutions of 21st century world. His philosophy is timeless and stands as legitimate because of eternal truth in the ideals of non-violence, self-respect and cooperation. His was a life of dedication totally committed for the amelioration of the weak and poor. He subscribed to human ideals of liberty, equality and justice up to the last moment, till the assassin's bullet did not silence him. The present day world is riddled with tensions and naturally his teachings of non-violence look increasingly relevant and useful. Perhaps Gandhian way is the only life for humanity, distressed and tortured by the so called development. Gandhi demonstrated in thought and deed that a warless, and a loving human society can be established with reasonable peace, security and prosperity. What is needed is a new approach – a pursuit of truth and non-violence.

Gandhi combines theory with practice. He was experimenting with truth and thereby investigating what should be the goal and how should it be attained. His all comprehensive philosophy consisted of three components: (1) Spirit, (2) Heart and (3) Head. Truth and non-violence stir all the three and will remain relevant to all humans in all cultures. He was not a saint, nor he preached or followed any religious sect. His main mission was to achieve political independence for India, but he stood for spiritual means. Freedom by hook or crook, he never imagined even in dreams. Freedom was his goal but means of non-violence and non-cooperation were equally important. He prepared a strategy that succinctly states 'Forgo the end if the means are unholy.' He kept Indian conditions and situations in mind and forged a tool which could be effective and practical in the contemporary conditions of India. The radicals, the extremist and the terrorist had brought the situation to ghastly violence of Jalianwala Bagh. Here come Gandhi and vowed that a pious goal like freedom cannot be achieved by blood baths.

He established a chain of Ashrams and taught people to lead a cooperative life in a non-violent way. This experiment in collective morality generated a discipline and volunteers were realised to suffer smilingly for a cause. His philosophy was that discipline, consciousness, simplicity and hard labour can shape character and such people can bring social reforms. He got his inspiration from ancient gurukuls, South African Christian Trappis Monastries, Swami Vivekanand, Ramakrishna Mission and Bharat Sevak Samaj of G.K. Gokhale. He wanted to have the versatile development of individuals. It required leaders and the Ashrams could be the schools for such leadership. He thought of formal institutes, but then preferred the Ashram system to teach rather than to preach about truth, love, self-sufficiency and civil disobedience. This experiment was informal, practical, voluntary and a selective education for mass mobilisation.

The Ashram management of Gandhiji explains his managerial skills. It was a laboratory where the experiments were designed and tested in time.

Gandhiji has left an indelible impact on India's national consciousness and political system. Apartheid and totalitarianism were also discouraged by his experiments. Even modern governments represent violence, the atomic proliferation has touched a new law. The world stands at a critical crossroad. This forces people to think why the rational humans are opting for this suicidal course. Science has conquered nature and technology represents a triumph of man. But the violent tendencies are taking mankind under its sway. The only answer to all this is human consciousness which should be awakened to make man capable to answer this challenge. This is the essence of Gandhism which shows the way.

Social Philosophy

Jean Paul Sartre once said 'If there is any philosophy which dreams of a warless world without any blooshed, it is the philosophy of Gandhi.' Gandhiji not only talked or dreamt about it but he practised it during the national movement of a society riven with communalism. He talked of his philosophy when freedom had not arrived. Most of these evils persist and people do not have the courage to profess and practise it. He was a Santani Hindu, who never supported the evils of Hinduism. Rather he struggled to reform them. He believed in truth and God and recited, *Raghupati Raghav Raja Ram* in his prayer meetings. His Ram was not the historical figure, the son of king Dasrath. He made Ram formless, an idea of abstract God.

He was a highly liberal and tolerant person. Today this philosophy seems relevant in the midst of increasing bitterness. He started from man as the basic unit of his thought and rebuilt him. His humans are not just flesh and blood, but they have spirit and beliefs. He believed in reincarnation and immortality of the soul. He used to say that even when dead I shall keep saying what I believe in the tomb of my graveyard. Each individual is capable to improve. So he should strive to become an ideal unto himself. Richness, rationality, knowledge are fine but what makes a man a man is his empathy. He is unhappy because others are not happy. He can help without being proud of his effort. This was his notion of a 'vaishnav'. Such people are needed everywhere, but these ethical values are getting extinct.

His advocacy of Varna System does not make him traditional. He studied it rationally and placed it in the context of liberalisation, privatisation and globalisation. The professional division of society is not harmful provided equality is practised. The family training in a profession does not make people low. Untouchability was a perversion. Ancient India was at the pinnacle of trade and commerce. The present era needs professional skills and some people have their training from childhood. He revised the system of caste and advocated it in functional form without perversions. He compared the groups with trade unions, who compete and protect citizen's interests.

Gandhiji could separate the system and its practising evils. He could see the evil and still defend the rationality of the system. He condemned untouchability because this evil is infectious. Nobody is a born Harijan. Man has the divine spark. He invented the term 'Man of god' and worked so hard for eradication of untouchability that the Hindu society got radically reformed. A number of welfare policies and projects of modern governments in India and outside reflect the urge with which he preached and professed these social reforms.

Equality of men and women is another area where Gandhi's progressive ideas have revolutionalised the traditional society. He gave parity and called women the incarnation of non-violence. She can teach peace, calm and reconciliation to violent men. Her motherhood directs not only children but men folk also cannot ignore her female power. No society can ever prosper if women are denied their due. He gave them higher positions in freedom movement. This belief revolutionised the leadership area and women came forward in every walk of life. Today it is a universally accepted truth that gender discriminations are irrelevant and mischievous.

Secularism in Gandhian Philosophy

Believing in truth and non-violence Gandhi started his political career supporting the Khilafat movement of Muslims in India.

He separated religion from Islam and supported Muslims because they were right. He looked at the question from a secular angle and a secular person should respect the religious positions no matter even if he may be a follower of a different religion. Politics cannot be devoid of religion because the separation will destroy both.

A look at the political situation explains that this position was too idealistic and too difficult to practise. Only a Gandhi could do it and in his exit it has been disappearing from Indian politics. Also politics is rarely Gandhian and has been thoroughly polluted by the people who profess Gandhian ideals. Gandhiji knew this stark fact about human nature. Politics is bound to degenerate when moral issues in politics are put on the backburner. After Gandhiji's assassination, politics in India slipped into the hands of power seekers who have created the present scenario of communalism and corruption. Nobody is interested in fulfilling the minimum needs. Even when there is a self-sufficiency in food, millions go to bed without two square meals. Poverty and ignorance apart, people are living in dirt and even water and air stand terribly polluted. The plans exist only on paper and bureaucracy is ruling the roost. Gandhiji had a premonition about these evils but he kept on reiterating his idealism, with the result that he was assassinated in 1948 and the country was partitioned in 1947.

Liberalisation, Privatisation and Swadeshi

Today Swadeshi is becoming out of date and globalisation is being advocated. Argument for global development is being paraded. Liberalisation, being a slogan has contributed to unemployment. The newly emerging nations of Asia and Africa have entered into a different kind of market slavery which makes political independence meaningless and harmful.

The developing countries are increasingly dependent on developed countries. They accept pressures. Gandhiji foresaw this danger. So he talked of Swadeshi and minimum machines to combat competitive economies by ignoring them. The policy of liberalisation and globalisation is harming weaker and backward nations. Gandhian philosophy prevents this economic slavery which is implicit in the advancement of technologies.

The spinning wheel economy implies a home economy not dependent on market forces. The needs are to be generated and fulfilled. Several kinds of college industries do not face any competition form global economies. People can be self-reliant in this cottage industry sector and rich nation will not be in a position to mortgage their economy. The multinationals will leave a developing nation if people wear home spun clothes.

Globalisation, Truth and Non-violence

Gandhiji was a contemporary of J. Stalin. When the Soviet Union was involved in a terrible violent civil war, Gandhiji said that the Marxist way of violence was detestable. He thrilled the whole world by demonstrating the power of non-violence.

A small boy, born in an ordinary family and who was not smart in studies could lead the world for ages was an inconceivable phenomenon. The childhood socialisation was so strong that in place of washing it away, he took inspirations from these teachings of early life. The story of Raja Harish Chandra and his truthfulness made him a devotee of सत्य (Satya) and अहिंसा (Ahinsa). He took truth to the position of God. There are millions of people who do not believe in God, but there will be none who does not accept truth as a fact of life. Truth comes earlier and an imperfect man should spend his life in searching the truth. Truth is an integral part of non-violence. He never claimed to be a blessed one, but maintained with pride that he is an experimenter with truth and discoverer of the path of non-violence.

People estimate Gandhiji's contribution as his teaching of truth. It is opposite of slavery and violence. His mission was not to propound the philosophy of truth, but to explain to the world that this world is based on goodwill, cooperation and mutual respect of human beings. His legacy is not only for India but also for the human kind which takes pride in what he said and literally believed. He worked in three continents, led agitations and struggles and successfully brought changes by consent and consensus. His maiden struggles made a dent in international relations. Albert Einstein, the greatest scientist of 20th century paid his tribute to Gandhiji in the following words:

> He was an Indian leader whose leadership was not based on power. His success was not a result of diplomatic strategies but a spontaneous impact of his personality. He opposed all sorts of violence tooth and nail. He was humble and a resolute man without inconsistencies. He sacrificed his entire life and energy for the emancipation of his countrymen. He proved his superiority after defeating the barbaric acts of Europeans. It is possible that future generations may not believe that such a human being ever walked on this earth in flesh and blood.

This estimate of the Mahatma makes him an extraordinary person. In the present day world mankind has become a shame for its own species. People dream of a world village but terrorist violence threatens to decimate human achievements. On 11 September 2001 the World Trade Centre was destroyed. Later the bomb on Pentagon and Indian parliament building made humanity weep and cry in pain. Today Gandhi's non-violence seems like the right answer to Islamic jehad and violence. The stark realities of violence look at us in the face. Gandhiji asked how long and why do you do all this. Love and brotherhood are better alternatives. Non-violence is an effective weapon. It defeats with out killing anybody. So his Satyagrah gives a message, an ideal weapon to fight and change the world without any cost of human blood. He said long ago in 1919 'Any victory that is achieved by violent killing is temporary and is equivalent to defeat.' Strong and weak have to be equals in a democracy. Peace is everybody's way. Friendship requires tolerance and tolerance is humanity in its ultimate. That is why Louis Fisher called him the greatest human being of last 1900 years.

Truth and non-violence represent the noblest virtues of man. He said that we should do our duty. Results should be left to the Almighty God. Man is partially maker of his destiny. There is a supernatural power, we fulfil our dreams and ambitions in a limited manner. Ram, Allah, God, Jesus is the power. I call it 'Truth'. This truth ultimately triumphs. Trust it with conviction and faith.

Gandhi's truth was dynamic. Only God knows the truth. We humans are capable to discover the partial truth. Like blind man defining an elephant, we know nothing about the elephant but keep fighting upon our experiences. The fights and bitterness obstruct our vision and truth is covered by falsehood. In 1926 while writing his autobiography he commented:

> I have been struggling to have actualisation of myself. I am not a scientist. I have delved deep in me and strived to come to conclusions. I do not claim to know the truth. In fact I call them true so long they conform to my logic or beliefs.

God is not truth, but truth alone is God proves Gandhi's philosophy. This truth does not change with the geography of South Africa or history of British India. He trusted the British but when convinced that they will never leave India, he took to his path of Satyagrah. He had an insight to discuss the truth and his techniques were non-violent. Satyagrah, fasting, dharana, inflicting pain on oneself are non-violent methods to filter out truth from falsehood. Even today they are effective. One may not comprehend the limits of time and space, but one should have deep faith in God and explore the truth non-violently, finally the light dawns and this is the glimpse of truth.

Gandhiji envisaged a social system which looks too idealistic or even unachievable. He maintained that this gulf between ideal and real is natural and inevitable. If you want to bridge it, then explore, research and experiment. You may or you may not succeed, but your effort will serve the truth, i.e. God. Hence struggle is a part of truthful life. Non-violence makes it honest and sincere. This is the service of God which permits man to actualise himself.

Gandhiji preached a non-violent response to violence. In his judgement violence pollutes your mental process. You cannot reach the truth with the hatred of revenge. Let violent man understand the cost of his false emotions. If you are non-violent this rate will remain contained and you may see the dawn of truth. Weapons create explosive situations. Soldiers do not discover truth. No one can save destruction if violence blinds our eyes. India has observed non-violent restraints against Pakistan's violence or aggressive behaviour. As a result we have an uneasy peace. Without the Gandhian non-violence super powers cannot coexist. Wars are immoral soldiers may belong to countries but they are human beings who leave their families behind. War creates more problems than it solves. Tormented by the problem of Palestine he wrote in *Harijan* in 1938:

> Arabs have a right on Palestine as much as Englishmen have on English soil. Imposing a Jewish rule on Muslims will be unfair. Palestinians have a right to live in peace and dignity. But then Jews should live where they were born and respect their land of birth.

In 1947 he advocated the liberation of Palestine. English empire was imposing itself on the basis of its military might. Non-violence is a better way and the problem can be resolved without shedding a drop of blood.

Sarvodaya

It was Gandhiji's ideal of developments, opposed to utilitarian and majority rule. He wrote:

> I work for an India, wherein the poorest of the poor may feel that he has a role in building of India. There are low or high groups or classes. All can live in peace and cordiality. Neither we exploit others nor we permit anybody to exploit us. Nothing short of it can satisfy me. I shall keep working for it.

The concept of a welfare state comes close to this dream. But there are weak and backward groups. They have to be brought to the mainstream. The present day ameliorative measures for weak women and disadvantaged people have this Gandhian principle to which Dr Ambedkar gave a constitutional shape. The Directive Principles of State Policy of the Indian Constitution has Gandhian contents of a Sarvodaya Samaj. They will keep reminding the succeeding generations of their responsibilities towards the backward and neglected people of the country. This agenda based on truth and non-violence is a constant reminder of progress. Laws, policies, programmes and government efforts must be directed to this end. A Sarvodaya is just not a plan, it is the pursuit of certain ideals for which Gandhiji worked, struggled and laid down his life.

From Gram Swarajya to World Government

In the millennium year the people and governments all over the world are talking of one world government. The information revolution has obliterated the distances. Mobility is drawing the countries nearer. This enhances the horrors of tragedies also. People are afraid of world war. Hence a one world government has become an imperative. Gandhiji was suspecting it and his panacea of decentralisation and non-violence can convince the governments to work on the ideal of one world government. A self-sufficient state will not be aggressive and such units can easily unite under a one world order.

Centralisation of last six decades in India has rendered the Indian polity monstrous and insensitive. All states have been demanding funds from centre and centre is forced to borrow from international organisations. This situation renders development a farce. Unless India takes to self-sufficiency and states decentralise their resources and programs, the disparities will continue and the way to world government will be obstructed by developed powers.

Education and Twenty-First Century

People all over the world are getting materialistic. Poor people think they can become rich by any means. To avoid wrong means people have to be educated. Gandhiji believed that without education no society can live in harmony and cooperation. Those who progress may unconsciously damage the over all progress of the world. Knowledge should combine action with education. His basic education was a plan of Nai Taleem in this direction.

He opposed the Macaulay scheme of education. It produced an army of babus who are still looking the society at lower levels.

He published a series of articles in *Harijan*. He asked Dr Zakir Hussain to prepare a blueprint of Buniyadi Shiksha (basic education). It was aimed at 'learning while earning'. It can reduce the gap between urban and rural India.

Gandhiji's scheme of education was productive and creative. The dependence on government employment is a bone of Macaulay education. It has crippled our youth and has rendered them invalid for creative physical labour. Gandhiji wanted children to learn crafts and make their living. The Macaulay education has failed to build character. On the contrary it has made our young people parasites who look to secure employment in all walks of life. Even our doctors and engineers are not creative professionals because they do not love physical labour. This education alienates educated citizens from the masses.

Charkha versus Atom Bomb

It was a paradox that the champion of non-violence and spinning wheel had to witness such a day when an atom bomb was dropped at Hiroshima in Japan. It decimated some 2,00,000 human beings in Nagasaki. More than 1,40,000 were killed in the attack. Gandhi called it a ghastly sin of science. His comment was 'If the world does not accept non-violence even now, then a global suicide is certain and is in the offering. Hatred and conflicts can be absorbed only by Ahimsa.'

The atomic race has made Gandhian principles more relevant and pertinent in the present day world. By possessing more bombs peace cannot be assured. Even small nations equipped with atomic arsenal will threaten world wars and will be less and less responsible. The big nations can end violence by demonstrating that non-violent nations have nothing to be afraid of. Bombs have no geographical boundaries. The political leaders who wield this atomic power are likely to abuse their atomic powers for personal greed or revenge. Hence only a message of love, peace and goodwill can conquer these hearts polluted by violence. Hatred cannot be reduced by more hatred. While love begets love, even the animals can be tamed by good behaviour. His message was that country which is non-violent will show the way to all those nations which can be provoked to universal destruction in the name of national honour and personal prestige. Disarmaments may be needed but rearmaments in scientific laboratories can only be checked by those who love peace and humanity. The world is sick of conferences and perennial wars. This unproductive venture needs a Gandhi and his non-violence.

Mechanisation and Industrialisation

Industrialisation causes scientific progress but its main evils are urbanisation, pollution and dehumanisation. These evils make city life hellish. The so called progress becomes a shame because the 'Man' himself becomes a machine. His sensitivities die and he forgets the bliss of family and fraternity. The rural folks have not been spoiled by urban dehumanisation. Their rural values are human and decentralisation can save them from this demonic path of progress through machines. Agriculture as a vocation has its blessings. The industrial employment system makes men and women mere cogs in the machine. The human relations which is the essence of human civilisation can be preserved by Gandhi's peace in poverty rather than by affluence under the spectre of violence and terror.

Industrialisation cannot be universal. Mere industry cannot feed people. The basic needs of survival apart from agriculture brings human beings close to nature. The cities become dirty by rain, while village life blooms and sprouts of periodic rains, wash the fields and irrigate the land for production and happiness. Machines have ruined the cities. Man has become invalid, a pygmy who does not realise the greatness with which God has endowed him. Unemployment is an urban problem. Employment should not be seen in numbers. Diversification and decentralisation of cooperative farms can produce enough for the need and the problem of urban greed will not be born. It can ensure universal good and welfare which the city life cannot even imagine or dream.

Swarajya or Ramrajya

'The Swarajya of my dream will ensure equality. The poor have a right to all those needs which rich people have. But if they live in palaces, we do not need palaces for the poor. But the minimum need of a dwelling has to be satisfied. No Swarajya can be complete unless the poor fulfil their minimum wants.'

Gandhi's Ramrajya is an ideal for the state. It seems like an impossibility to abolish affluence, but abolishing poverty is the basic need of a human society. It is difficult to achieve but efforts should continue in this direction. Gandhiji was not a mere visionary like Plato or Shankaracharaya. As a Karamyogi he strived to materialise his dream. His Satyagrah in South Africa, Champaran, Kheda, Civil Disobedience and Quit India Movement demonstrate that he knew how to fight for his dreams. He could humble down a mighty British empire. It was the power of the poor people whom he could galvanise and energise.

Gandhi did not merely preach but he acted. 'Be the change, you want to see in this world.' It was his watch word. It made him conscious of his own limitations. He did not want others to act. Even governments must only help. The rural development is a villager's responsibility. This message of self-help is Gandhi's Swarajya or Ramrajya.

Swarajya is only a conducive condition. Peace and non-violence create these conditions. According to him social change needs only two incentives: (1) to be free from greed and (2) to get rid of fear. To this he later added love and sacrifice. This gave birth to Satyagrah and people became powerful enough to fight the imperial power. Injustice increases when people succumb and accept injustice.

Gandhiji built a bridge between individual and the society, which can be called micro and macro. He knew that individual without society cannot develop. Two people start society or family. So he talked of eleven vows which can change entire relationships. His constructive programme had a multiple dimension from Satyagrah to the Khadi of spinning wheel. This could take consciousness to the rural huts and shepherds of India. It offered a code of conduct – which was an attempt to build a non-violent society in all its permutations.

Humanity can avoid total annihilation by following Gandhiji. Terrorism is the manifestation of violence. The world is scared. अहिसां परमोधर्म: (non-violence is the basic duty) is the cure whether one finds it convincing or not. The message is eternal.

Martin Luther King in US and Nelson Mandela in South Africa also demonstrated that Gandhi's message was eternal and universal. They achieved an unprecedented success and the Nobel Prize has been awarded to them for world peace. Aung San Suu Kyi is showing the way to her people. These Gandhian leaders all over the world explain that Gandhi was a global leader, a universal man and a citizen of the world.

Gandhiji followed Jesus in letter and spirit. He rose against the prejudices of his times. He was talking in India but the message was for the world which is yet to be born and appreciate his deeds.

Martin Luther King used to say 'those who live by sword perish by sword. Let us love our enemies. Do not use weapons. We shall overcome. It is justice. God is with us.' These words look like Gandhiji's preaching in a prayer meeting. He openly confessed that he learnt the ideals from Jesus Christ but he developed the techniques from Mahatma Gandhi. The whole of Africa which is resurgent today remembers him as a Messiah of liberation. Nkrumah, Kaunda and a host of others have inspired their people with Gandhi's message of nationalism, love and non-violence. He attacked upon colonialism but struggled without any bloodshed or any civil war.

The most unique character of Gandhian thought is the notion of freedom. All schools of thought – capitalist, socialist or Marxist put restraints and curtail liberty. Today democracy is popularly professed and practised, but people everywhere complain about the end of liberty under one excuse or another. People are unemployed and loss of freedom is a common experience. The political truth is the emergence of elitism in all democracies. The elites rule and enjoy in the name of masses. The elective institutions are a farce and even judicial institutions are far away from the reach of the people. Fear, exploitation, corruption and poverty have deprived the people of their fundamental human rights. This scenario can be changed only by practising what the Mahatma preached and practised. Social change is coming in a big way. Both law and violence have failed to channelise it. So the only way available to mankind is non-violence and self-rule of the poor. Love, compassion, self-sacrifice and abnegation are an effective way to change people's heart. Gandhiji brought freedom, it is a partial truth. The reality of history is that he taught the methodology. The fight was not against enemies but against our own perversions of human nature. Improvements are not possible with abundance or with atom bomb. Love, truth, and non-violence are the answers.

Bibliography

Ambedkar, B.R., *Gandhi and Gandhism*, Jalandhar: Bheem Patrika Publications, 1943.

Andrews, Charles Freer, *Mahatma Gandhi's Ideas*, London: Allen & Unwin, 1929.

Ansbro, John J., *Martin Luther King Jr.: The Making of a Mind*, Maryknoll, NY: Orbis, 1983.

Ashe, Geoffrey, *Gandhi: A Study in Revolution*, London: Heinemann, 1968.

Athalye, D.V., *The Life of Mahatma Gandhi*, Poona: Swadeshi Publishing Co., 1923.

Ayyar, P.A. Subrahmanya, *Our Mahatma*, Madras: Kariraja Publishers, 1949.

Bahuguna, Sunderlal, 'Gandhi's Betis', *Save Himalaya*, pp. 1–4. (n.d.)

Balasubramanian, K., *Directory of Gandhian Constructive Workers*, New Delhi: Gandhi Peace Foundation, 1996.

Bandyopadhyaya, Jayantanuja, *Social and Political Thought of Gandhi*, Bombay: Allied Publishers, 1969.

Banerjee, D.N., *India's Nation Builders*, Calcutta: Mukherjee & Co., 1961.

Barash, David P., *Introduction to Peace Studies*, Belmont, Calif.: Wadsworth, 1991.

Barr, F. Mary, *Mahatma Gandhi: His Life and Teaching*, Allahabad: Radhakrishan Lal, 1934.

Bartolf, Christian (ed.), *Letter to a Hindoo: Taraknath Das, Leo Tolstoi and Mahatma Gandhi*, Berlin: Gandhi-Informations-Zentrum, 1997.

Baruah, Upendra Kumar, *Portrait of a Gandhian: Biography of Dr. Martin Luther King, Jr.*, Guwahati: The Author, 1985.

Basham, A.L., *The Wonder That was India*, Delhi: Rupa and Co., 1971.

Bedi, B.P.L. (ed.), *The Saint of Human Rights: Gandhi*, Delhi: Unity Book Club of India, 1948.

Bhave, Vinoba and Jayaprakash Narayan, *Gramdan for Gramswaraj*, Varanasi: Sarva Seva Sangh Prakashan, 1967.

Bhave, Vinoba, *Bhoodan Yagna*, Ahmedabad: Navajivan, 1957.

Birla, G.D., *In the Shadow of the Mahatma*, Bombay: Vakils, Feffer & Simons, 1968.

Bishop, Peter D., *A Technique for Loving: Non-violence in Indian and Christian Traditions*, London: SMC Press, 1981.

Bolton, G., *Tragedy of Gandhi*, London: Allen & Unwin, 1934.

Bondurant, Joan V., *Conquest of Violence: Gandhian Philosophy of Conflicts*, Princeton, NJ: Princeton University Press, 1958; Bombay: Oxford University Press, 1959; Berkeley: University of California Press, 1967.

Bose, Amalendu, 'Gandhi and Ruskin: Ideological Affinities', in C.D. Narasimhaiah (ed.), *Gandhi and the West*, Mysore: University of Mysore, 1969, pp. 128–44.

Bose, Nirmal Kumar, *My Days with Gandhi*, Calcutta: Nishana, 1953.

——, *Studies in Gandhism*, Calcutta: Indian Associated Publishing Co., 1947; Ahmedabad: Navajivan, 1972.

Briggs, George W., *The Power of Non-violence in India*, NJ: Madison, 1943.

Brown, Judith M., *Gandhi and Civil Disobedience: The Mahatma in Indian Politics, 1928–1934*, London: Cambridge University Press, 1977.

——, *Gandhi: Prisoner of Hope*, New Haven, CT: Yale University Press, 1989.

——, *Gandhi's Rise to Power: Indian Politics 1915–1922*, London: Cambridge University Press, 1972.

Buch, M.A., *Rise and Growth of Indian Nationalism, Non-violent Nationalism: Gandhi and His School*, Baroda: Baroda College, 1939.

Burning, Gillian, *Gandhi Letters: From Upper House to Lower House, 1906–1914*, Durban: Local History Museum, 1994.

Butler, Dom E.C., 'Monasticism', in *The Cambridge Medieval History*, Vol. 1, London: Cambridge University Press, 1911.

Case, Clarence Marsh, *Non-violent Coercion: A Study in Methods of Social Pressure*, London: George Allen & Unwin, 1923.

Catlin, George, *In the Path of Mahatma Gandhi*, London: Macdonald, 1948.

Chakrabarti, K. Chandra, *The Philosophy of Gandhi*, Imphal: M. Chakraborty, 1958.

Char, K.T. Narasimha (ed.), *A Day of Thoughts from Mahatma Gandhi*, Calcutta: Macmillan, 1951.

Chatterjee, Margaret, *Gandhi and his Jewish Friends*, London: Macmillan, 1992.

Chatterjee, Nandlal, *Mahatma Gandhi: A Torch Bearer of Humanity*, Allahabad: Indian Press, 1958.

Chaudhary, P.C.R., *Gandhi and His Contemporaries*, Delhi: Sterling, 1972.

Chitambar, Jaswant Rao, *Mahatma Gandhi: His Life, Work and Influence*, Chicago: John C. Winston Co., 1933.

Dange, S.A., *India from Primitive Communism to Slavery*, Bombay: People's Publishing House, 1949.

Das Gupta, Arun Chandra, *Non-violence: The Invincible Power*, 2nd edition, Calcutta: Khadi Pratisthan, 1946.

Datta, D.M., *The Philosophy of Mahatma Gandhi*, Madison: University of Wisconsin Press, 1953.

De Ligt, Bart, *The Conquest of Violence: An Essay on War and Revolution*, London: George Routledge & Sons, 1937.

Desai, A.R., *Social Background of India Nationalism*, Bombay: Popular Books, 1959.

Desai, Kantilal S., *Gandhi and Gandhism: The Future Voice for India*, Ahmedabad: Sakarlal Bulakhidas, 1931.

Desai, Mahadev, 'Apartim Sadhak', in Navajivan Trust, Ashram No Pran, pp. 50–67.

——, *Day to Day with Gandhi: Secretary's Diary*, 9 Vols, Rajghat, Varanasi: Sarva Seva Sangh, 1968–74.

——, *The Gita According to Gandhi*, Ahmedabad: Navajivan, 1946.

——, *The Story of Bardoli: Being a History of the Bardoli Satyagraha of 1928 and Its Sequel*, Ahmedabad: Navajivan, 1929; 1957.

Desai, Narayan, *My Gandhi*, Ahmedabad: Navajivan, 1999.

Deshpande, Gangadhar Rao, 'Ahimsa in Action', In *Gandhiji* Bombay: Kaihatak Publishing House, 1945.

Deshpande, M.S., *Light of India: The Message of the Mahatma*, Bombay: Wilco Publishing House, 1950.

Devanesen, D.S., *The Making of the Mahatma*, New Delhi: Orient Longmans, 1969.

Devas, S., *Gandhiji and Some of His Thoughts*, Madras: Good Pastor Press, 1949.

Dhawan, G.N., *The Political Philosophy of Mahatma Gandhi*, Bombay: Popular Book Depot, 1946; Ahmedabad: Navajivan, 1951.

Dhebhar, U.N., *Gandhian Thought*, Kurukshetra: Kurukshetra University, 1961.

Diwakar, R.R., *Gandhi's Life, Thought and Philosophy*, Bombay: Bhartiya Vidya Bhawan, 1963.

——, *Satyagraha: Its Technique and Theory*, Bombay: Hind Kitabs, 1946.

Doctor, Adi H., *Sarvodaya: A Political and Economic Study*, Bombay: Asia Publishing House, 1967.

Doke, Joseph J., *M.K. Gandhi: An Indian Patriot in South Africa*, London: London Indian Chronicle, 1909.

Dumont, Louis, *Homo Hierarchicus: The Caste System and its Implications*, London: Paladin, 1972.

Dutt, R. Palme, *India Today*, Calcutta: Manisha, 1970.

Eaton, Jeanette, *Gandhi: Fighter Without a Sword*, New York: William Morrow, 1950.

Einstein, Albert, *Ideas and Opinions*, London: Alvin Redman, 1954.

Embree, A.T., *India's Search for a National Identity*, New York: Knopf, 1972.

Erikson, Erik H., *Gandhi's Truth: On the Origins of Militant Non-violence*, New York: Norton, 1969; London: Faber & Faber, 1970.

Fischer, Louis, 'Miscellaneous Notes from a House Guest', in Norman Cousins (ed.), *Profiles of Gandhi: America Remembers a World Leader*, New Delhi: Indian Book Co., 1969, pp. 54–64.

——, *The Life of Mahatma Gandhi*, Bombay: Bharatiya Vidya Bhavan, 1956; New York: Collier, 1962.

——, *Gandhi, His Life and Message for the World*, New York: The New American Library, 1954.

Fraser, Kenneth C., The Politics of Gandhi's Constructive Programme, Bachelor of Arts Thesis, La Trobe University, 1976.

Fry, A. Ruth, *Victories Without Violence*, London: Dennis Dobson, 1939.

Gandhi, Arun and Sunanda Gandhi, *The Forgotten Woman: The Untold Story of Kastur Gandhi, Wife of Mahatma Gandhi*, Huntsville, AR: Ozark Mountain Publishers, 1998.

Gandhi, M.K., *All Men are Brothers: Life and Thoughts of Mahatma Gandhi as Told in His Words*, New York: Columbia University Press, 1958.

——, *An Autobiography: The Story of My Experiments With Truth*, Ahmedabad: Navajivan, 1940.

——, *Ashram Observances in Action*, Ahmedabad: Navajivan, 1955.

——, *Bapu's Letters to Mira, 1924–1948*, Ahmedabad: Navajivan, 1949.

——, *Collected Works of Mahatma Gandhi*, Vols 1–100, New Delhi: Publications Division, Government of India, 1958–91; CD-ROM version, New Delhi: Publications Division, Government of India, 1999.

——, *Gandhian Gems*, Ambala: Standard Publishing Co., 1954.

——, *Glorious Thoughts of Gandhi*, New Delhi: New Book Society of India, 1965.

——, *Hind Swaraj* or *Indian Home Rule*, Ahmedabad: Navajivan, 1939.

——, *My Non-violence*, Compiled and edited by Sailesh Kumar Bandyopadhyaya, Ahmedabad: Navajivan, 1960.

——, *Non-violence in Peace and War*, Ahmedabad: Navajivan, 1948.

——, *Ruskin: Unto This Last: A Paraphrase*, Ahmedabad: Navajivan, 1951.

——, *Sarvodaya: The Welfare of All*, Ahmedabad: Navajivan, 1954.

——, *Satyagraha in South Africa*, Madras: S. Ganesan, 1925.

Gandhi, Madan, *Gandhian Aesthetics*, Chandigarh and Delhi: Vikas Bharati, 1969.

Gandhi, Prabhudas, 'Magankaka', in Navajivan Trust, Ashram No Pran, pp. 4–41.

——, *My Childhood with Gandhi*, Ahmedabad: Navajivan, 1957.

Gandhi, Rajmohan, *Patel: A Life*, Ahmedabad: Navajivan, 1991.

Ganguli, B.N., *Gandhi's Social Philosophy*, New Delhi: Vikas Publishing House, 1973.

Ghosh, Atulya, *Ahimsa and Gandhi*, Calcutta: Congress Bhavan, 1954.

Green, Martin, *Gandhi: Voice of a New Age Revolution*, New York: Continuum, 1993.

——, *The Challenge of the Mahatmas*, New York: Basic Books, 1978.

——, *The Origins of Non-violence: Tolstoy and Gandhi in Their Historical Settings*, University Park, PA: Pennsylvania State University Press, 1986.

Gregg, Richard B., *A Discipline for Non-Violence*, Ahmedabad: Navajivan, 1941.

——, *The Power of Non-violence*, London: George Routledge & Sons, 1938; Ahmedabad: Navajivan, 1949.

——, *The Psychology and Strategy of Gandhi's Non-violent Resistance*, Madras: Ganesan, 1929.

Gupta, Nagendra Nath, *Gandhi and Gandhism*, Bombay: Hind Kitabs, 1948.

Harris, Ishwar C., *Gandhians in Contemporary India: The Vision and the Visionaries*, Lewiston, NY: The Edwin Mellen Press, 1998.

Hingorani, Anand T. and Ganga A. Hingoraini, *The Encyclopedia of Gandhian Thoughts*, New Delhi: AICC [I], 1985.

Holmes, John Haynes, *My Gandhi: A Personal Portrait of a Man Who Shook the World*, London: George Allen & Unwin, 1954.

Hunt, James D., 'The Kallenbach Papers and Tolstoy Farm', unpublished working paper presented to the Association for Asian Studies meeting in Washington, DC, 6–9 April 1995.

——, *Gandhi and the Nonconformists: Encounters in South Africa*, New Delhi: Promilla and Co., 1986.

——, *Gandhi in London*, New Delhi: Promilla and Co., 1978.

Hussain, S. Abid, *The Way of Gandhi and Nehru*, London: Asia Publishing House, 1959.

Ingram, Catherine, *In the Footsteps of Gandhi: Conversation with Spiritual Social Activities*, Berkeley: Parallax, 1990.

Iyer, Raghavan N., *The Moral and Political Thought of Mahatma Gandhi*, New York: Oxford University Press, 1973.

Joshi, Chhaganlal, *Satyagraha Ashram and Gandhi Parivar*, Ahmedabad: Sabarmati Ashram Suraksha and Smarak Trust, 1975.

Kabadi, Waman P., *The Immortal Mahatma*, Bombay: Yeshanand Publications, 1950.

Kalelkar, Kaka, *Stray Glimpses of Bapu*, Ahmedabad: Navajivan, 1950.

Kamath, M.V., *Gandhi's Coolie: Life and Times of Ramakrishna Bajaj*, Ahmedabad: Allied Publishers, 1988.

Karunakaran, K.P., *New Perspectives and Gandhi*, Shimla: Indian Institute of Advanced Studies, 1969.

Keer, D., *Mahatma Gandhi: Political Saint and Unarmed Prophet*, Bombay: Popular Prakashan, 1973.

Khanna, G.D., 'Mahatma Gandhi', in his *Great Men of India*, Madras: Macmillan & Co., 1947.

Kothari, Rajni, *Caste in Indian Politics*, New Delhi: Orient Longmans, 1970.

Kripalani, J.B., *Gandhian Thought*, New Delhi: Gandhi Smarak Nidhi, 1961.

——, *The Latest Fad*, Wardha: Hindustani Talimi Sangh, 1946.

——, *Gandhian Philosophy*, Gandhi Memorial Lectures, Agra University, 1951; Aligarh: Dwadash Sheni & Co., 1952.

——, *Non-violent Resolution*, Bombay: Vora & Co., 1938.

——, *The Gandhian Way*, Bombay: Vora & Co., 1945.

Krishnadas, *Seven Months with Mahatma Gandhi*, Ahmedabad: Navajivan, 1951.

Kumar, R. (ed.), *Essays on Gandhian Politics: The Rowlett Satyagraha of 1919*, Oxford: Clarendon Press, 1971.

Lacombe, Olivier, 'The Future of Non-violence', in his *The Emerging World*, Jawahar Lal Nehru Memorial Volume, Bombay: Asia Publishing House, 1964.

Lanza del Vasto, J.J., *Gandhi to Vinoba: The New Pilgrimage*, London: Rider, 1956.

Lewis, M.D. (ed.), *Gandhi: Maker of Modern India?*, Boston: D.C. Heath and Co., 1965.

Mahadevan, T.K. (ed.), *Truth and Non-violence: A UNESCO Symposium on Gandhi*, New Delhi: Gandhi Peace Foundation, 1970.

Mashruwala, K.G., *In Quest of Truth*, Ahmedabad: Shravana, 1983.

——, *Gandhi and Marx*, Ahmedabad: Navajivan, 1951.

——, *Practical Non-violence and Ideology of Non-violence*, Ahmedabad: Navajivan, 1946.

Mazumdar, Haridas T., *Mahatma Gandhi: Peaceful Revolutionary*, New York: Charles Scribner's Sons, 1952.

McLaughlin, Elizabeth T., *Ruskin and Gandhi*, Cranbury, NJ: Associated University Presses, 1974.

Mehta, Ashoka, *Studies in Socialism*, Bombay: Bharatiya Vidya Bhavan, 1951.

Mehta, Ved, *Mahatma Gandhi and His Apostles*, Middlesex: Penguin Books, 1977.

Miller, William Robert, 'Experimentation in Non-violence: The Next Phase', in G. Ramachandran and T.K. Mahadevan (eds), *Gandhi: His Relevance for Our Times*, New Delhi: Gandhi Peace Foundation, 1967.

Mukherjee, Hiren, *Gandhiji: A Study*, New Delhi: People's Publishing House, 1958.

Murthi, V.V. Ramana, *Non-violence in Politics: A Study of Gandhian Techniques and Thinking*, Delhi: Frank Bros., 1958.

Murthy, K.S. and A.C. Bouquet, 'Gandhi's Philosophy of Non-violence', in their *Studies in the Problems of Peace*, Bombay: Asia Publishing House, 1960.

Myrdal, Gunnar, *Asian Drama: An Inquiry into the Poverty of Nations*, 3 Vols, New York: The Twentieth Century Fund, 1968.

Nag, Kalidas, *Tolstoy and Gandhi*, Patna: Pustak Bhandar, 1950.

Nair, Sankaran, *Gandhi and Anarchy*, Madras: Tagore & Co., 1922.

Namboodiripad, E.M.S., *The Mahatma and the Ism*, New Delhi: People's Publishing House, 1958.

Nanda, B.R., *Gokhale, Gandhi and the Nehrus: Studies in Indian Nationalism*, London: Allen & Unwin, 1974.

——, *In Gandhiji's Footsteps: The Life and Times of Jamnalal Bajaj*, New Delhi: Oxford University Press, 1990.

——, *In Search of Gandhi: Essays and Reflections*, New Delhi: Oxford University Press, 2002.

——, *Mahatma Gandhi: A Biography*, London: Oxford University Press, 1981.

——, *Gokhale: The Indian Moderates and the British Raj*, Princeton, NJ: Princeton University Press, 1977.

——, *Mahatma Gandhi*, London: Allen & Unwin, 1965.

Narayan, Shriman, *Jamnalal Bajaj: Gandhiji's Fifth Son*, New Delhi: Publications Division, Ministry of Information and Broadcasting, Government of India, 1974.

——, *Mahatma Gandhi: The Atomic Man*, Bombay: Somaiya Publications, 1971.

Nayar, Kuldip, *India: The Critical Years*, Delhi: Vikas Publishing House, 1971.

Nayar, Sushila, *Mahatma Gandhi, Volume IV: Satyagraha at Work*, Ahmedabad: Navajivan, 1989.

——, *Mahatma Gandhi, Volume V: India Awakened*, Ahmedabad: Navajivan, 1993.

——, *Mahatma Gandhi, Volume VI: Salt Satyagraha: The Watershed*, Ahmedabad: Navajivan, 1995.

Nehru, Jawaharlal, *An Autobiography*, London: John Lane, The Bodley Head, 1936.

——, *Non-violence and the Doctrine of the Sword*, London: Nodlay Head, 1955.

——, *The Discovery of India*, New York: Anchor Books, 1960.

Parulekar, N.B., *The Science of Soul Force or Mahatma Gandhi's Doctrine of Truth and Non-violence*, Bombay: Hind Kitabs, 1962.

Parvate, T.V. and Jamnalal Bajaj, *A Brief Study of His Life and Character*, Ahmedabad: Navajivan, 1962.

Payne, Robert, *The Life and Death of Mahatma Gandhi*, London: The Bodley Head, 1969.

Polak, H.S.L., H.N. Brailsord and Lord Pethick-Lawrence, *Mahatma Gandhi*, London: Odhams Press, 1949.

Polak, H.S.L., *Mahatma Gandhi*, Madras: Natesan, 1931.

Polak, Millie Graham, 'In the South African Day's', in C. Shukla (ed.), *Incidents of Gandhiji's Life*, Bombay: Vora and Co., pp. 247–51.

——, *Mr. Gandhi: The Man*, Bombay: Vora and Co., 1949.

Power, Shahed, 'Gandhi and Deep Ecology: Experiencing the Nonhuman Environment', unpublished PhD thesis, Environmental Resources Unit, University of Salford, 1991.

Prabhu, R.K. and U.R. Rao, *The Mind of Mahatma Gandhi*, Ahmedabad: Navajivan, 1967.

Pradhan, Benudhar, *The Socialist Thought of Mahatma Gandhi*, Vol. I, Delhi: GDK, 1980.

Prasad, Mahadev, *Social Philosophy of Mahatma Gandhi*, Gorakhpur: Vishwavidyalaya Prakashan, 1958.

Prasad, Rajendra, *At the Feet of Mahatma Gandhi*, London: Asia Publishing House, 1961.

——, *Satyagraha in Champaran*, Ahmedabad: Navajivan, 1949.

Prasad, Vilma, *Socialism, Sarvodaya and Democracry: Selected Works of Jaiprakash Narain*, Bombay: Asia Publishing House, 1964.

Puri, Bindu (ed.), *Mahatma Gandhi and His Contemporaries*, Shimla: Indian Institute of Advanced Study, 2001.

Pyarelal, Mahatma Gandhi, *The Early Phase*, Vol. I, Ahmedabad: Navajivan, 1965.

——, *The Last Phase*, Vol. X, Ahmedabad: Navajivan, 1958.

Pyarelal and Sushila Nayer, *In Gandhiji's Mirror*, Delhi: Oxford University Press, 1991.

Radhakrishnan, S. (ed.), *Mahatma Gandhi: Essays and Reflections on His Life and Work*, London: Allen & Unwin, 1939; Bombay: Jaico, 1956.

——, *Mahatma Gandhi: 100 Years*, New Delhi: Gandhi Peace Foundation, 1968.

Rai, Ganpat, *Mahatma Gandhi: Builder and Liberator*, Ambala Cantt.: National Publisher's Corpn., 1952.

Rajagopalachari, C., *Gandhi's Teachings and Philosophy*, Bombay: Bhartiya Vidhya Bhawan, 1963.

Ray, Sibnarayan (ed.), *Gandhi, India and the World*, Philadelphia: Temple University Press, 1970.

Reynolds, Reginald, *To Live in Mankind: A Quest for Gandhi*, London: Andre Deutsch, 1951.

Rolland, Romain, *Mahatma Gandhi: The Man Who Became One with the Universal Being*, London: Allen & Unwin, 1924.

Rothermund, Indira, *The Philosophy of Restraint*, Bombay: Popular Prakashan, 1963.

Rudolph, Lloyd I. and Susanne Hoeber Rudolph, *The Modernity of Tradition: Political Developments in India*, Chicago: The University of Chicago Press, 1967.

Schumacher, E.F., *Small is Beautiful: A Study of Economics as if People Mattered*, London: Abacus, 1974.

Sen, Priyaranjan, *Mahatma Gandhi's Sayings*, Calcutta: Orient Book Co., 1948.

Sethi, J.D., *Gandhi Today*, Sahibabad: Vikas Publishing House, 1979.

Sharma, Bishan Swarup, *Gandhi as a Political Thinker*, Allahabad: Indian Press, 1956.

Sharp, Gene, *The Meaning of Non-violence*, London: Housmans Bookshop, 1957.

——, *Which Way to Freedom? A Study in Non-violence*, Cardiff: Plaid Cymru [n.d.].

——, 'Gandhi's Political Significance Today', *Gandhi Marg*, Vol. 9, 1965, pp. 47–56.

——, *Gandhi Wields the Weapon of Moral Power: Three Case Histories*, Ahmedabad: Navajivan, 1960.

Shridharni, Krishnalal, *War Without Violence: A Study of Gandhi's Method and its Accomplishments*, New York: Harcourt, Brace and Co., 1939.

Shrimali, K.L., *The Wardha Scheme*, Udaipur: Vidya Bhawan Society, 1949.

Shukla, Chandrashankar (ed.), *Gandhiji as We Know Him*, Bombay: Vora & Co., 1945.

——, *Incidents of Gandhiji's Life*, Bombay: Vora and Co., 1949.

——, *Reminiscences of Gandhiji*, Bombay: Vora and Co., 1949.

Simons, Earnest J., *Tolstoy*, London: Routledge and Kegan Paul, 1973.

Singh, Balwant, *Under the Shelter of Bapu*, Ahmedabad: Navajivan, 1962.

Sinha, Srikrishna, 'Ahimsa is Our Creed', in his *Speeches and Writings*, Patna: Director of Public Relations, Bihar, 1956.

Sinuta, J.E., 'Gandhi's Political Method', in C.F. Andrew's (ed.), *Mahatma Gandhi's Ideas*, London: George Allen, 1949.

Sitaramayya, B.P., *Gandhi and Gandhism: A Study*, Allahabad: Kitabistan, 1942.

——, 'Gandhi in His Many Aspects', in C.F. Andrews (ed.), *Mahatma Gandhi's Ideas*, London: George Allen, 1949.

Slade, Madeleine [Mirabehn], *The Spirit's Pilgrimage*, London: Longmans, 1960.

Spratt, P., *Gandhism: An Analysis*, Madras: The Huxley Press, 1959.

Sundram, I., *Gandhian Thought*, Delhi: Malhotra Bros., 1961.

Sutherland, Bill and Matt Meyer, *Guns and Gandhi in Africa: Pan African Insights on Non-violence, Armed Struggle and Liberation in Africa*, Trenton, NJ: Africa World Press, 2000.

Swan, Maureen, *Gandhi: The South African Experience*, Johannesburg: Ravan Press, 1985.

Tagore, R.N., *Mahatmaji and the Depressed Humanity*, Calcutta: Visva Bharati, 1932.

Tarachand, *History of the Freedom Movement in India*, New Delhi: Publications Division, 1973.

Tendulkar, D.G. (ed.), *Gandhiji: His Life and Work*, Bombay: Keshav Bhikaji Dhawale, 1944.

Tendulkar, D.G., *Gandhi in Champaran*, New Delhi: Publications Division, Government of India, 1957.

——, *Mahatma: Life of Mohandas Karamchand Gandhi*, 8 Vols, New Delhi: Publications Division, Ministry of Information and Broadcasting, Government of India, 1960–63.

Thomson, Mark, *Gandhi and His Ashrams*, Bombay: Popular Prakashan, 1993.

Unnithan, T.K.N., *Gandhi and Free India*, Amsterdam: J.B. Walters-Graningen, 1956.

Varma, V.P., *The Political Philosophy of Mahatma Gandhi and Sarvodaya*, Agra: Lakshmi Narayan Agarwal, 1959.

Vaswani, K.N., *Glimpses of Gandhi and Gandhism*, New Delhi: Sterling, 1955.

Vepa, Ram K., *New Technology: A Gandhian Concept*, New Delhi: Gandhi Book House, 1975.

Watson, Francis and Hallam Tennyson, *Talking of Gandhi*, New Delhi: Sangam, 1976.

Weber, Max, *The Protestant Ethic and the Spirit of Capitalism*, Translated by Talcott Parsons, London: Unwin University Books, 1930.

Weber, Thomas, *Conflict Resolution and Gandhian Ethics*, New Delhi: Gandhi Peace Foundation, 1991.

——, *Gandhi as Disciple and Mentor*, New Delhi: Cambridge University Press, 2007.

——, *Gandhi's Peace Army: The Shanti Sena and Unarmed Peacekeeping*, Syracuse, NY: Syracuse University Press, 1996.

——, *On the Salt March: The Historiography of Gandhi's March to Dandi*, New Delhi: Harper Collins, 1997.

Woodcock, George, *Anarchism*, Middlesex: Penguin Books, 1963.

——, *Gandhi*, London: Fontana, 1972.

Yagnik, Indulal K., *Gandhi as I Know Him*, Part I, Bombay: Advocate of India Press, 1933; Part II, New Delhi: Danish Mahal, 1943.

Periodicals

Aiyar, S.P., 'Gandhi, Gokhale and the Moderates', in Sibnarayan Ray (ed.), *Gandhi, India and the World*, Melbourne: Hawthorn Press, 1970, pp. 99–118.

Andrews, Charles Freer, 'Mr. Gandhi at Phoenix', *Modern Review*, Vol. XV, No. 5, May 1914.

Ansbro, John J., The Ark: Elements of a Non-violent World, pamphlet [n.p., n.d.].

Atreya, B.L., 'A Plea for Ahimsa in Human Life', in his *Moral and Spiritual Foundations of Peace*, Banaras: International Standard Publications, 1952.

Bajaj, Jamnalal, 'In Search of a Guru', in K. Kalelkar (ed.), *To a Gandhian Capitalist*, Bombay: Sevak Prakashan, pp. 9–12.

Barratt, Barnaby B., 'The Alternative Village', *South Asian Review*, Vol. 7, No. 4, July 1974.

Bedekar, V.M., 'Ahimsa in the Mahabharata and Gandhi', *Gandhi Marg*, Vol. 2, No. 2, April 1958.

Benoit, Madhu, 'The Mahatma and the Poet', *Gandhi Marg*, Vol. 19, 1997, pp. 304–23.

Bhana, Surendra, 'The Tolstoy Farm: Gandhi's Experiment in Cooperative Commonwealth', *South African Historical Journal*, Vol. 7, No. 1, 1975, available at www.anc.org.za/andocs/history/people/gandhi/bhana.html

——, 'Tolstoy Farm: A Satyagrahi's Battleground', *Journal of Indian History*, Vol. LVII, August–December 1979.

Bharatiya, L.K., 'Gandhiji's Ashram: Institution and its Significance', *Lok Rajya*, Vol. 26, No. 12, 16 October 1970.

Bhattacharya, N.C., 'Is Non-violent State Possible?', in B.B. Majumdar (ed.), *Gandhian Concept of State*, Calcutta: M.C. Sarkar and Sons Private Ltd., 1957.

Bondurant, Joan V., 'Force, Violence and the Innocent Dilemma', *Gandhi Marg*, Vol. 9, No. 3, July 1965.

Bose, N.K., *Satya and Ahimsa [Truth and Non-violence]: Mahatma Gandhi's Interpretation*, Calcutta: Committee for World Meeting, 1949.

——, 'Gandhi and Gandhism', *Visva Bharati Quarterly*, Gandhi Memorial Peace Number, 2 October 1949.

Bristol, James, 'Non-violence as a Positive Concept', *Gandhi Marg*, Vol. 8, No. 1, January 1964.

Brown, D. Mackenzie, 'Mohandas Karamchand Gandhi, Face to Face with Ahimsa', in his *Indian Political Thought from Ranade to Bhave*, Berkeley: University of California Press, 1961.

Caveeshar, Sardul Singh, *Non-violent Non-co-operation*, Lahore: National Publications, 1934.

Chatterji, Nandlal, 'Mahatma Gandhi's Conception of Politics', in his *India's Struggle for Freedom*, Allahabad: Indian Press, 1958.

Church, Roderick, 'Vinoba Bhave, Jayaprakash Narayan and Indian Democracy', *Gandhian Perspectives*, Vol. 2, No. 2, 1980, pp. 89–129.

Dasgupta, A.C., 'A Dose of Gandhism', in *The Indian Culture: Mahendra Jayanti Volume*, Calcutta: Bharat Sanskrite Parisat, 1951.

Dellinger, Dave, 'The Future of Non-violence', *Gandhi Marg*, Vol. 9, No. 3, July 1965.

Desai, Morarji, 'Gandhian Concept', in his *Selected Speeches*, Edited by Chandrakant Mehta, Bombay: Hind Kitabs, 1956.

Devdutt, 'Vinoba and the Gandhian Tradition', *Gandhi Marg*, Vol. 5, 1983, pp. 600–15.

Diwakar, R.R., 'Democracy and Non-violence', *Gandhi Marg*, Vol. 3, No. 4, October 1959.

——, 'Gandhian Non-violence: A Landmark', *Gandhi Marg*, Vol. 1, No. 4, October 1951.

——, 'The Creative Thought of Gandhi', *Gandhi Marg*, Vol. 7, No. 4, October 1963.

Frank, J.D., 'Human Nature and Non-violent Resistance', in Quincy Wright (ed.), *Preventing World War III*, New York: Simon and Schuster, 1962.

Gandhi, Arun, 'Gandhi Ashrams: No Gandhian Spirit', *The Illustrated Weekly of India*, 1 February 1976.

Gandhi, M.K., *Non-violent Way to World Peace*, Compiled by R.K. Prabhu, Ahmedabad: Navajivan Publishing House, 1959.

Galtung, Johan, 'Gandhi's Views on the Political and Ethical Preconditions of a Non-violent Fighter', in Pran Chopra (ed.), *The Sage in Revolt: A Remembrance*, New Delhi: Gandhi Peace Foundation, 1972, pp. 203–16.

Goldie, Fay, 'Last of the Gandhis in South Africa', *The Illustrated Weekly of India*, 3 October 1971.

Groom, Donald G., 'Impressions of Gandhi', *Gandhi Marg*, Vol. 13, No. 3, July 1969.

Guha, Ramachandra, 'Radical American Environmentalism and Wilderness Preservation: A Third World Critique', in Nina

Witoszek and Andrew Brennan (eds), *Philosophical Dialogues*, Lanham: Rowman and Littlefield, 1999, pp. 313–24.

Hay, Stephen N., 'Jain Influences on Gandhi's Early Thought', in Sibnarayan Ray (ed.), *Gandhi, India and the World*, Melbourne: Hawthorn Press, 1970, pp. 29–38.

Hendrick, George, 'Gandhi and Dr. Martin Luther King', *Gandhi Marg*, Vol. 3, No. 1, 1959, pp. 18–22.

——, 'Influence of Thoreau and Emerson on Gandhi's Satyagraha', *Gandhi Marg*, Vol. 3, No. 3, 1959, pp. 165–78.

——, 'Influence of Thoreau's "Civil Disobedience" on Gandhi's Satyagraha', *New England Quarterly*, Vol. 29, No. 4, 1956, pp. 462–71.

Herman, Ted, 'Adding Gandhi to Galtung for Peace Work', *Peace, Environment and Education*, Vol. 5, 1994, pp. 23–27.

Hermann, A.L., 'Satyagraha: A New Indian Word for Some Old Ways of Western Thinking', *Philosophy East and West*, Vol. 19, No. 2, 1969, pp. 123–42.

Hoda, Surur, 'Schumacher on Gandhi', in Manmohan Choudhary and Ramjee Singh (eds), *Mahatma Gandhi: 125 Years*, Varanasi: Sarva Seva Sangh/Gandhian Institute of Studies, 1995, pp. 95–105.

Horsburgh, H.J.N., 'Non-violence and Impatience', *Gandhi Marg*, Vol. 12, 1968, pp. 355–60.

Hunt, James D., 'Experiments in Forming a Community of Service: The Evolution of Gandhi's First Ashrams, Phoenix and Tolstoy Farm', in K.L. Seshagiri Rao and Henry O. Thompson (eds), *World Problems and Human Responsibility: Gandhian Perspectives*, Barrytown, NY: Unification Theological Seminary, 1988, pp. 177–203.

——, 'Gandhi and the Theosophists', in V.T. Patil (ed.), *Studies on Gandhi*, New Delhi: Sterling, 1983, pp. 163–76.

——, 'Thoreau and Gandhi: A Re-evaluation of the Legacy', *Gandhi Marg*, Vol. 14, No. 4, 1970, pp. 325–32.

Hussain, Zakir, 'The Emergency of Non-violence', *Gandhi Marg*, Vol. 6, No. 3, July 1962.

Jack, Homer A., 'Henry S.L. Polak', *Gandhi Marg*, Vol. 3, No. 4, 1959, pp. 289–92.

Kalelkar, Kaka, 'Gandhiji's Cottage in Sevagram', *Lok Rajya*, 1 October 1971.

——, 'Jamnalalji as I Knew Him', in his *To a Gandhian Capitalist*, Bombay: Hind Kitabs, pp. 13–20.

——, 'Tapasvi Jivan', in Navajivan Trust (ed.), *Ashram No Pran*, Ahmedabad: Navajivan, pp. 78–82.

Kaur, Rajkumari Amrit, Gandhiji's Moral and Spiritual Contribution to Indian Life and Thought in 'What Gandhiji has Done for India', 1946.

Kumarappa, Bharathan, 'The Roots of Gandhi's Politics', *Gandhi Marg*, Vol. 1, No. 2, April 1957.

Mannin, Ethel, 'Non-violence and the Modern World: Gandhiji's Mission of Reconciliation', *Para-Bharati Quarterly*, 2 October 1949.

——, 'Some Reflections on Violence', *Gandhi Marg*, Vol. 8, No. 3, July 1963.

Menon, K.P. Sarkara, 'Ahimsa and Respect for Life', *Gandhi Marg*, Vol. 2, No. 4, October 1958.

Miller, William Robert, 'Notes on the Theory of Non-violence', *Gandhi Marg*, Vol. 5, No. 4, October 1962.

Moore, Charles A., 'Ahimsa [Non-violence] as the Supreme Ethical Principle', in S. Radhakrishnan and Others (eds), *A.R. Wadia: Essay in Philosophy*, Madras: G.S. Press, 1959.

Narayan, Jayaprakash, 'The Relevance of Gandhi', *Asian Studies*, Vol. 7, No. 3, December 1969.

Nargolkar, Vasant, 'Vinoba and Satyagraha', *Gandhi Marg*, Vol. 2, No. 12, 1981, pp. 661–72.

Nelson, Stuart, 'The Tradition of Non-violence and its Underlying Forces', *Gandhi Marg*, Vol. 4, No. 1, January 1960.

Nigam, Saling Ram, 'Ahimsa or Non-violence', in his *World Peace and the New Order*, Lucknow: Universal Publishers, 1947.

Orwell, George, 'Reflections on Gandhi', in *The Collected Essays, Journalism and Letters of George Orwell, Volume 4: In Front of Your Nose*, Harmondsworth: Penguin, 1970, pp. 523–31.

Polak, H.S.L., 'Appendix II', in C.F. Andrews (ed.), *Speeches and Writings of M.K. Gandhi*, Madras: Natesan, 1922, pp. 38–44.

——, 'Satyagraha and its Origin in South Africa', in Kshitis Roy (ed.), *Gandhi Memorial Peace Number*, Shantiniketan: The Visva-Bharati Quarterly, 1949, pp. 111–20.

——, 'Some South African Reminiscences', in C. Shukla (ed.), *Incidents of Gandhiji's Life*, Bombay: Vora and Co., 1949, pp. 230–47.

Prasad, C. Shambu, 'Gandhi and Maganlal: Khadi Science and the Gandhian Scientist', in B. Puri (ed.), *Mahatma Gandhi and His*

Contemporaries, Shimla: Indian Institute of Advanced Study, 2001, pp. 228–51.

Pyarelal, 'Gandhiji's Last Experiment: Sevagram Ashram', *The Illustrated Weekly of India*, 2 December 1962.

Raghuwanshi, V.P.S., 'Gandhi and Gandhism', in his *Indian Nationalist Movement and Thought*, Agra: Lakshmi Narain Agarwal, 1959.

Rao, P. Kodanda, 'Gokhale and Gandhi', in G. Ramachandran and T.K. Mahadevan (eds), *Quest for Gandhi*, New Delhi: Gandhi Peace Foundation, 1970, pp. 343–51.

Rao, U.S. Mohan, 'Introduction', in K. Kalelkar (ed.), *To a Gandhian Capitalist*, Bombay: Sevak Prakashan, 1979, pp. 23–64.

Sharp, Gene, 'A Study of the Meanings of Non-violence', *Gandhi Marg*, Vol. 3, No. 4, October 1959.

——, *Gandhi as a Political Strategist: With Essays on Ethics and Politics*, Boston: Porter Sargent, 1979.

——, 'Gandhi's Political Significance Today', *Gandhi Marg*, Vol. 9, No. 1, January 1965.

Spodek, Howard, 'On the Origins of Gandhi's Political Methodology: The Heritage of Kathiawad and Gujarat', *Journal of Asian Studies*, Vol. 30, No. 2, 1971, pp. 362–72.

Vine, John C., 'Interview with Mrs. Millie Graham Polak', 2 May 1960, in S. Durai Raja Singam, 'They Were Ready to Talk About Gandhi', unpublished manuscript [n.d.], pp. 16–20.

Wadia, A.R., 'Philosophy of Mahatma Gandhi', in his *Philosophy of Mahatma Gandhi and Other Essays*, Mysore: University of Mysore, 1958.

Walker, Charles C., 'Non-violence in Eastern Africa, 1962–64: The World Peace Brigade and Zambian Independence', in A. Paul Hare and Herbert H. Blumberg (eds), *Liberation Without Violence: A Third Party Approach*, Totowa, NJ: Rowman and Littlefield, 1977, pp. 157–77.

Weber, Thomas, 'Gandhi is Dead. Long Live Gandhi: The Post-Gandhi Gandhian Movement in India', *Gandhi Marg*, Vol. 18, No. 2, 1996, pp. 160–92.

——, 'Gandhi, Deep Ecology, Peace Research and Buddhist Economics', *Journal of Peace Research*, Vol. 36, No. 3, 1999, pp. 349–61.

——, 'Gandhi's "Living Wall" and Maude Royden's "Peace Army"', *Gandhi Marg*, Vol. 10, No. 4, 1988, pp. 199–212.

——, 'Gandhi's Salt March as Living Sermon', *Gandhi Marg*, Vol. 22, No. 4, 2001, pp. 417–35.

——, 'Gandhian Philosophy, Conflict Resolution Theory and Practical Approaches to Negotiation', *Journal of Peace Research*, Vol. 38, No. 4, 2001, pp. 493–513.

——, 'Legal Ethics/Gandhian Ethics', *Gandhi Marg*, Vol. 7, No. 10, 1986, pp. 692–706.

——, 'Non-violence is Who? Gene Sharp and Gandhi', *Peace and Change*, Vol. 28, No. 2, 2003, pp. 250–70.

Wellock, Wilfred, 'Is there a Non-violent Road to a Peaceful World?', *Gandhi Marg*, Vol. 101, January 1963.

West, Albert, 'In the Early Days with Gandhi', *The Illustrated Weekly of India*, 3 October 1965, pp. 30–31.

Wynne-Tyson, Esme, 'The True Significance of Gandhi', *Gandhi Marg*, Vol. 2, No. 4, October 1958.

Zunes, Stephen, 'The Role of Non-violent Action in the Collapse of Apartheid', *Gandhi Marg*, Vol. 20, No. 4, 1999, pp. 398–429.

Zutshi, C.N. Ashimsa, 'The Only Way to World Peace', *India and World Peace*, Lahore: Hero Publications, 1934.

Index